READING AND THE SPECIAL LEARNER

edited by
Carolyn N. Hedley
John S. Hicks

Fordham University

Ablex Publishing Corporation
Norwood, New Jersey

Library of Congress Cataloging-in-Publication Data

Reading and the special learner / edited by Carolyn N. Hedley, John S. Hicks.
    p. cm.
    Includes bibliographies and indexes.
    ISBN 0-89391-495-9.   ISBN 0-89391-517-3 (pbk.)
    1. Handicapped children—Education—Reading. 2. Learning disabled children—Education—Reading.   I. Hedley, Carolyn N.
II. Hicks, John S.
LC4028.5.R4   1988   88-4118
371.9′044—dc19   CIP

Ablex Publishing Corporation
355 Chestnut St.
Norwood, NJ 07648

Table of Contents

PART II: THE SPECIAL LEARNER AND THE READING TASK

PART III: SPECIFIC PROGRAMS FOR THE SPECIAL LEARNER

To our students
in the Reading/Special Education Institute
who inspired our work and that of our fellow contributors

Preface

The annual Reading/Special Education Institute at Fordham University was truly a conference of the participants. We endeavored to have special educators, and language and reading development educators in equal numbers from both fields with regard to the speakers; by the same token, students from both special education and reading education were represented equally. Thus, the two groups gathered to find that we had much in common, and that the needs of the youngster with learning problems, whether designated as special learning or reading problems were not truly distinct. In fact, the development of reading, writing and language abilities for the special learner do not pose a whole new set of skills for the teacher, whether that teacher functions in the regular classroom or the self-contained special education class. Language development, including reading and writing, is seen as a naturally occurring cognitive process involving information processing, best developed in social and interactive environments. What forms of developmental language difficulty inhibit learning for the mildly handicapped learner – whether that learner is learning disabled, physically handicapped, hard of hearing, visually impaired, perceptually impaired, memory and language impaired, a slow learner or a learner with a combination of learning problems? In addressing questions, which derive from this concern, we considered theoretical issues and practical concerns that affect teachers, parents, students, and support personnel.

As editors, we owe the greatest debt to our students who helped us with their enthusiastic and intelligent involvement in the Institute. It is to them—the Brooklyn Diocese educators, the special educators, the Tarrytown contributors, the doctoral students, as well as those less well identified—that we dedicate this book. Thank you for giving us a vision. To our contributor/speakers we owe the greatest thanks, since they created a wonderful institute and a fine book.   The best contributor/speakers are always the busiest; what we asked them to do took earnest academic commitment and physical, intellectual, and personal-social sacrifice. We wanted you to know that we knew that. We wish to acknowledge, as ever, our families, for putting up with the travail of publication. Thanks, folks. Then, too, we want to thank our editor, whose praises have gone unsung for too long—Barbara Bernstein. Our thanks also to the Office of Research Services of Fordham University, particularly to the Director, Dr. Judith Ginsberg, who supported us with her encouragement and with financial aid in the preparation of the manuscript. Finally and not least, our appreciation to Anne Goldstein for her word processing capability!

Carolyn N. Hedley
John S. Hicks

The Authors

PATRICIA ANTONACCI. Patricia Antonacci is on the faculty of Fordham University at Lincoln Center and at Tarrytown, New York. She is a teacher in the Yonkers public schools. She has developed a reading curriculum and participated in test development in the Yonkers schools. Dr. Antonacci is professionally active in the International Reading Association and the New York State Reading Association, serving on the Board of Directors. She has published in *Reading Horizons*.

CARL BEREITER. Carl Bereiter has long been interested in the special learner. His early studies at the University of Illinois were done with underachieving children. Currently, Dr. Bereiter is a professor at the Ontario Institute for Studies in Education, where he works in educational psychology. His latest book, written with Marlene Scardamalia, is *The Psychology of Written Composition*.

BERTRAM BRUCE. "Chip" Bruce is a division scientist and researcher at Bolt, Beranek, and Newman, where he writes and develops educational software. Dr. Bruce collaborates with the Center of Reading at the University of Illinois, where he develops computer programs, QUILL as one, that aid in the writing and reading task. He is co-editor of the book *Theoretical Issues in Reading Comprehension*. Dr. Bruce received his Ph.D. from the University of Texas at Austin in computer sciences. Dr. Bruce, with his wife, has two small children: his primary focus right now is being a good father.

JANET EMIG. Janet Emig teaches and does research at Rutgers University where she is a professor of English. She was a forerunner in the developmental approach to the process of writing. She has written book chapters such as "Non-Magical Thinking: Presenting Writing Developmentally in the Schools" (Frederiksen and Dominic, *Writing: The Nature, Development, and Teaching of Written Composition*), and the book, *The Web of Meaning*. Currently, she is doing cross-cultural research using case studies of writers from Holland and Italy. Additionally, she is researching the composing processes of aging.

ROSA HAGIN. Rosa Hagin is a professor in the Division of Psychological and Educational Services in the Graduate School of Education at Fordham University, and Research Professor in Psychology in the Department of Psychiatry at New York University Medical Center. Her research interests have centered on prevention, diagnosis, and treatment of learning disorders in children and adults. Her publications include longitudinal studies of learning-disabled children, investigations of neuropsychological development of children, and assessment of models of intervention programs. She is co-author of the *Search and Teach* program. She was principal investigator in a Handicapped Children's Model program funded by the U.S. Office of Education, titled *Links in Education: Emotionally Disturbed Children and Youth.*

CAROLYN N. HEDLEY. Carolyn Hedley is a professor and the Director of Reading Programs at Fordham University Graduate School of Education. She has been involved in the development of the doctoral program in Language Literacy and Learning at Fordham. Dr. Hedley is the co-editor of the books *Contexts of Reading* and *Home & Schools: Early Language and Reading* and she has published widely in journals of reading (*Reading Horizons, Educational and Psychological Measurement, Elementary English,* as examples). She has contributed articles to several books, on such topics as "Career Education and the Language Arts" and "Reading Difficulties." Dr. Hedley is a co-author of the Scott Foresman *Life Long Series in Adult Education: Reading Comprehension,* which includes 24 books. Dr. Hedley received her doctorate from the University of Illinois.

JOHN S. HICKS. John Hicks is an associate professor at Fordham University, where he is director of Programs in Special Education. He was co-director and workshop leader in the Reading/Special Education Institute. Dr. Hicks is co-author of the book *How to Teach Reading to the Special Learner,* to be published in early 1988. He recently wrote "Reading and Learning Problems of Special Children." His interest in evaluation has led to publication of *A Rating Scale for Rehabilitation Programs for*

Adults; currently he is developing and conducting studies for a pre-school rating scale.

SHARON JAMES. Sharon James is a professor at Syracuse University, where she works in special education, researching children's language development. She is widely published in this area. Her works include *Assessing Children with Language Disorders.* Currently, Dr. James is on leave, working at the University of Wisconsin at Madison doing research on language development and the special learner.

JANET LERNER. Dr. Lerner was our keynote speaker. Her work, *Reading Problems: Diagnosis and Remediation,* co-authored with Lynn List and Margaret Richek, is a classic, in that it was one of the first efforts of reading specialists and special educators to write on the common concerns of the learner in difficulty. Dr. Lerner has brought out her own book on the young child who is a special learner, just this year. She continues to publish prolifically, with great professional benefit to her colleagues.

ANDEE RUBIN. Andee Rubin is a senior scientist at Bolt, Beranek, and Newman. She has degrees from Massachusetts Institute of Technology in computer science and artificial intelligence. She has published several articles and chapters with Dr. Bruce. Her own work includes "Learning with Quill: Lessons for Students, Teachers and Software Designers" and "Reading Comprehension: From Research to Practice." Her most recent book is *Reading and Writing: How Are the First Two R's Related?*

CORINNE SMITH. Corinne Smith is a professor at Syracuse University in the Department of Special Education. She believes in the ecological approach to teaching reading to the special learner and has written a book titled *Learning Disabilities: Interaction of the Learner, Task and Setting.* She is active as a presenter in such professional organizations as American Psychological Association, National Association for School Psychologists, and the Council for Exceptional Children. Her publications have occurred in *Journal of Learning Disabilities, the Teaching of Exceptional Children,* and *Child Development.*

MARILYN COCHRAN SMITH. Marilyn Cochran Smith is a professor and researcher at the University of Pennsylvania, where she works in the Graduate School of Education. Her book *The Making of a Reader* was among the first studies in education to use ethnographic techniques to analyze classroom interaction and the reading and languaging processes of the preschool and kindergarten. It was Dr. Cochran Smith who developed such terms as *literacy event* and *contextualized* reading—terms which direct current thinking in reading today.

BETTY VAN WITSEN. Betty Van Witsen is an adjunct professor at Fordham University. Dr. Van Witsen runs a resource center in the Hewlett Woodmere Schools in her "other life." She has written several books, which include: *Perceptual Training Activities Handbook, Teaching Children with Severe Behavior/Communication Disorders,* and *Listen and Learn.* This last publication is a group of stories and listening activities for primary children with learning disabilities.

Introduction

Someone coming into a strange country will sometimes learn the language of the inhabitants from ostensive definitions that they give him; and he will often have to *guess* the meaning of these definitions; and will guess sometimes right, sometimes wrong.

And now, I think, we can say: Augustine describes the learning of human language as if the child came into a strange country and did not understand the language of the country; that is, as if it already had a language, only not this one. Or again: as if the child could already *think*, only not yet speak. And "think" would here mean something like "talk to one's self."

Ludwig Wittgenstein
Philosophical Investigations
Paragraph 32

This book is the result of an academically rewarding and happy experience of a number of professionals at many levels. The chapters presented here are the outgrowth of the presentations at the annual Reading/Special Education Institute that occurs every summer at Fordham University at Lincoln Center. The position taken by the authors on reading and the special learner is that reading would be learned in normative ways, were not some factor intervening in the

1

learning processes that would naturally take place. Thus the special learner learns in much the same way as the normative learner, except that the child with learning problems needs compensatory methods and adaptive means to provide for his or her special need. Therefore, the discussion in this book deals with usual strategies and methods that have adapted and reconsidered in the light of what we can observe about the needs of the learner with problems.

The book is divided into three parts, one on assesssment and intervention, the next on the dimensions of the reading task; the last section contains specific programs for the special learner. Janet Lerner was our keynote speaker; her opening chapter stresses methods that can be adapted to work with the special student, as well as special methods that may be useful. She stresses the notion of top-down teaching and reading as a holistic process. In Chapter 2, Carl Bereiter, with his background in psychology, points out that the learner with reading disability is, in fact, accommodating his or her difficulty in highly intelligent ways, but that these adaptive measures may prove counter-productive in the long run. Bereiter asks that we look at disability as a way of coping in the classroom context, so that we may construct more productive ways of meeting the student's long range needs. The third chapter in this section is Corinne Smith's, who recommends ecological approaches to reading assessment. Her chapter is the logical response to Dr. Bereiter's concerns, since she acknowledges the insufficiency of traditional assessment and instruction methods that do not take into consideration the nature of the learner, task, and setting. Moreover, she indicates methods which may be adapted for the special learner's immediate needs as well as his or her well-being in the long run. In Chapter 4, Dr. Rosa Hagin reports on her research on preventing reading failure. Why allow failure in reading, when the sensible approach is to prevent failure from occurring in the first place? Principles and procedures for a program for the prevention of reading failure are described. Long-term positive effects in reading achievement, motivation, and interpersonal adjustment are demonstrated when preventive measures are taken.

Part 2 deals with the special dimensions of the reading task. In Chapter 5, Sharon James writes that "children with reading disabilities have been found to have deficits in their primary linguistic abilities." Dr. Smith analyzes what these difficulties may be and how to reach special students. Marilyn Cochran Smith presents her position on mediated text experiences for children in Chapter 6. She recommends a great deal of story reading, combined with read-aloud and reading-along strategies, as a primary method of mediating text with the special learner. Writing is also part of her method. Chapter 7, developed by Carolyn Hedley, presents dimensions of the reading act in which the special learner often excels, that is, reading for daily living. She suggests how such reading may developmentally lead to other kinds of successful reading. In her discussion, she deals with *intentionality* and with the *affect* dimensions of reading. In Chapter 8, Patricia Antonacci provides instructional methods for the special learner for teaching comprehension as meaning construction.

Part 3 contains special programs for the handicapped learner. In Chapter 9, Betty Van Witsen, a highly successful teacher of the learning disabled, presents a specific program for the special learner in the self-contained classroom, which is both practical and beneficial. Janet Emig, in Chapter 10, views the special writer as a constructionist, a maker of worlds through text; ultimately she provides a set of recommendations for teachers of writing in the special setting. John Hicks, in Chapter 11, is more specific than Dr. Emig in his advocacy of computers to teach reading, writing, and spelling to the learner in the self-contained special classroom. Finally, in Chapter 12, "Chip" Bruce and Andee Rubin describe a computer program for the special learner, namely QUILL, with lessons for students, teachers, and software designers. QUILL is one of the more flexible, adaptable, and individualized writing programs for students, and was developed by Drs. Bruce and Rubin.

PART I

READING ASSESSMENT AND READING INTERVENTION

Chapter 1

Theories for Intervention in Reading

Janet W. Lerner

Northeastern Illinois University

Reading disability continues to be a serious problem for many children, adolescents, and adults in the United States and throughout the world. Without interventive help, these individuals are destined to be handicapped throughout their lives. As a primary cause of school failure, poor reading ability leads to a lowered self-esteem and serious emotional overlays. However, reading problems prevent individuals from reaching desired career goals, as well as robbing them of the opportunity to read for pleasure and enjoyment. Because illiteracy is associated with many social problems, society as a whole suffers the consequences of poor reading among its citizenry (Richek, List, & Lerner, 1988).

How serious is the problem of illiteracy in America? About 23 million adult Americans are functionally illiterate—with basic skills at fourth grade level or below. Another 35 million are semi-literate with skills below the eighth grade level. Illiterate adults account for 75% of unemployed, one third of the mothers receiving Aid to Families with Dependent Children, 85% of the juveniles who appear in court, 60% of prison inmates, and nearly 40% of minority youth. Of people in the workforce, 15% are functionally illiterate—11% of professional and managerial workers, and 30% of semi-skilled and unskilled workers (Orton Dyslexia Society, 1986).

This chapter reviews intervention strategies—ways to teach people who encounter serious difficulty learning to read. Many of these teaching techniques have a long-established tradition and have been widely used for many years. Other strategies reflect more recent ideas about teaching reading and are based on current research of the reading process. It is important for teachers who work with problem readers to develop competencies in both the traditional teaching methods and some of the newer methodologies for teaching reading. Often the new knowledge obtained through research confirms old beliefs about how to teach reading. The old and the new methods can be synthesized in a workable and practical way.

Becoming a Nation of Readers: The Report of the Commission on Reading

Extensive research has been conducted about ways to teach reading. To synthesize this extensive body of research, a study was sponsored by the National Institute of Education. The goal of the final report of this study, *Becoming a Nation of Readers,* was to summarize the knowledge acquired from research in the last decade and to draw implications for reading instruction (Anderson, Hiebert, Scott, & Wilkinson, 1985). The report reached the following generalizations about the nature of the reading as observed in skilled readers:

1. *Skilled reading is constructive.* No reading passage is completely self-explanatory. To bring meaning to the printed text, readers draw upon their existing store of knowledge and their prior experiences. Thus, readers *construct* the meaning of the written passage by filling in the gaps with pieces of information they possess. For example, when reading about computer software, a reader came across the word, "utilities." Using his prior knowledge, he constructed the meaning of this text to be about "electric power companies."

2. *Skilled reading is fluent.* This refers to the ability to identify individual words easily. If the reader must concentrate on figuring out the words, he or she is unable to focus on meaning. Therefore, the reader must be able to fluently "break the code," to readily relate the spelling to the sound. Moreover, for fluent reading, this word identification process must become automatic, not a conscious, deliberate process. Research consistently shows that children who earn the best scores on reading comprehension tests in the early grades are those who made the most progress in fast and accurate word identification skills. Thus, there is a payoff for teaching beginning readers skills in phonological word analysis (phonics), sight word identification skills, and the

ability to rapidly and accurately read words as they appear in organized text.

3. *Skilled reading is strategic.* Skilled readers are flexible. They change and direct their reading style depending upon the purpose for reading, the complexity of the text and their familiarity with the topic. Unlike poor readers, skilled readers assess their knowledge in relation to the task and monitor their reading comprehension. If something in the reading is puzzling, they will go back and use fix-up strategies, such as re-reading or rephrasing the text to improve comprehension, or looking ahead to discover the answer to the problem.

4. *Reading requires motivation.* Sustained attention over a long period of time is required to learn to read. It takes several years to learn to read well. Teachers must plan to sustain the attention of beginning and poor readers. Many studies show that poor readers have lost motivation. While reading, they are listless, inattentive, do not complete their work, and give up easily. It is important that teachers make the reading lesson enjoyable and convey a belief that the student will learn to read.

5. *Reading is a lifelong pursuit.* Reading is a continuously developing skill, one that continues to improve through practice. It is not a skill that is mastered once and for all. At all stages of reading, from the beginning on, it is important the learner has sufficient opportunities to practice and engage in the process of reading. Teachers must search for strategies that will offer many reading opportunities.

Overview of Intervention Methods

Reading is the most researched area of the school curriculum, as well as one of the most controversial. There are many suggested methods for teaching reading. A single method often has its strong supporters as well as its critics. To provide an overview of the major intervention strategies for the teaching of reading, the various strategies are grouped into the following: (a) adaptations of developmental methods, (b) traditional remedial methods, (c) cognitive learning strategies, (d) schema theory and holistic methods, and (e) microcomputer methods for teaching reading.

Adaptations of Developmental Methods

Developmental methods are methods and materials that are normally used by the regular classroom teacher. They include: basal readers, sight words, phonics, and language experience approaches. Methods and materials intended for students progressing normally in reading can be successfully adapted for pupils with reading and learning disabilities. Adaptation techniques to make developmental methods more successful include: Increasing the amount of repetition, allotting more time for the completion of work, providing more examples or activities, providing more review, introducing the work more slowly, expanding the background information, and providing more work on vocabulary development. Sometimes a developmental method that may have failed in the past seems to work because it is taught at another time, or in another place, or by a different teacher—one who has that magic clinical touch.

Basal Readers

Basal readers are a sequential and interrelated set of books and supportive materials intended to provide the basic material for the development of fundamental reading skills. A basal reading series consists of graded readers that gradually increase in difficulty, typically beginning with very simple readiness and first-grade books and going through the sixth- or eighth-grade level. The books increase in difficulty in vocabulary, story content, and skill development. Most basal reading series incorporate many procedures to teach readiness, vocabulary, word recognition, comprehension, and the enjoyment of literature.

The basal reader is the major tool for reading instruciton in the elementary grades (Anderson et al., 1985). Most young adults vividly remember the chief characters in the basal reader series which they used in the early grades. The basal reader provides a wealth of opportunities for instructing the student with reading problems. It is an extremely flexible, useful tool. It is better for the special teacher to obtain basal readers that are not being used in the mainstream classroom, but to find another series—one that gives the student a fresh start. In addition, teachers could use a basal series especially produced for remedial instruction (Richek et al., 1988).

Word Recognition Skills

The skill of recognizing words quickly and accurately is basic to all other aspects of reading. Readers use a number of ways to recognize or identify words, including the skills of sight words, phonics, structural analysis, and context clues. Sometimes all are used simultaneously. Since readers need all of these strategies to achieve independence and flexibility, teachers need methods for teaching them to students having difficulty in learning to read. Two of these word recognition methods—sight words and phonics—are briefly discussed.

Sight words.   Sight words are words that can be recognized immediately, without need for further analysis. Instruction is focused on helping the pupil build a sight vocabulary. By mastering a core of words that are recognized easily and quickly, the reader is able to process and understand a printed selection more easily. To accomplish this, beginning readers need much practice recognizing these sight words. The average student needs many exposures to a word before the student fully possesses it and it becomes a sight word; the student having difficulty learning to read will need even more exposures to attain ownership of the word. A variety of instructional strategies can help that beginning reader develop a sight vocabulary: Using basal readers, library books, and language experience stories, games, flash cards, computer drill and practice. The words selected for sight word instruction can include high frequency words or words that have meaning for the student.

Phonics.   The skill of recognizing the relationship of sounds to printed letters is recognized as an essential element of learning to read. Research shows that children who are taught phonics have a better start in learning to read than children who are not taught phonics (Anderson et al., 1985). There is no question about *whether* phonics should be taught, but rather about *how* it should be taught.

For many youngsters having difficulty learning to read, auditory perceptual problems make learning phonics particularly troublesome. They find it confusing to remember isolated sounds, to match them to letter shapes, and also to differentiate one sound from a similar one. Learning short vowels may be particularly confusing for these youngsters. Yet these youngsters must learn letter–sound relationships in order to break the code and become independent and self-reliant readers. Instruction should be simple, provide ample practice, and the opportunity for transferring the phonics skills to contextual reading.

1. *Phonics and segmentation.* A strong research basis for the importance of phonics instruction has been developed over a number of years by Liberman (1984) and her colleagues in their research on phonemic segmentation. Their research shows that readers do not recover speech from print on a letter-by-letter basis. Instead, they combine the particular string of segments that in ordinary speech would be produced as a unit. The unit is commonly a syllable. Learning to combine letters into a speakable unit is a vital part of learning to read. This process is called

"segmentation." Poor analytic linguistic abilities are consistently found to be related to and predictive of poor reading achievement. .

According to Liberman (1984), a word is something apart from its meanings. Print represents the words of the language—not meaning. Before one can get to the meaning of the word presented by the print, one must first get from the print to the word. Neither children nor skilled readers go directly from print to meaning. Rather, the reader gets to the meaning via the language, by dealing in distinctively linguistic ways with the units of language (phonological segments, words, and sentences). Beginning readers, therefore, should be encouraged to take advantage of the phonological and morphophonological information in a printed word.

Liberman's research stresses that the way English is represented in print (the alphabetic orthography) has a relationship to word recognition. In order to understand the reading process and its disabilities, it is critical to understand exactly how an orthography represents a language and what cognitive demands that kind of presentation makes on the would-be reader. Further, the cognitive demands for learning to read in English (an alphabetic orthography) are different from that of a language like Chinese (a logogram orthography). If children are taught that words represent experiences, they are treating the alphabet written word as if it were a logogram—a printed pattern like the dollar sign, which bears no relation to the internal segmental structure of the word "dollar." The whole word strategy loses all the remarkable benefits of the alphabetic system and children are taught like Chinese children (Liberman and Shankweiler, 1985).

2. *Intervention strategies based on segmentation.* To make best use of an alphabetic orthography, both skilled and beginner readers must apprehend the internal structure of the word. Skilled readers do it quite automatically; and beginners, though it may be difficult for them, should be given direct instruction from the start as to just how the orthography represents words. Liberman recommends that teachers help children as early as possible to become aware of the segmentation of speech—using activities such as nursery rhymes, word play and word games. Also, teachers should help children learn segmental structure—first in words, then in syllables, and finally phonemes. Then teach letters of the alphabet, their names and sounds. Emphasize the creation and re-creation of the sound form of the word from its practical representation, segmenting syllables in phonemes, words into syllables, concepts of the number and order of sounds within a spoken pattern.

Language Experience Methods

Language experience stories provide a very personal way of teaching reading. The raw materials are the experiences and language of the students themselves. They therefore develop a sense of authorship of the text (Ringler & Weber, 1984). The approach is successful with many kinds of students—young beginning readers, adolescents, and bilingual students. The process begins by having the student personally experience some event. The student then dictates the story to the teacher who writes it down. This story then becomes the basis of the student's reading experiences.

The language experience approach is a natural approach in learning to read. It encourages the student to conceptualize the relationships in language (Lee and Allen, 1963):

> What I can think about, I can talk about. What I can say, I can write (or someone can write for me). What I can write, I can read. I can read what others write for me to read.

The language exprience approach to reading integrates all of the communication modes—listening, speaking, writing, and reading. Pupils read their own language instead of the language of a text author. This is an important intervention strategy for all teachers of reading.

Traditional Remedial Methods

There are a number of intervention strategies that are considered special approaches for students having difficulty in learning to read. These methods are not considered developmental approaches nor are they typically used in the regular classroom. Knowledge and skill with these special methods should be considered among the competencies of teachers working with problem readers. Several of the major remedial methods are presented in this section.

VAKT

The letters V, A, K, T, stand for the *visual, auditory, kinesthetic,* and *tactile* channels of learning.The underlying rationale for this strategy is that using several modalities during the learning situation tends to reinforce that learning. Thus, the reader is asked to (1) see the word, (2) hear the teacher say the word, (3) say the word themselves, (4) hear themselves say the word, (5) feel the muscle movement as they trace the word, (6) feel the tactile surface under their fingertips, and (7) hear themselves say the word. Two special remedial approaches that are based on a multisensory approach which have been used for many years are the Fernald and the Gillingham methods.

Fernald

The Fernald (1943) method was reported as successful by Grace Fernald over 40 years ago. It is a multisensory approach to teaching reading which involves four sensory avenues: visual, auditory, kinesthetic, and tactile. Whole words to be learned are selected by the student. Although the method consists of four stages, it is the first stage which is unique. In the first stage, the teacher writes the word to be learned with a crayon on a large piece of paper. The student then traces the word with his or her fingers making contact with the paper (visual, tactile, and kinesthetic senses). As the student traces the word, the teacher says the word aloud (auditory). This process is repeated until the student can write the word correctly without looking at the sample. When that task is accomplished, the word is placed in a file box. Words thus learned are accumulated in the word box until the student writes a story using the words.

Gillingham

This method also has roots that go back about 40 years (Gillingham & Stillman, 1966). An outgrowth of the biological studies of dyslexia conducted by Samuel Orton (1937), this method is a highly structured approach to the teaching of reading. Initial activities focus on the learning of individual letter sounds and then the blending of these sounds. It is multisensory in that the student uses a tracing technique to learn single letters and their sound equivalents. These single sounds are later combined into larger groups and then into short words. There are many advocates of the Gillingham method. This method and other topics concerning dyslexia are the focus of an organization known as the Orton Dyslexia Society (1986).

Neurological Impress Method

Perhaps this method could be more aptly called the "read-along" method. Briefly, it consists of unison reading by the pupil and the instructor. The pupil sits slightly in front of the instructor and both read together using one book. The voice of the instructor is directed into the ear of the student at a fairly close range. The student or teacher uses a finger as a locator as the words are read. When the student is reading well, the rate of the instructor's reading is slightly slower than that of the student. If the student begins to falter, the instructor reads a bit faster and louder to pull the student along. No preliminary preparations are made. The premise underlying the method is that the auditory feedback from the reader's own voice and the voice of someone else reading the same material establishes a new learning process. For many severe readers, this is the first time that they experience reading as a continuous process rather than a word-by-word experience.

Cognitive Learning Strategies

In the field of learning disabilities, there is a growing conviction that a primary characteristic of learning disabled students with reading comprehension problems is that these students are inefficient learners. That is, they do not know how to go about the business of learning.

Studies of the behavioral characteristics of successful learners show that efficient learners know how to use and direct their own cognitive and thinking processes to facilitate learning and to deal with the abstract concepts needed for academic work. Efficient learners ask themselves questions and organize their thoughts; they connect and integrate the new materials they are trying to learn with the experience and knowledge they already possess. They try to predict what is to come and monitor the relevance of new information. In short, efficient learners have learned how to go about the business of learning and have at their disposal a repertoire of cognitive strategies that work for them. Their behavior reflects an active interest in learning and solving problems (Deshler, Schumacher, & Lenz, 1984).

In contrast, learning disabled students lack such cognitive learning strategies. They do not know how to control and direct their thinking to learn, how to gain more knowledge, or how to remember what they learn. They approach learning in a dependent, passive manner, waiting for the teacher to do the work, a style that has been referred to as "learned helplessness."

Fortunately, research shows that cognitive learning strategies can be taught and that learning disabled students do improve after instruction in specific strategies for learning (Deshler et al., 1984). Some of the instructional strategies for teaching reading comprehension from this perspective are:

Self-Questioning

In this strategy (also referred to as verbal mediation), the students quietly ask themselves questions about the material. The internal language, or covert speech, helps organize material and behavior. Students ask themselves the questions such as:

What is the problem? What am I supposed to do?
What is my plan? How can I do about doing it?
Am I using my plan? How did I do?

Predicting and Monitoring

In predicting, the students guess about what they will learn in the lesson or what will come next in the story. In monitoring, they check on whether their guesses were correct and monitor whether what they have learned is reasonable and fits in with previous learnings.

Self-Rehearsal

The students practice and review what they have learned. This self-initiated verbal rehearsal helps them remember. People easily forget when the brain trace fades away. Recitation and verbal review of material to be learned helps the student understand and remember.

Cognitive Behavior Modification

This strategy requires self-instruction, self-monitoring, and self-evaluation. The steps include: (a) the teacher models the desired behavior while providing an explanation, (b) the student performs the task while the teacher describes it, (c) the student talks the task through out loud, (d) the student whispers the task to himself or herself, and finally (e) the student performs the task with nonverbal self-cues.

Schema Theory: Reading as a Holistic Process

A perspective for teaching reading which evolved from research on "schema theory" treats reading comprehension as a holistic process. Reading is viewed as a unitary, whole process entailing cognitive and psycholinguistic behavior. This view of reading suggests that all readers must be able to bridge the gap between the information presented in the written text and their own personal knowledge in order to understand what they read. Further, readers must actively combine their existing schemata (conceptual structure and knowledge that they already possess) with the new information in the printed text.

Suggested instruction from this perspective includes: (a) getting students actively involved in reading, (b) encouraging students to make use of information they already possess, (c) teaching students to work at reconstructing the author's message, and (d) increasing the quantity of material that the students actually read (Richek et al., 1988). A few of the specific teaching strategies stemming from the holistic perspective are:

DR-TA (Directed Reading-Thinking Activity)

In the Directed Reading-Thinking Activity, teaching reading becomes a way of teaching thinking. Teachers ask important questions that direct the reading-thinking process and require cognitive activity: What do you think? Why do you think so? Can you prove it? The teacher guides the student to think about the reading. Specifically, teachers ask students to (a) examine the reading material, (b) hypothesize or speculate about what will happen, (c) find proof of evidence to support the hypothesis, (d) suspend judgment, and (e) make decisions.

Predictable Books

In this strategy books that have a repeated refrain are used. Examples are *The Little Red Hen* and the *Three Billy Goats Gruff*. As the teacher reads the book out loud, the children participate in the predictable passages.

Written Conversations

Instead of saying what they wish to communicate to friends, students write the message in a note and send it to their friends. The responses are also written notes. This strategy makes the reading very personal and meaningful.

Using Themes

The theme approach requires the teacher to find a topic that interests the student and then gather reading material on that topic. By capturing the student's interest, the teacher encourages an active involvement in the reading, and lessons can build on the student's background knowledge and experience.

Using the Microcomputer for Teaching Reading

Teachers of reading and learning disabilities are discovering all kinds of interesting curriculum applications and exciting ways to use the microcomputer to teach reading. The use of the microcomputer as a pedagogical tool is based upon familiar and sound principles of learning; including individualization of instruction, sufficient review and repetition, sequential steps of presentation, and opportunities to learn through experimentation. Several applications are:

Drill and Practice Programs

Perhaps the most common and familiar uses of microcomputers for problem students are drill and practice programs (about 60–85% fall into this category). These programs are designed to provide motivating opportunities for the pupils to increase mastery of already introduced concepts and skills. It allows them to practice and review skills in an interesting context.

Tutorial Programs

Tutorial programs are designed to teach a new skill to the pupil. The quality of tutorial software programs is rapidly improving and beginning to take advantage of the many innovational, instructional strategies available for use with the microcomputer, such as graphics, animation, enlarged print, use of color in both graphics and print, and branching to adjust the presentation to meet specific learner needs.

Learning to Read by Writing

Chomsky (1979) suggested that writing may be easier than reading, and it may actually develop earlier. Writing is a more self-involving task than reading since the meaning of a writer's message originates from within the writer and is known to the writer in advance. On the other hand, reading requires the reader to be able to penetrate someone else's use of language and meaning, which is a more difficult task for the beginner. The physical aspect of writing literally forces active involvement upon the writer. While children are attempting to put their meaning into print, they are learning about the alphabetic nature of the conventions of written English. Writing, then, is an active task that involves children in their own learning.

The problem is that writing has proved to be such an arduous task for many learning disabled students that this approach has not been feasible. The opportunity to work at a computer may be that missing key. The computer is a motivator for most children. Wordprocessing is the writing tool of the present and future classroom.

Word Processing

Teachers increasingly report the successful use of word preocessing programs to help exceptional children develop a variety of language skills, including reading, writing, spelling, and grammar. Word processing is proving to be an innovative and motivating way to learn a variety of written language skills. With the use of a speech synthesizer, it can also be used to learn oral language skills. About 25% of the special education instructional use is wordprocessing.

Wordprocessing can strengthen the relationship between reading and writing. The writing process consists of PREWRITING (60–80%), WRITING, and REVISION. Wordprocessing can be used in all three.

In research on wordprocessing, Rust (1986) found that children who used wordprocessing did better in writing and reading than a comparison group who wrote by hand. Rust found: (a) the physical act of composing was easier, (b) students whose handwriting could never be deciphered before were given a fair chance for the first time, (c) revision was easier (sentences could be rearranged, expanded or combined; entire paragraphs were moved by a few keystrokes), (d) printing another copy of the revised version was easy, and (e) quantity as well as quality of writing increased.

Summary

This chapter examined theories for intervention in reading. The chapter first reviewed the conclusions reached by the Commission on Reading which synthesized the body of research on the teaching of reading. The chapter also presented groups of intervention strategies, including adaptation of developmental methods, traditional reading methods, cognitive learning strategies, schema theory/holistic methods, and using the microcomputer for teaching reading.

Teachers who work with problem readers need competencies in many intervention methods. They must be able to use many strategies to meet the varying needs of their students.

References

Anderson, R. D., Hiebert, E. H., Scott, J. A., & Wilkerson, I. A. (1985). *Becoming a nation of readers: The report of the Commission on Reading*. Washington, DC: National Institute of Education.

Chomsky, C. (1979). Approaching reading through invented spelling. In L. B. Resnick & P. A. Weaver (Eds.), *Theory and practice of early reading* (Vol. 2, pp. 43–65). Hillsdale, NJ: Lawrence Erlbaum Associates.

Deshler, D., Schumacher, J., & Lenz, B. (1984). Academic and cognitive intervention for learning disabled adolescents. Part I. *Journal of Learning*

Disabilities, 17, 108–119.

Fernald, G. (1943). *Remedial techniques in basic school subjects.* New York: McGraw-Hill.

Gillingham, A., & Stillman, B. (1966). *Remedial training for children with specific difficulty reading, spelling, and penmanship* (7th ed.). Cambridge, MA: Educators Publishing Services.

Lee, D., & Allen, R. (1963). *Learning to Read Through Experience.* New York: Appleton-Century Crofts.

Liberman, I. Y. (1984). A language-oriented view of reading and its disabilities. *Thalamus: International Academic for Research in Learning Disabilities, 4,* 1–42.

Liberman, I. Y., & Shankweiler, D. (1985). Phonology and the Problems of Learning to Read & Write. *Remedial & Special Education, 6*(6), 8–17.

Orton, B. (1937). *Reading, writing and speech problems in children.* New York: Norton.

Orton Dyslexia Society. (1966). *Annals of Dyslexia, 36.*

Orton Dyslexia Society. (1986). Some facts about illiteracy in America. *Perspectives on Dyslexia, 13*(4), 1.

Richek, M., List, L., & Lerner, J. (1988). *Reading problems: Diagnosis and remediation.* Englewood Cliffs, NJ: Prentice-Hall.

Ringler, L., & Weber, C. (1984). *A learning-thinking approach to reading: Diagnosis and teaching.* San Diego, CA: Harcourt Brace Jovanovich.

Rust, K. (1986). Wordprocessing: The missing key for writing. *The Reading Teacher, 39,* 611–612.

Chapter 2

A Cognitive Adaptational Interpretation of Reading Disability

Carl Bereiter

Ontario Institute for Studies in Education

Does an injured foot cause one to limp? Not exactly. The limp is, at least in part, an adaptation to the injury. Although the limp may be the most visible evidence that something is wrong, it is not the problem or even an integral part of the problem. In fact, it is a *solution* to a problem—the problem of how to move about while minimizing pain and further damage to an injured foot.

In this paper we develop a similar interpretation of the reading comprehension strategies of disabled readers. Passive, low-comprehension reading strategies may be a conspicuous characteristic of disabled readers (Torgensen, 1982; Wong & Jones, 1982). But these strategies, we shall argue, have adaptive value. They are a way of coping with school demands, given that one has poor word-recognition ability. What we shall call the *minimal comprehension strategy* is, like limping, a way of getting along while minimizing pain and further damage. It is a *cognitive* adaptation, in that the adaptation largely involves mental rather than physical adjustments to a situation, but its adaptive significance remains very much like that of the limp. It is an adaptation both to internal conditions (the child's initial reading disabilities, whatever those might be) and to external conditions (in particular, the conditions of classroom life as they are experienced by a child with reading difficulties).

Cognitive Adaptation in Reading

One type of cognitive adaptation has been fairly definitely identified in reading, although it is not usually described in those terms. Readers who are weak in automatic word recognition tend to compensate by making greater use of inferential process based on context (Stanovich, 1980). This adaptive response is evidently available to good readers as well, who use it when dealing with degraded print that interferes with automatic recognition (Perfetti & Roth, 1981). This adaptation illustrates several typical features of adaptation that are worthy of special notice:

1. Adaptation typically shows many-to-one convergence of causes on outcomes. It does not matter whether the interference with automatic word recognition is external (in the form of bad print) or internal (in the form of any number of possible neurological or psychological conditions that might affect word recognition). The adaptive response (resort to inferential processes) is the same, because it represents one of a limited number of possible solutions to the problem of how to identify words rapidly when graphical information does not suffice. The same kind of convergence is found in the biological realm, when both aquatic mammals and fish evolve the same body shape: The fish-type architecture represents one of a limited number of solutions to the problem of how a large body can propel itself efficiently through water.

2. The adaptations that are of special interest are those that develop without deliberation or awareness. Intelligent beings, of course, also achieve adaptations that are deliberate and conscious. But these we deal with as examples of planning, problem solving, creative thinking, and the like. Adaptiveness (more specifically, rationality) is presupposed in such cases, and so there is nothing further to gain by applying an adaptationist heuristic.

3. Adaptations are assumed to be *locally optimal*. Implicit in Stanovich's (1980) compensatory theory is the assumption that readers use a mixture of automatic and inferential processes so as to achieve some optimal balance of speed, accuracy, and effort—optimal, that is, in relation to goals of the individual and to the limitations within which the individual functions. To say that the adaptation is *locally* optimal, however, is to say that it may not be optimal in relation to more remote or long-term goals or with respect to some wider set of conditions. For instance, the balance of automatic and inferential processes that a child uses might not be optimal for the child's future development as a reader. There is no way the child can adapt to future or unknown conditions (That is where outside intervention by a teacher might be relevant.) Local optimality will be an important idea in the discussion that follows, because a major point of the argument will be that disabled readers

develop comprehension strategies that are adapted to classroom conditions but that are radically unsuitable for real-world literacy demands.

The cognitive adaptation that we have been discussing deals specifically with word recognition. In the ideas to be developed in the next section, this adaptation forms one part of a more comprehensive adaptation by disabled readers. We will call this part *top-down emphasis in word recognition,* referring to the poor reader's tendency to rely on top-down, knowledge-based processes. The more comprehensive adaptation, of which top-down emphasis is a part, is what we shall call the *minimal comprehension strategy.*

Minimal Comprehension as an Adaptive Strategy

The following analysis greatly simplifies what is undoubtedly a complex and highly variable process by which individual children come to cope with their individual reading problems. But the heuristic value of adaptationist theorizing lies very much in its ability to capture a certain simplification that is believed to exist in real life. This is the many-to-one convergence referred to previously, whereby multiple causes converge on a common problem that has only a limited range of possible solutions.

Such a convergence of multiple causes on a single adaptive outcome is depicted in Figure 1. The question-mark boxes on the left side of the diagram refer to the variety of possible causes contributing to the condition that we define objectively as *slow and inaccurate word recogniton.* Children having this characteristic are not, of course, all slow and inaccurate in the same way. A large experimental literature is devoted to differences in the specific kinds of word recognition difficulties that poor readers manifest (Doehring, Trites, Patel, & Fiedorowicz, 1981). Regardless of the precise nature of a child's difficulties, however, slow and inaccurate word recognition represents an objective condition to which the child must adapt, and that is the important point in the present analysis.

Slow and inaccurate word recognition, then, is treated here not as a symptom or defining characteristic of reading disability (although it may be those as well) but as one of the salient conditions to which most reading disabled children must adapt. The condition need not be irremediable; it need only persist over a long enough period of time that a stable adaptation to it can develop. That seems to be a reasonable assumption about most children who get themselves labeled as reading disabled. Also, where intelligent adaptation is concerned, it may be relevant that the child *believes* that the condition will persist.

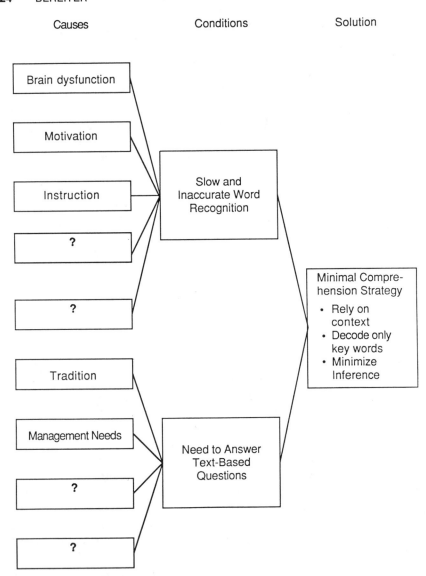

Figure 2.1 Model showing convergence of multiple causes on a single adaptive strategy.

The other major condition to which the reading disabled child must adapt is identified in Figure 1 as "Need to answer text-based questions." Here we refer to the questions teachers ask during reading lessons and in most other academic subjects and also to the varieties of text-based questions commonly posed in workbook exercises and other kinds of assigned seatwork. Why single out this particular feature of classroom life? There are several reasons:

1. Question-asking is by far the prevalent mode of instruction in schools (Bellack, Kliebard, Hyman, & Smith, 1966). As far as instruction in reading comprehension is concerned, it comes close to being the *only* mode of instruction (Durkin 1979). Therefore it is reasonable to expect that children will develop reading strategies adapted to the requirements of question-answering.

2. Learning disability classes are evidently no exception to the preceding generalizations. Leinhardt, Zigmond, and Cooley (1981) found students in LD classes to be averaging about 50 minutes a day on indirect reading activities, which presumably consist mainly of question-answering—considerably more time than was spent on actual reading.

3. If children read outside of class for pleasure or for information, their reading strategies should be at least partly adapted to the requirements of these kinds of reading. But poor readers tend to do little or no reading beyond what is explicitly required of them in school (Fielding, Wilson, & Anderson, 1986). If this reading is always concerned (insofar as comprehension is concerned) with answering questions, then the requirements of question-answering become the central and perhaps the only requirements to which comprehension strategies must adapt.

Disabled readers may face more stressful problems, such as having to read aloud in class, but having to answer text-based questions stands out as an enduring problem likely to have a formative influence on reading comprehension strategies. Children may, of course, develop noncognitive strategies, such as copying, that free them from having to read anything at all (Anderson, 1984). The question we shall consider, however, is what would constitute a locally optimal *reading* strategy? That question is important because it has a bearing, not merely on children's classroom behavior, but on the kind of literacy that they carry with them into later life.

As suggested in Figure 1, the optimal reading strategy for dealing with text-based questions, given that one is poor at word recognition, has three components. The first has already been discussed—top-down emphasis in word recognition. Classroom conditions set a premium on both speed and accuracy in word recognition. Following Stanovich (1980), we assume that, for most reading disabled children, the optimal adaptation to these conditions will involve an above-average reliance on top-down processes. The second component of the optimal strategy is to concentrate decoding efforts on important words. The rationale for this component is obvious. Decoding all the words would take too much time and might overload working memory. Therefore it makes sense to focus attention on those words that carry the most information. (How the student knows which words those are is another problem, which we shall say a word about later.)

The final component of the strategy is the most speculative but also the most central to local optimality. It is now widely recognized that even the most literal comprehension of a text requires a good deal of inference (Collins, Brown, & Larkin, 1980; van Dijk & Kintsch, 1983). Readers differ in the amount of inference they carry out, however, and poor readers are found to do significantly less of it than good readers (Franks et al., 1982). The common view seems to be that this is maladaptive—that poor readers would be better off if they did more inferencing when they read (cf. Gaskins & Baron, 1985). Undoubtedly this is true from a life-span perspective, but it is not necessarily true as far as adapting to classroom conditions is concerned.

Consider the reading disabled child who, in keeping with the first two components of the optimal strategy, has rather shakily identified a limited number of words in a text passage and, on the basis of this, must inferentially construct a meaning to assign to the passage. To be concrete, suppose the child has identified the words, "Long ago," "Robin Hood," "Little John," "Sherwood Forest," and a few other words of lesser note. What is the best inferential strategy the child could use in order to be ready to answer a question about this passage? One fairly reasonable strategy would be to do nothing at all. Just try to remember the words, and do all of the inferring after the question is asked. If, for instance, the question is "Where did Robin Hood live?" a quick search of memory should easily identify "Sherwood Forest" as the best candidate for an answer. Because this strategy requires remembering a number of isolated items, however, it is probably not as effective as a strategy that establishes a meaningful connection among the words. Such a connection would be provided by inferring that there was some relationship between Robin Hood and Little John, and that they were in Sherwood Forest at some time in the distant past. This is the essence of the *minimal comprehension strategy*—limiting inference to just what is required to establish coherence among the recognized words in a text.

But why should inference stop at this minimum? The reason is that, when only a limited number of the words in a text have been identified, there are not enough constraints on possible interpretations of the text. For instance, in the present example, there is nothing in what the child has decoded to refute the inference that Little John was a boy who fled from his cruel master, Robin Hood, and got lost in Sherwood Forest. But inferences that go that far are risky. They can lead to foolish answers and embarrassment. All readers have to restrain their inferencing, and how this is done has proved to be a problem for artificial intelligence researchers (Schank, 1979). It is not clear how one finds the line between too much inference and too little. For the reading disabled child coping with classroom questions, however, the safest strategy would seem to be to err on the side of too little inference.

According to an adaptationist line of thinking, if the minimal comprehension strategy is indeed the locally optimal strategy for disabled readers under classroom conditons, then we should expect disabled readers of a variety of kinds to gravitate toward this strategy. Not all disabled readers will necessarily arrive at this strategy, however. One way to check the claim that it is optimal is see how children fare who do not follow this strategy. In a group of nine reading disabled students whom I observed recently over a 6-week period, two deviated in one or another respect from the minimal comprehension strategy. One failed to follow the top-down emphasis part of the strategy. He relied on letter-by-letter decoding to identify unfamiliar words, even in context. As a result he was by far the slowest reader, and in general the least successful. Another student violated the minimal inference part of the strategy. He engaged in wildly imaginative inferencing that carried him far beyond the text, and he could not distinguish between what he had read and what he had imagined. As a result, he initially gave the impression of being psychotic, although with a few weeks of work on comprehension strategies he was able to being his inferencing within reasonable bounds. None of the students violated the principle of focusing on important words, but is is easy to see how doing so would lead to trouble either by slowing reading down too much or by overlooking key information.

It should also be evident,however, that the minimal comprehension strategy is only locally optimal. Indeed, for real-word survival, it would seem that reading disabled people would be better off adopting the *opposite* of the minimal comprehension strategy on every count. Faced with a document to sign, an important notice to read, or any such practical demand on literacy, one needs to adopt a *maximal* comprehension strategy—maximal in the sense of making use of all available resources to increase comprehension. For the disabled reader, this would probably mean trying to decode every word, using as much bottom-up information as possible so as to avoid risky guessing, and carrying out extensive, careful inferential analysis to arrive at understanding. The maximal comprehension strategy, in other words, is much like that which a tourist would be likely to adopt when trying to deal with notices or official documents in an unfamiliar language.

The Minimal Comprehension Strategy as Self-Limiting

Normal readers all become proficient in phonic skills, as indicated by their ability to decode nonwords. Although disabled readers are notoriously poor in decoding nonwords (Doehring et al., 1981), it is seldom the case that disabled readers are altogether incapable of learning to use grapho-phonemic information. They progress slowly, but developmental studies show that year-by-year disabled readers progress in their ability to decode nonwords (Siegel, 1985). From an adaptationist standpoint, therefore, we have to ask why it is that children who have at least some resources for phonic skills do not somehow manage to put those resources to more effective use.

The question, however, is perhaps better asked the other way around. How do normal readers manage to acquire phonic skills even when they receive little or no instruction? Here it is worth noting that the knowledge of spelling-to-sound patterns that people eventually acquire far exceeds anything that is taught in even the most thorough of phonics programs. So it seems fair to say that all normal readers acquire phonics skills in part without instruction. A reasonable guess, from an adaptationist standpoint, is that comprehension drives the process. Decoding rules that lead to sensible interpretations of text are retained while those that produce nonsense are dropped, and over time this results in a set of rules that produce about as good a mapping of spelling on to pronunciation as the language permits. (The term *rule* is used here in a purely functional sense; seldom would people be aware of or be able to state the rules they use.)

From this standpoint the minimal comprehension strategy can be seen to have a very undesirable side-effect. Because it involves severely limiting the effort to make sense of text, comprehension fails to drive the acquisition of decoding skills the way it does for the normal reader. The minimal comprehension strategy is thus a kind of developmental dead end. Such dead-end strategies have been identified in other areas of school learning (Bereiter & Scardamalia, 1985; Brown, Bransford, Ferrara, & Campione, 1983). These are strategies that adapt to immediate school conditions in such a way as to avoid the problems and challenges that would lead to development of strategies adapted to the wider set of real-world conditions. Undoubtedly such self-limiting strategies exist in everyday life as well. For instance, neurotic defenses may be thought of as adaptations that avoid ego damage but that in the process also avoid experiences that would promote development of a stronger ego (Vaillant, 1977).

The fact that local optimization can prove maladaptive in the long run is, of course, one reason why societies have things like parents, teachers, doctors, and prophets. Human beings are highly adaptive to the conditions in which they find themselves, but their long-term welfare often requires that this adaptation be tempered by factors lying outside the immediate situation. Adaptationist theorizing has practical value insofar as it can reveal both what is locally optimal about people's adaptations (so as to understand what causes and maintains them) and what is globally suboptimal about them (so as to bring more far-sighted wisdom to bear).

Educational Implications

When the preceding analysis is examined for educational implications, it turns out not to yield any single dramatic idea. But when its implications are put together, they suggest a fairly radical reorientation of educational treatment of disabled readers.

1. *Etiology and classification may be even less relevant to educational treatment than critics have supposed.*   Much of the most sophisticated research on reading disabilities deals with underlying causes and psychodiagnostic categories. Discussions of this kind of research almost always conclude with hopeful remarks about improvements in treatment that will eventuate from scientific progress along these lines (e.g., Fisk, Finnell, & Rourke, 1985; Mattis, 1981). Even though empirical results have overwhelmingly failed to support these hopes (Arter & Jenkins, 1979), they continually rise from the ashes. The reason seems to be that etiological and classificatory approaches have the great appeal of science, theory, and complexity on their side. Against this, arguments in favor of just teaching children what they don't know sound simple-minded and crudely empirical (note, for instance, the contemptuous tone of Thies, 1985, p. 101).

An adaptational approach makes it possible to understand why, on the one hand, there can be a complex system of causes resulting in a seemingly endless variety of reading difficulties, while on the other hand the problems that must be dealt with instructionally reduce to a few major challenges, and why knowledge of etiology may not be very helpful in figuring out how to meet those challenges. On theoretical grounds, an adaptationist approach can incorporate the discoveries of psychoneurological research into an explanatory network that takes account of the human capacity for intelligent adaptation. It thus makes for a scientifically defensible alternative to syndrome analysis and other psychometrically or medically inspired approaches.

2. *Treatment must somehow alter the conditions of adaptation.* This is the most fundamental idea to emerge from an adaptationist analysis. The minimal comprehension strategy cannot be expected to change so long as it remains a locally optimal adaptation to conditons.

According to the model shown in Figure 1, conditions could change in either of two main ways. The child's word recognition skills could improve. This would make it advantageous for the child to make greater use of bottom-up processes and to decode more of the words in a text, and this in turn might boost comprehension to the point where a minimal inference strategy was no longer the most adaptive. Alternatively, classroom conditions could change so that answering questions was no longer such a formative influence on comprehension strategies. For instance, shifting the emphasis from question-answering to summarization would mean that minimal inference was no longer an effective way to meet classroom demands.

3. *Educational treatment of reading disabilities should be opportunistic but not prescriptive.* This idea follows naturally from the preceding implications. In trying to decide what educational treatment to apply with a given child, an attempt to diagnose the child's underlying problem is not likely to prove very helpful, because it is the child's overall adaptation to reading that has to be dealt with, and this adaptation is likely to show only an indirect relation to etiology. More important is to discover, for any particular child, where the greatest opportunities for change lie. One child might show an ability to catch on to decoding rules, and so that would be a way to move. Another might show a willingness to tackle puzzle tasks calling for detailed comprehension. Another might show an inclination to read for pleasure, given sufficiently easy material. Another might be relatively unsusceptible to any direct change in reading behavior, but might be susceptible to isolated training in a strategically relevant subskill (Frederiksen, Warren, & Roseberry, 1985). This is not to propose an eclectic, multi-everything approach to instruction. Rather, it is to suggest that finding *any* way to break out of the child's self-limiting pattern of adaptation should be seized upon, with some reason to hope that this will increase the child's readiness to change in other respects.

4. *Training in spelling-to-sound skills is potentially valuable for most disabled readers, but gains from it will tend to be slow and effortful.* There is empirical support for this conclusion. Successful instructional programs almost always involve specific teaching of spelling-to-sound operations, but the success tends to be limited and hard-won (Naidoo, 1981). The preceding analysis provides an explanation that is not simply an aptitude deficit explanation. As suggested previously, an alternative or supplementary explanation is (a) that children following the minimal comprehension strategy tend not to use all the spelling-to-sound skills they actually possess (in keeping with

their reliance on top-down processes and the strategy of decoding only important words), and (b) that comprehension does not drive the evolution of better spelling-to-sound rules. Inasmuch as it would be impossible to teach a child all the context-sensitive spelling-to-sound rules that apply in English (see Venezky, 1976), an effective program must discover some way to get reading disabled students to begin developing such rules by themselves.

5. *Training aimed at deeper comprehension should improve decoding as well.*   This inference also follows from the idea that in normal reading development the effort to comprehend drives the development of decoding skills.

6. *Treatment should promote more intelligent, self-directed adaptation.*   It is understandable that disabled readers, given the way they are treated, should develop an attitude of helplessness (Butkowsky & Willow, 1980). But is is also clear that trying to engender in them an attitude of "I can do it if I try" may prove unrealistic (Licht, 1983). Unless children have some understanding of their cognitive strategies and of their consequences, there is nothing they can do but adapt to immediate contingencies. In a variety of experiments with children as young as 10, it has been found possible to engage them actively as coinvestigators into their cognitive processes (Scardamalia & Bereiter, 1983). A case study reported by Brett and Bereiter (1986) illustrates how coinvestigation was used with a disabled reader to help him develop an alternative to his existing self-limiting reading strategy.

Conclusion

There is one dangerous misapplication of an adaptationist view that must be guarded against. The danger is that it will be used as an excuse for doing nothing to remedy children's reading difficulties. Of course, any explanatory theory runs the risk of being abused in this way. But with an adaptationist approach there is the special risk that people will mistakenly believe it to imply that reading disabilities themselves are adaptive and therefore not to be tampered with. NO such idea has been advanced in this chapter.

There may indeed be cases in which reading disability itself represents an adaptation for some child. Not learning to read might, for instance, be a way of coping with intolerable parental pressures for achievement. But that is not the kind of adaptation that this chapter has been about. The children we have been talking about are ones who have some serious reading difficulty that they experience as a handicap and not as a benefit. The argument has been, however, that, in attempting to solve the problem of how to get along in school with this reading difficulty, many children employ adaptive strategies that give the appearance of being *additional* reading disabilities. So indeed they may prove to be, when it comes to making headway in the world at large. But unless we understand the adaptive significance of those reading strategies *within the immediate school context*, we may never succeed in helping the child develop reading strategies that are genuinely adaptive to the larger life contexts in which literacy matters.

References

Anderson, L. (1984). The environment of instruction: The function of seatwork in a commecially developed curriculum. In G. G. Duffy, L. R. Roehler, & J. Mason (Eds.), *Comprehension instruction: Perspectives and suggestions* (pp. 93–103). New York: Longman.

Arter, J. A., & Jenkins, J. R. (1979). Differential diagnosis – Prescriptive teaching: A critical appraisal. *Review of Educational Research, 49,* 517–555.

Bellack, A., Kliebard, H. M., Hyman, R. T., & Smith, F. L., Jr. (1966). *The language of the classroom.* New York: Teachers College Press.

Bereiter, C., & Scardamalia, M. (1985). Cognitive coping strategies and the problem of "inert knowledge." In S. F. Chipman, J. W. Segal, & R. Glaser (Eds.), *Thinking and learning skills: Research and open questions* (Vol. 2, pp. 65–80). Hillsdale, NJ: Erlbaum.

Brett, C., & Bereiter, B. (1986, April). *Cognitively based remediation in reading.* Paper presented at the annual meeting of the American Educational Research Association, San Francisco.

Brown, A. L., Bransford, J. D., Ferrara, R. A., & Campione, J. C. (1983). Learning, remembering, and understanding. In J. H. Flavell & E. M. Markman (Eds.), *Handbook of child psychology: Vol. 3. Cognitive development* (4th ed., pp. 77–166). New York: John Wiley & Sons.

Butkowsky, I. S., & Willows, D. M. (1980). Cognitive-motivational characteristics of children varying in reading ability: Evidence of learned helplessness in poor readers. *Journal of Educatioanal Psychology, 72,* 408–422.

Collins, A., Brown, J. S., & Larkin, K. M. (1980). Inference in text understanding. In R. J. Spiro, B. C. Bruce, & W. F. Brewer (Eds.), *Theoretical issues in reading comprehension.* Hillsale, NJ: Erlbaum.

Doehring, D. G., Trites, R. L., Patel, P. G., & Fiedorowicz, A. A. (1981). *Reading disabilities: The interaction of reading, language, and neuropsychological deficits.* New York: Academic Press.

Durkin, D. (1979). What classroom observations reveal about reading comprehension instruction. *Reading Research Quarterly, 14,* 481–533.

Fielding, L. G., Wilson, P. T., & Anderson, R. C. (1986). A new focus on free reading: The role of trade books in reading instruction. In T. E. Raphael & R.

Reynolds (Eds.), *Contexts of school-based literacy.* New York: Random House.

Fisk, J. L., Finnell, R., & Rourke, B. P. (1985). Major findings and future directions for learning disability subtype analysis.In B. P. Rourke (Ed.), *Neuropsychology of learning disabilities* (pp. 331–341). New York: Guilford Press.

Franks, J. J., Vye, N. J., Auble, P. M., Mezynski, K. J., Perfetto, G.A., Bransford, J. D., Stein, B.S., & Littlefield, J. (1982). Learning from explicit vs. implicit text. *Journal of Experimental Psychology: General, 111,* 414–4222.

Frederiksen, J. R., Warren, B. M., & Roseberry, A. S. (1985). A componential approach to training reading skills: Part I. Perceptual units training. *Cognition and Instruction, 2,* 91–130.

Gaskins, I. W., & Baron, J. (1985). Teaching poor readers to cope with maladaptive cognitive styles: A training program. *Journal of Learning Disabilities, 18,* 390–393.

Leinhardt, G., Zigmond, N., & Cooley, W. W. (1981). Reading instruction and its effects. *American Educational Research Journal, 18,* 343–361.

Licht, B. G. (1983). Cognitive-motivational factors that contribute to the achievement of learning-disabled children. *Journal of Learning Disabilities, 16,* 483–490.

Mattis, S. (1981). Dyslexia syndromes in children: Toward the development of syndrome-specific treatment programs. In F. J. Pirozzolo & M. C. Wittrock (Eds.), *Neuropsychological and cognitive processes in reading* (pp. 93–107). New York: Academic Press.

Naidoo, S. (1981). Teaching methods and their rationale. In G. T. Pavlidis & T. R. Miles (Eds.), *Dyslexia research and its application to education* (pp. 263–287). Chichester, England: Wiley.

Perfetti, C.A., & Roth, S. (1981). Some of the interactive processes in reading and their role in reading skill. In A. M. Lesgold & C. Perfetti (Eds.), *Interactive processes in reading* (pp. 269–297). Hillsdale, NJ: Erlbaum.

Scardamalia, M., & Bereiter, C. (1983). Child as co-investigator: Helping children gain insight into their own mental processes. In S. Paris, G. Olson, & H. Stevenson (Eds.), *Learning and motivation in the classroom* (pp. 61–82). Hillsdale, NJ: Erlbaum.

Schank, R. C. (1979). Interestingness: Controlling inferences. *Artificial Intelligence, 12,* 273–297.

Siegel, L. S. (1985, August). *Phonological deficits in children with reading disabilities.* Paper presented at American Society for Research in Child Development, Toronto.

Stanovich, K. (1980). Toward an interactive-compensatory model of individual differences in the development of reading fluency. *Reading Research Quarterly, 16,* 32–71.

Thies, A. P. (1985). Neuropsychological approaches to learning disorders. *Review of Research in Education, 12,* 91–119.

Torgensen, J. K. (1982). The learning disabled child as an inactive learner: Educational implications. *Exceptional Education Quarterly, 1,* 45–52.

Vaillant, G. E. (1977). *Adaptation to life.* Boston: Little, Brown.

van Dijk, T. A., & Kintsch, W. (1983). *Strategies of discourse comprehension.* New

York: Academic Press.

Venezky, R. L. (1976). *Theoretical and experimental base for teaching reading.* The Hague, Netherlands: Mouton.

Wong, B. Y. L., & Jones, W. (1982). Increasing metacomprehension in learning-disabled and normally achieving students through self-questioning training. *Learning Disability Quarterly, 5,* 228–240.

Chapter 3

Ecological Approaches in Reading Assessment

Corinne Roth Smith

Syracuse University

What makes for reading success and what makes for reading failure are very complicated matters. Reading success, as well as reading failure, are the result of the interaction of specific characteristics of the child with the school and home goals that the child is expected to meet, and the school and home environments in which the child is to "learn to live" and "learn to learn." Therefore, when we're so proud of little Allison because she could read before entering kindergarten, and in Grade 2 is still a year above grade level, we have many factors to laud besides just Allison. Her success has something to do with her family background, the type of school environment that has encouraged such growth, and the nature of the tasks her family and teachers have expected her to accomplish.

Conversely, when we're concerned about Sara's lack of progress in reading, it's seldom that she is altogether responsible for this poor achievement. Children don't grow up in a vacuum, they don't learn in a vacuum, and consequently their successes and failures do not occur in a vacuum. Therefore, in evaluating what contributes to Sara's reading difficulties, we have to go way beyond assessing just Sara. We have to study her home and school settings as well, in order to fully understand what may be aggravating some of Sara's delays and also what may be

ameliorating other problem areas so that these difficulties are minimized.

What if Sara comes from a very supportive home, has had superb
teaching, and still has difficulty learning to read because, at birth the
placenta was wrapped around her neck, she was deprived of oxygen,
and needed to be resuscitated? Her neural maturation has never caught
up with that of other children her age, and her achievement lags seem
to get greater year to year. One might argue that, in this case, Sara, "The
Learner," is to blame for her problems. But again, if all we paid attention
to was "what is *wrong inside* of Sara," we would be limiting opportunities
to accelerate her growth and development. Why? Can educators facilitate
Sara's educational and psychological growth by changing her directly?
No. If we pause to think about it, what we really do is change *task* and
setting variables so as to encourage Sara's development. Sara will change
only as a result of modifications in *what* we do with and expect of her,
how we do it and expect it, *who* does it and expects, and *where* it's done
and expected. In other words, when we try to help, our focus is really
on what, how, who, and where *we can change* so as to promote Sara's
development. Our focus is not on how we can instantly change Sara.
Sara will only change as *we* change all these what, how, who and
wheres.

If you are a parent, do you remember your struggle with toilet
training? It was you who did all the planning, rewarding, agonizing,
and running, so that in the end your child would succeed. It's the same
with school learning. When a child in our classroom cannot learn from
a phonics approach to reading, we experiment with a linguistic approach; if our student has difficulty attending when seated in clusters,
we move the child closer to our desk or to a study carrel; and when
Tommy cannot copy the first letter in his name, it is we who decide to
backtrack and teach drawing vertical and horizontal lines. In other
words, *we* are changing *what* we are expecting him to learn by altering
instructional objectives, and we are changing *how* he is expected to learn
by modifying our teaching approaches.

Clearly, whenever we try to assess why things are going well with a
student, and why some things aren't going well, we must turn the
looking glass both inward and outward. We have to identify what in our
tasks and settings is well matched to student characteristics, thereby
facilitating their development; then we recommend more of the same.
We also have to identify what in our tasks and settings aggravates
learning problems because they are mismatched with what the child is
ready to learn and how he or she learns best; then these need to be
changed.

This chapter builds a model of learner, task, and setting factors that we need to consider when assessing children's strengths and weaknesses and recommending intervention approaches (see Figure 1). We shall discover that this is not an easy matter. The reading-disabled group is extremely heterogeneous, with multiple causes, characteristics, and intervention needs. Therefore, each reading-disabled student is likely to be unique. It's no wonder, then, that research in reading disorders is so hard to conduct. Since it is hard to find very similar groups to study, contradictory findings abound and we don't know precisely to which children our results can be generalized. No wonder too that assessment measures and valid intervention methods must be specially tailored to each individual student's unique characteristics and circumstances.

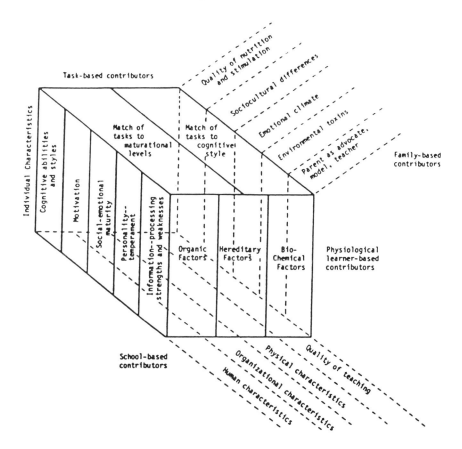

Figure 1. Learner, task, and setting contributors to learning success and failure

From Smith, C. R., (1985), Learning disabilities: Past and present. *Journal of Learning Disabilities, 18,* 513–517.

In taking an ecological approach to reading assessment, we must fully explore each face on Figure 1's cube. Once we have come to grips with the specific learner, task, and setting characteristics that interact to influence reading failure, we can better direct our intervention efforts. We shall explore the implications for assessment of physiological, individual, task-based, family-based, and school-based contributors to reading disabilities.

Physiological Learner-Based Contributors

Many physiological factors can cause slowed or uneven patterns of brain maturation. These, in turn, result in slowed or uneven learning progress. In our assessments, it is important to examine children's medical histories and to ascertain whether the reading-disabled student appears to be quantitatively or also qualitatively different from his or her peers. There are many students with reading disabilities who, due to slow brain maturation, are quantitatively behind their peers in reading ability, yet qualitatively very similar in learning needs and styles to younger typical children. For these students, a curriculum geared toward the readiness level of a younger child is very appropriate. In contrast, there are other students who, in addition to being quantitatively behind expectancies, have such uneven brain development that they are very different types of learners from even younger typical children. These students' qualitatively different styles of development require individually designed instructional methods that differ substantially from typical developmental reading approaches. Among the causes of such quantitative and qualitative discrepancies in learning ability are organic, hereditary, and biochemical influences.

Organic Factors

Brain differences can be related to structural brain deviations from normalcy or injury to an otherwise intact brain. Structurally, there is evidence that some individuals' reading disabilities are related to incomplete migration of brain cells to the gray matter during the second trimester of gestation. Autopsy findings report reduced density of brain cells, atypical cell types, unusual webbing of neuron endings, insufficient glial cells that provide structural/nutritional support to the brain's neurons, and right temporal lobes larger than the left when the reverse is more often the norm. Clearly, a brain structure not set to support the type of learning expected in our schools can lead to a wide gamut of delays in early childhood development and later school learning.

Injury to brain tissues also may result in developmental delays. Nevertheless, brain injury and reading disabilities are not the same thing. Brain injury, even to large areas, does not always deter learning to read, comprehend, and write; and reading disabilities can be caused by many other factors. The brain is "plastic"; undamaged areas can take over for those that have become less efficient. Therefore, the nature and extent of learning impairment caused by brain insults are hard to predict. Due to the brain's plasticity, and the fact that many brain injury indicators (e.g., birth difficulty, head injuries, EEGs, neurological hard and soft signs) do not tap brain areas involved in higher-level academic reasoning, we find nearly as many positive indicators of brain dysfunction among typical learners as among poor learners. The mere knowledge that a child may be brain injured tells us nothing about his or her learning strengths, weaknesses, and appropriate instructional strategies.

A more fruitful way for explorations of brain-behavior relationships to guide our instructional recommendations is by learning from the neuropsychological patterns that differentiate individuals with unique strength/weakness patterns. Through such new techniques as positron emission tomography, computer averaged EEGs, and nuclear magnetic resonance, we have found that typical learners have a dynamic interrelationship between brain areas. Their brain regions rarely work in isolation. Instead, the areas are intimately interconnected, any type of information processing generally activating several regions, each to a different degree. Differences in degree of specialization between corresponding areas in each hemisphere influence learning efficiency and styles. Reading aloud, for example, may activate as many as seven areas in each hemisphere, with the left hemisphere usually being somewhat more active. In contrast, reading-disabled students often underuse both hemispheres, or they overuse one, rather than sharing a great deal of activity between the same locations in both hemispheres. They do not develop the normal asymmetry between left and right areas of specialization. Children who overuse right-hemisphere strategies, for example, tend to prefer attending to wholes rather than analyzing and sequencing parts. This strategy is incompatible with the phonetic analysis and linguistic sequencing required in reading. On the other hand, those who overuse left hemisphere, analytic, sequential strategies tend to have difficulty quickly recognizing whole words by sight or revisualizing irregular spelling words.

We find that a large number of children with reading disabilities have motor weaknesses. While misarticulations can interfere with phonic acquisition, hand movement difficulties can interfere with the ability to put down on paper what one knows. The EEGs of these children often are immature, approximating those of younger, normal students. As typical children pay greater attention, their brain wave amplitudes usually increase, and the time needed for the brain to respond to new stimuli decreases. For some reading-disabled students, however, brain wave amplitudes are lower than normal; therefore, they have to put far greater than normal energy into attending to information. Their nervous systems are slow to respond, and slow up even more as the task continues. It makes sense that these students require longer time than is typical to process information and perform tasks.

Finally, neuropsychological studies report that inhibiting a response to something that has caught one's attention takes more neural energy than reacting. Because inhibition is harder, it is understandable that some children with reading disabilities can't help attending to distractions even when trying so hard to do their work.

Neuropsychological research is still in its infancy. It is not sophisticated enough to clarify the strength/weakness patterns involved in different forms of reading disabilities nor to prescribe specific interventions. Nevertheless, this research is beginning to shed light on some factors that can differentiate good from poor learners, offering us useful hypotheses regarding intervention. For example, if in the classroom or assessment session words that were correctly read 5 minutes earlier are now read incorrectly, or if handwriting deteriorates markedly as the child nears the end of a paragraph, one might wonder if this is one of those children for whom attention attenuates as effort continues. Trying an approach that recaptures attention with novel tasks and requires only a few minutes of practice at a time would shed light on whether this child "could do better if only he tried" or "can't do better because he's already using all the energy he has."

Hereditary Factors

Different brain structures, patterns of brain maturation, biochemical irregularities, or susceptibility to diseases that impair brain functioning may be genetically transmitted. There is a strong relationship in reading disorders among parents and siblings. Knowing that reading difficulties can be hereditary, it is imperative that we focus on the family's learning history during the assessment process. This involves grandparents as well as aunts, uncles, and cousins. If the family history shares some features in common with a child's developmental patterns, then perhaps this history also will shed light on prognosis and teaching approaches that were successful with similarly handicapped relatives.

Biochemical Factors

Some of the children we see suffer from biochemical irregularities which result in hyperactive or hypoactive behavioral states that make attending to learning tasks difficult. The activity level is not the important factor; but the inattention that it represents is. Knowing more about how these irregularities impact on attention can help guide our observations during assessment and impact our intervention plans.

Current thought is that hyperactivity of biochemical origin is due to an inability to inhibit distractions, which then deters focusing and sustaining selective attention. The neurochemical activity needed to inhibit attention to distractors seems to be deficient. The short attention span and distractibility in turn lead to poor impulse control, restless, and inappropriate, non-goal-directed body movements. The child's mind is by no means blank. Instead it is busy learning things that the parent or teacher find irrelevant. Research has found that stimulant medication acts on the brain's neurotransmitters to energize inhibitory mechanisms so that distractions can be screened out. Medication also seems to sensitize specific brain systems to incoming stimuli. In a large majority of students, stimulants seem to facilitate attention and behavior management in structured situations. They do, however, have negative side effects and seldom produce long-term social or academic gains. In addition, there is some evidence that learning in these children may be state-dependent. That is, if information has been learned while on medication, then it might be recalled efficiently only if on medication at the time of testing. This body of knowledge influences evaluators to attend to whether children are on or off medication at the time of testing, and whether their inconsistency in performance may relate to see-sawing medication levels. Most importantly, educators are influenced to actively plan very special educational interventions for students on medication, rather than hoping that the medication itself will produce a cure.

In contrast with the biochemically hyperactive child, it seems that the hypoactive youngster's learning may be deterred by overactive inhibitory mechanisms. This child is overfocused, ponders too long, is lethargic, overly attentive to details, can't arrive at rapid decisions, needs more sleep, asks few questions, and often commands little attention in the classroom because he is not disruptive. Some research suggests that sedatives tone down these children's inhibitory mechanisms, thereby allowing more stimuli to come to attention. Again, understanding the etiology of these behaviors helps us explain and plan for these children's slower work speed, poorer performance on timed tests, or less-than-expected comprehension.

Other biochemical irregularities about which we need to be knowledgeable include thyroid and calcium imbalances. Excess thyroid hormone results in hyperactivity, while thyroid deficiencies result in listlessness, placid behavior, and reduced motivation to put energy into learning. Abnormal elevation in calcium levels can result in personality alterations and permanent intellectual deficits. Finally, there is a great deal of controversy about whether periodic episodes of low blood sugar disrupt some children's behavior because the level of glucose required by the brain to efficiently process information has been reduced. We need to be alert to these possibilities and work with physicians to minimize the negative effects of biochemical irregularities on learning.

Individual Characteristics

In assessing students with reading disabilities, it is very important that we focus on their cognitive abilities and styles, motivation, social-emotional maturity, personality-temperament, and information-processing strengths and weaknesses. Once these factors are well understood, we can better explore which aspects of our curriculum, home, and school settings are well matched to a student's needs, and which are exacerbating his or her difficulties.

Cognitive Abilities

The measurement of cognitive abilities involves studying a child's intellectual capabilities and contrasting these with his or her achievement level in various areas. Due to the high correlation between IQ and academic achievement, intelligence testing has traditionally played a key role in assessment. IQ certainly is important to consider in predicting reading achievement and understanding reading delays. Nevertheless, its influence must be tempered by consideration of many other variables, because more than IQ goes into predicting achievement. IQ is an imperfect yardstick by which to set academic goals, correlating only 50% with achievement. Intelligence and achievement test performance seem to share in common such attributes as general knowledge and speed/quality of problem solving. The 50% of achievement that does not correlate with IQ appears related to such personality attributes as motivation, eagerness to accept challenges, perseverance, willingness to try hard, and optimism. These factors are of equal importance in judging what a child's ultimate reading expectancy might be.

More important than intellectual capabilities, the influence of experiential background must be considered when determining the level of reading a child may be capable of achieving. While IQ correlations do increase with genetic similarity, what has been laid down by the genes can be strongly modified by the environment. In other words, a child's potential may be set by genetics, but whether or not he or she reaches the limits of his or her potential depends on the environment. Therefore, it becomes our responsibility to encourage environmental modifications that will help the child achieve to the limits of his or her potential.

The intelligence testing situation offers a perfect opportunity to explore just how modifiable one's intelligence is. Intelligence measures can be selected that capitalize on a child's strengths and minimize the interfering effects of weaknesses (e.g., tests on which slow processing speed will not disadvantage the child, visual stimuli will heighten attention, motor demands are limited). The limits of one's potential can also be explored with nonstandard, testing-of-limits procedures. These procedures assume that errors on standardized intelligence tests tell us only what the child "did not do," and not what he "could not do." By hypothesizing about what is interfering with performance, and then modifying the task to accommodate this interference, a great deal can be learned about a child's intellectual potential and methods by which this potential can be realized. For example, when a 10-year-old girl's high anxiety level seemed to be interfering with problem solving on an intelligence test, we showed her the age markings on the protocol and praised her for responding to some questions above the 16-year-age indicator. The resulting pleasure in her achievements and enhanced self-confidence helped this child attack and solve many problems on which she had previously erred. These gains raised the question of how much low self-esteem and high anxiety were interfering with reading acquisition. For another child raised in a home devoid of blocks, puzzles, sequence-type activities, or the kind of verbal stimulation that would require her to think about similarities and differences, standard testing was followed with playing preschool games that involved similar types of reasoning. Later retesting reflected tremendous gains and shed light on the need to expand this little girl's experiential base in order to help ready her for formal instruction.

The second aspect of cognitive abilities that must be evaluated is the level of achievement in all areas, not just reading. If there are some academic areas in which the student demonstrates particular strengths, then we must analyze ways in which these strengths can be built on in reading instruction. Conversely, it is important to evaluate whether reading disabilities are creating disabilities in other achievement areas as well (e.g., written expression, math word problems, content area instruction) so that reading is not permitted to be the only avenue through which the child can become knowledgeable.

Cognitive Styles

Cognitive style refers to a child's preferred way of perceiving and interacting with the world. Many reading-disabled children's styles are inappropriate to classroom demands, thereby interfering with progress. These children are different from others in their styles of attending to information, organizing it, and rehearsing it for memory. Yet they may learn very well when tasks are modified to match their preferred style, or when taught more efficient learning strategies.

Three of the more frequently studied cognitive styles include impulsivity–reflectivity, high–low conceptual learning styles, and poor learner strategies. Many children with reading delays are impulsive in their approach to learning. They are underfocused and make decisions prematurely. Because they prefer to scan wholes, impulsive students often have an advantage over more reflective children in quickly overviewing situations, being open to incidental learning and a wide array of information, being sensitive to social cues, and solving inferential problems. But teachers seldom say "Hurry up, skim, and find the main idea." More often they teach toward the reflective youngster's more focused, analytic style. Although each child learns well through his or her own style, our schools prefer the reflective student who is more task oriented, takes more time to arrive at solutions, and likes to analyze and memorize details. If, during the assessment process, we feel that impulsivity is interfering with performance, then perhaps we might try covering the pictures in the child's text (so he or she has fewer cues with which to guess words), using a repeated reading procedure (so that comprehension rather than phonetic analysis can guide the child's decoding), or highlighting and underlining (in order to draw attention to details). In other words, assessment is not satisfactory if it merely documents a child's level of underachievement and describes his or her cognitive style. We must also use the assessment process to attempt modifications in how we present learning tasks to students, thereby discovering exactly what might work.

The second style, high–low conceptual level, reflects the child's nondirected or directed instructional needs. High conceptual level learners can generate their own concepts and alternatives for problem solving, provide their own rules, and consider different views. They are more inquiring, self-assertive, and capable of independently handling complex conceptual material. Unfortunately, the student with a reading disability often is a low conceptual learner: a categorical thinker who is dependent on rules, less capable of generating his or her own concepts and considering alternatives, and who has difficulty directing his or her own learning. If this is the type of student we are observing, then it is important for us to recognize that learning will be faster if a lecture rather than discovery approach is utilized. These children prefer rules before rather than after examples, because they need to be informed about the key concepts to be looking for. When asked open-ended questions such as "What do you think?" they often respond, "I don't know." If instead, however, they are given the choices to think about, these students often demonstrate ability to reason at much higher levels and with a great deal more cognitive flexibility. Therefore, if we are evaluating a youngster with reading comprehension difficulties who may be a low conceptual level student, it may be wise to repeat the comprehension measures, but this time offer direction by reading the comprehension question just before the youngster reads the corresponding paragraph. We might be surprised to find that, with guidance regarding precisely what to look for and think about, this student's comprehension is markedly enhanced.

Finally, we find that most children with learning difficulties exhibit very poor learner strategies. They tend to be inefficient in their learning, inactive, disorganized, and aware of neither their own cognitive processes on tasks nor of task demands. Since they put little energy into learning, no sustained, organized approach is evident. At times they seem unaware that memory is possible or desirable, and that there are strategies that might help them to learn. What happens when, during our evaluation sessions, we actually give these students a strategy for memorizing (e.g., revisualizing the faces of presidents when trying to recall their names; verbal associations to aid memory for vocabulary words; mnemonic tricks to recall the 13 colonies)? Often we find that, when given an efficient strategy to use, many of these students memorize very well. They do not have basic deficits in ability to learn. Rather, it is their inefficient learning strategies that prevent them from using their basic abilities to best advantage. Once we have discovered a memory strategy in the evaluation setting that helps a student deal more successfully with material, it is important to test its efficacy in the classroom as well.

Motivation

The best form of motivation comes from within the child. High motivation, engaging in tasks with responsibility, creativity, and effort, can help children achieve equivalent to students at least one standard deviation higher in intelligence. These types of students are internally controlled and feel personal responsibility for success and failure. Therefore, they put effort into work. If they fail, they blame their efforts rather than intelligence: "I went to the movies instead of studying, so I deserve what I got."

Unfortunately, low motivation often characterizes the reading-disabled and seriously hampers intervention efforts. Being externally controlled, these students hold outside, seemingly unalterable factors, or their own low ability, responsible for failure (e.g., "I failed because the teacher hates me; she smudged the dittos; I'm dumb anyway"). Any successes are attributed to luck, not to personal ability. These children may see themselves as inferior humans, expecting so little of themselves that it's worthless to even try. After years of failure, they have learned that it's safer to be helpless. Clearly, such self-attributions must be modified by helping the child become more successful and by praising his or her efforts rather than outcome. If effort is reinforced, it will increase and likewise augment chances for success. The evaluation situation is the perfect time to ascertain just how motivation affects progress and the types of rewards, privileges, student-paced learning, high interest materials, or other variables that could make the classroom a more exciting place to exert effort.

It is important to point out that there are many students with reading disabilities who are very highly motivated to succeed. Their efforts result in near grade level achievement, and their motivation masks the constant struggle, frustration, and inordinate effort to keep up. Observers need to be sensitive to this possibility and ready to suggest ways to make learning a more enjoyable experience.

Social-Emotional Maturity

Our students' feelings about themselves and how they get along with others are very key concerns, perhaps even more important than the ultimate reading levels they achieve. Social-emotional maturity is so very critical because often it impacts on adult job, family, and leisure time adjustment to an even greater extent than low intelligence or achievement levels. Unfortunately, behavioral disturbances are far more frequent among reading-disabled than nondisabled students. Their social relationships are deterred by their learned helplessness, their social imperceptions (e.g., not knowing how close to stand to others or how to read others' feelings), and their language disabilities (e.g., poor syntax and semantics in conversation, not knowing how to enter conversations or not asking questions to keep conversations going, being too egocentric in discussions, being so slow in conjuring up the words with which to communicate that the other party has lost interest). Their information processing inefficiencies may make them seem out of sync, not listening or looking on the same wave length as others. Such additional factors as inattentiveness, physical activity and restlessness, strong cognitive styles, maturational lags, unique temperaments, misarticulations, poor athletic ability, sloppy dress, disorganization, and the poor self-esteem engendered by others' responses further deter social relationships. When these youngsters try so very hard to succeed socially, and don't understand the reactions and rebuffs they get from others, it is no wonder that emotional difficulties set in. An ecological assessment must give priority to identifying those individuals and activities within a student's life that can begin to alter these self-perceptions. Equally important is the need to identify the student's deficient social skills and plan very structured lessons to address this area just as seriously as one would address reading. If the student achieves a very high degree of reading success, but still feels unaccepted and a failure, then job acquisition, maintenance, and pleasure with one's life circumstances will be severely compromised.

Personality-Temperament

Every child enters the family with behavioral characteristics that are uniquely his or her own. Some are easy children, others are difficult children, and yet others are slow-to-warm-up. Often, students with reading disabilities fall into the latter two categories. Their temperaments can make teaching difficult. Nonetheless, temperament can be modified by a good fit between the parent/teacher and child. A warm, supportive home and school environment which adapts to the child's temperament may help avoid such secondary emotional problems as depression or poor self-image. On the other hand, a home or school that is too hostile or critical, harbors expectations beyond the child's capabilities, or does not adapt its own temperament and interactions to the child's behavioral style, will only exacerbate the child's difficulties. Therefore, it is imperative that our ecological assessments include observation of the student in his or her natural settings, the home and classroom. These observations, together with interviews of individuals most closely connected with the child, will suggest ways in which interactions with the child can be modified so as to promote a more positive, appropriate personality-temperament for learning and social interaction.

Information Processing

Memory is affected by the efficiency with which information is processed and how this processing interacts with the youngster's cognitive, social, and motivational characteristics. Since, by definition, reading-disabled students are not remembering what we have tried to teach them, it is very important that our evaluation process address the visual, motor, language, and attention factors that may be interfering with progress.

Research has found that visual perceptual weaknesses present mild to moderate, but not severe obstacles to reading progress. They account for approximately 10% of reading problems, seeming to interfere most with reading acquisition at the kindergarten and first grade reading stages. Children with visual perceptual difficulties seem to have difficulty mastering the initial phases of reading, which rely on perception of words as gestalts. As they get older, these youngsters may have difficulty rapidly recognizing sight vocabulary, or spelling irregular words that require revisualization. Consequently, they often need to sound out words or guess from the passage's content. These children seem to process visual information very slowly. In some cases, visual images linger longer than usual, thereby limiting the time available to transfer this information to short-term storage before moving on. For example, if the eye moves too quickly to a second letter in the word, without the first image being properly stored, the two images may overlap and cause confusion. Sensitivity to such difficulties should help guide trial teaching efforts during assessment: reading words could be attempted again, but with more time permitted to scan each letter; irregular words could be pronounced the way they're spelled in order for phonetic strengths to aid memory.

Motor weaknesses are common to 75% of poor learners. Rather than interfering with skill acquisition, these weaknesses make it difficult for children to show what they've mastered. Verbal communication is inhibited my misarticulations, written communication is deterred by fine-motor weaknesses, and acceptance on the playground is diminished by incoordination. While these weaknesses are being remediated, the classroom teacher needs to compensate for their interference with demonstrating knowledge. There is no better place than the actual classroom to ascertain whether dictating answers might be more beneficial than writing them down, or being soccer scorekeeper more satisfying than goalie. The occupational and physical therapist are important consultants who can offer valuable insights and recommendations for remediation.

Language weaknesses often become the focus of evaluation, because over 60% of reading and spelling delays seem to be language based. Dealing effectively with language symbols is necessary for mastering reading, spelling, reading comprehension, written expression, foreign languages, poetry, and even high level math. Reading disabled children who have higher verbal skills are the ones likely to improve fastest in reading, because auditory processing is second only to IQ in contributing to reading success. By third grade, auditory perceptual, rather than visual perceptual skills, become more highly correlated with reading success, because higher level reading relies on the comprehension of a language system more so than the visual analysis of its symbols.

Slow auditory processing time characterizes many of these children. They seem to require longer time intervals between auditory stimuli to process them, or they need the stimuli to last longer. As brief stop consonants (e.g., b and t vs. m and s) can not be sustained, these present the most difficulty in decoding and comprehension. While vowel sounds can be sustained and present little difficulty, unfortunately it is the consonants that carry the meaning and pass by unprocessed.

Auditory retrieval weaknesses also contribute to reading disabilities. These children are slower and less accurate at naming common objects, so what they see or hear often doesn't get verbally labelled, rehearsed, or stored for recall. Difficulty searching their memories for letter sounds interferes with decoding progress. These word-finding difficulties are very similar to "blocking" on our best friend's name, and seem only to get worse as memory scanning continues. Consequently, a word read correctly at the beginning of a paragraph may no longer be recognized 10 lines later. If it appears that auditory processing deficits underlie a child's reading difficulties, the evaluation setting should be used to try out compensatory techniques: e.g., using only sustainable sounds in decoding exercises, aiding comprehension by speaking more slowly and pausing between phrases, enhancing memory by allowing time for verbal rehearsal.

Children who have not made the transition from the earlier gestalt phase of reading acquisition to the more analytic, sequential approach required for word analysis often experience difficulty segmenting words into their component sounds and sequencing comprehension information. Language weaknesses at the syntactic or semantic levels further interfere with comprehension, decoding clues, and written expression. Consultation with a speech pathologist can be helpful in developing programs that will aid language development and impact on reading acquisition and comprehension.

Poor attention can interfere just as severely with reading success as a language delay. Children with attention deficits focus insufficiently on relevant stimuli and find it hard to ignore the irrelevant. Catching attention seems to be easy. Sustaining it is the hard part. These children have many atypical physiological indices for attention: EEG response rate and peaks, heartrate deceleration, skin conductance and resistance. They are slow to notice stimuli and respond, and their attention wears down over time. This type of child needs to be given longer to respond, and can not take long work periods. If the attention deficit is very severe, it can actually cause visual and auditory processing deficits. Other children manifest attention deficits that are not of physiological origin, but rather reflect their impulsive cognitive style or weak verbal mediation skills. As part of the assessment process, it is important to sort these out, because the nature of the attention deficit will lead the examiner to try different kinds of compensatory approaches.

Task-Based Contributors

Exploration of the physiological and individual characteristics that contribute to students' reading disabilities is only the first step in developing intervention strategies that will enhance their development. Children's weaknesses may be aggravated by curriculum materials and methods that make demands on them that they are unable to meet. These methods and materials frequently are mismatched with children's maturity levels and learning styles. When appropriate matching of task characteristics to these children's uneven ability patterns and unique learning styles occurs, progress can be markedly facilitated. Teachers must continually ask, "In which way must I change *what* I am expecting students to learn and *how* I am asking them to learn it?"

Match of Tasks to Maturational Levels

We have seen that some students' reading disabilities reflect slow maturation in the visual, motor, language, and attention processes that underlie higher cognitive development. Each of these children has different sets of immaturities, with different rates and styles of passing through developmental stages. While many selective immaturities co-exist, each may appear at different times as both the cognitive demands of tasks and the child's strengths/weaknesses change. For example, Andrew was an excellent math and art student in kindergarten and first grade but had difficulty learning to decode words. The decoding difficulty was resolved by fourth grade; however, in ninth grade it once again surfaced in difficulty mastering French. In contrast, Sally was an excellent student in the first three grades, until writing demands increased and her painfully executed letter formations decreased both her motivation to write and the level of ideation she communicated. Developmental theorists conceptualize these students' delays as due to a time lag in the neurodevelopmental maturation of certain brain areas. They observe that, if our curriculum forges ahead too quickly, if we teach too much, too soon, too fast, these children are forced into faulty learning. They learn errors, are confused, and need to later spend time unravelling their thinking and unlearning their errors. If, in our zeal to educate children, we push those who are unready into error, we are likely to even further aggravate their delays.

After reaching an understanding of the student's individual characteristics, it is important for us to turn to the curriculum and, with equal scrutiny, question whether the academic tasks are geared precisely to what children are ready to master, rather than to their age and grade expectancies. If a good match occurs, the need for very special teaching techniques is reduced. Often a slowed rate of instruction geared to the typical development of a younger child is appropriate.

Developmentalists tend to advocate delayed school entry if a child is not ready to profit from the curriculum of the grade. Research finds that, although by the upper elementary grades children may catch up with their peers on such "low threshold" skills as copying and letter reversals, the threshold for such complex skills as speed of naming and language reasoning keeps rising so that catch up on these complex skills is difficult. Several studies report that those children who enter kindergarten, despite being unready, usually are retained by the sixth grade or placed at the bottom of their classes. Those who were very ready for kindergarten tend to be at the top of their classes 7 years later. Boys seem to be more immature than girls at the time of school entry, and most are at risk for not keeping up with the work of the grade. The ideal program is one that gears the curriculum toward each individual's needs and allows each child to progress at a comfortable pace. With current pressures for minimum competencies and teacher accountability, we need to be all the more sensitive to mismatches between curriculum demands and our students' readiness.

Our society is a pressure cooker and does not allow children time to catch up. While physicians all too often advise parents, "Don't worry, he'll catch up," we now know that we can't afford to take that chance. Intervention must begin as early as possible.

How do we begin to assess exactly *what* our student is ready to be taught so that our academic *content* can be appropriately matched? Smith (1983) and Sperry's (1974) work suggests nine parameters to follow in analyzing assessment, trial teaching, and observational data so as to decide on exactly what to teach.

1. *Evaluate previous learning opportunities.*   It is hard to evaluate the academic attainments of a child without knowing the nature and intensity of his or her previous learning experiences. Steven, a bright 15-year-old from a New York City private school, illustrates the importance of examining past teaching attempts. Referred because of his spelling difficulties, we found that Steven could easily learn new spelling patterns and generalize these to new words (e.g., learning "commercial" generalized to "superficial"). Despite his underachievement, Steven did not seem to be learning-disabled, because he did not

require a more intensive level of instruction than that available in a typical curriculum. When his teachers were consulted regarding recommendations for spelling instruction, they responded, "But we never teach spelling as a subject; these children just pick it up." Clearly, Steven did not just sponge it up. He had directed learning needs in spelling and had not been given the opportunity to learn. His school setting was a great contributor to what at first glance looked like a serious "learner-based" deficit. Steven subsequently received private tutoring in a typical developmental spelling curriculum. He went on to college, where he was not the best speller but nevertheless maintained a B average even in spontaneous written work.

2. *Consult the child.*   It is impossible to know what's going on in the child's mind. We can observe task execution in fine detail and analyze successes and errors, yet our conclusions are still only hypotheses. Why not make the youngster a partner in the evaluation process? We learn a great deal from asking how the child has gone about solving a problem. Shawn is a case in point. Shawn was a junior in high school with excellent comprehension skills. His decoding was slow but accurate. Shawn often analyzed words because he had trouble recognizing them by sight. His spelling was at a second grade equivalency, all misspellings being good phonetic equivalents. It was hypothesized that a visual memory problem interfered with spelling and sight recognition. On all memory for digit, letter, or object tasks, Shawn could recall at most three symbols that he had seen. Aurally, he could recall as many as seven or eight items. On a visual perceptual measure, Shawn earned 8-year-age equivalencies on all but one subtest, which required recall of a series of up to 12 designs. On this task, Shawn earned a perfect score, outperforming the average senior in high school. Having difficulty understanding this performance, we asked Shawn to explain how he recognized which of the four sequences matched the sample. Shawn's response was an eye opener: "I only looked at the two designs at the far right of the sample and became lucky; only one of the four choices had the same two designs on the right!" Knowing now that Shawn could visually process only two symbols at once, we designed a remediation program dealing initially with no more than three-letter sequences. A word family approach was used in order to provide Shawn sound clusters to expand memory capacity. Tracing/fading methods and visual discrimination exercises on which Shawn filled in missing letters were constructed. Finally, oral spelling was encouraged in order to utilize Shawn's strengths in working around his weaknesses.

3. *Expressive versus receptive task requirements.*   Often children fail to demonstrate their knowledge at an expressive level, yet we ignore

the fact that they may have good skill mastery at the receptive level. For example, we always ask children to give letter names, but we seldom dictate the names and ask children to point to the correct letter. By changing the letter naming task into an easier receptive task, we might in fact find that the child has mastered this information, but at a level different from that required in the classroom. The challenge then becomes designing a program that capitalizes on receptive expression of knowledge while building facility with sound retrieval. Similarly, teachers often refer students to the psychologist due to spelling difficulties, yet the psychologist reports back that spelling is at grade level. If we were to analyze the spelling measure, we might find that the student was asked to point to the one word among four that seemed correctly spelled. Back in the classroom, the student continues to fail because recall, rather than recognition, is being required. Taken in perspective, the assessment data are helpful in indicating the type of content with which the student is knowledgeable. The student's good visual recognition skills could be creatively utilized to help the student move from a receptive to expressive level of functioning.

4. *Social versus nonsocial settings.*   After an assessment, one might be tempted to say, "She can do it; she did it for me." However, this is not always so. Testing situations often overestimate what the child is capable of handling when back in the classroom. In a one-to-one situation, children receive more frequent praise, are more motivated to put energy into work, and have fewer distractors. We might unfairly pressure the youngster if we expect the same quality and consistency of performance in a busy classroom. For similar reasons, individually administered tests are prone to overestimate performance levels. Therefore, when administering a formal reading battery, it is very important that the grade equivalency be used only as a rough guide for where to begin an Informal Reading Inventory within the child's curriculum. It is the level at which the student is 95% successful decoding in his or her textbook, and 75% successful in comprehension, that should dictate appropriate placement. The formal reading test score can never be allowed to be the final determiner of program placement.

5. *Abstract versus concrete materials and responses.*   At times we require children to demonstrate skills at such an abstract level that we mistakenly conclude that the student is deficient in that ability. For example, in order to determine if auditory discrimination difficulties are interfering with phonics acquisition, we often dictate two similar words to a child and ask whether they are the "same" or "different." If the child fails, we may conclude that he or she requires auditory discrimination

training. Yet it could be that it was the abstractness of our measure, rather than the skill itself, that was hard for the child. If instead we dictate similar sounding words, but ask the child to point to the corresponding picture, we would be evaluating the same skill in a more concrete manner and reaching a more valid determination of the child's need for discrimination training.

6. *Verbal versus nonverbal tasks.*   For some children, capturing attention aurally tends to be more difficult than visually. In contrast, others are overloaded when scanning too many visual stimuli. Likewise, nonverbal responses such as pointing and copying are easier for some children, whereas verbal responses are easier for others. Therefore, in order to accurately determine what a child is able to handle, it is important to assess the area of weakness both verbally and nonverbally. For example, one may wrongly hypothesize that a semantic language deficit underlies a reading comprehension problem because the child performs poorly on a language measure involving verbal questions and responses. On a measure with picture cues, however, the student may exhibit much greater linguistic processing capacity. Therefore, the comprehension deficit seems to be specific to the modality used for information processing, rather than semantic facility itself. Such dis- crepancies in performance suggest the way in which classroom materials can be made more meaningful in order to enhance comprehension.

7. *Symbolic versus nonsymbolic tasks.*   Often we assess child- ren's abilities at the most symbolic level, and, therefore, do not accu- rately determine the precise content the child is capable of handling. For example, we usually evaluate a high school student's ability to recall details, sequences, and make inferences or generalizations after he or she reads the textbook material. In this case, the symbolic level at which we are presenting the information may deter ability to process it. Had we taken comparable material and read it to the student, we would have eliminated the need to deal with symbols and more accurately examined his or her ability to master class content.

8. *Sequential versus static items and responses.*   Dealing with each element in a series is much harder than dealing with each in isolation. For instance, if a youngster can't recognize the alphabet when all 26 letters are presented on one sheet, it would be important to try presenting fewer letters at a time. If the student is successful, there are clear implications for choosing a reading program that reduces the number of letters dealt with at one time. Likewise, research suggests that spelling lists might be mastered more quickly by reviewing only a

few words per day rather than the entire list. These types of hypotheses should be systematically tested in order to determine exactly what the child can handle.

9. *Long-term recall versus short-term recall versus no memory requirement.* Students may need to be tested at different recall levels in order for us to appreciate what they have learned and understood. For those who retain information well, essay exams or dictated responses seem not to be a problem. For many of our students, however, organized retrieval of information is difficult, and tasks that require recognition of information (e.g., multiple choice tests) or locating information (e.g., open book exam) more accurately reflect current comprehension levels. The challenge is to channel this comprehension into more efficient long-term recall. For example, if a student cannot independently link personal experiences with the reading content when using a top-down reading approach, the teacher may need to explicitly draw these associations from the student, or even engage in an experiential activity to build these associations.

Match of Tasks to Cognitive Style

Sensitivity to the impulsive–reflective styles, directed learning needs, and poor strategies that characterize many students with reading disabilities heightens the importance of modifying our teaching approaches to match these children's styles. Once we understand the way in which each child prefers to go about learning, we must scrutinize our teaching methods and modify them to be congruent with the child's preferred style. We also must encourage the development of more appropriate strategies.

The assessment of child–task matches becomes a very individualized, ongoing process for several reasons: not all methods work for all children; the same method may not work in all curriculum areas for any one child (e.g., the method required to comprehend a novel differs from that required to comprehend a science text); and the same materials or methods may, after some time, no longer work for a given child (e.g., we hear, "I used these reading materials for 6 months and she made such rapid progress; I don't understand why progress has stopped").

Where do we begin to assess *how* our student will best profit from instruction, so that teachers can appropriately match the *processes* required by their lessons? Let us discuss eight parameters to follow in analyzing assessment, trial teaching, and observational data so as to decide on the style most suited for teaching a particular child.

1. *Matching tasks to attending strategies.*   Students with reading disabilities often become overloaded when required to attend to
more than three or four elements at once. If this seems to be the case,
then we need to experiment with teaching the identical content by
breaking it into smaller chunks. Suzie, for example, stopped failing
weekly spelling tests when she was given four words to learn on each of
5 days, rather than 20 to practice daily. Similarly, Suzie mastered new
sight words very efficiently if five were taught at once. However, if she
was pushed to deal with six or more new sight words simultaneously,
she generally could recall only two or three.

Structuring tasks so as to draw attention to distinctive features,
reducing stimulus complexity, and reducing competing responses may
markedly improve the retention of children with attention deficits. For
example, if a child is impulsively guessing at words on an Informal
Reading Inventory, the examiner might cover the pictures to minimize
cues for guessing. If this works, it becomes a useful approach to attempt
in the classroom when the teacher's goal is phonetic analysis. For
children with b/d discrimination difficulties, the examiner might try
placing the letters on top of one another to see if this formation aids
discrimination. If so, this becomes a recommended way to organize class
worksheets. For children who can think of no strategy with which to
recall rote information, the examiner might try building association
value into material (e.g., note that Pennsylvania, the Keystone State, is
key-shaped, while Oklahoma is like a Panhandle; Eisenhower is pasted
on an army background, while Carter is recalled on his peanut farm and
Roosevelt in a wheelchair). Testing out whether encouraging imagery,
clustering of information, or mnemonic tricks aid recall also readily
translates into recommendations for how a teacher might present
content in the classroom. Similarly, by arranging eight words one per
index card we may be able to reduce stimulus complexity and aid recall.

One of the basic goals of assessment is to determine the optimal unit
size per pupil and optimal arrangement of learning materials. If we limit
material accordingly and arrange it in a fashion that grabs and sustains
attention, learning is likely to maximized.

2. *Matching time limits to information processing speed.* Recognizing that some students need longer time periods to process visual
and auditory information, in our assessment sessions we need to
experiment with such things as longer pause times or using sustainable
sounds for decoding instruction. We need to wait more patiently for
responses, and we need to permit time for the slow word finder to label,
verbally rehearse, or chunk what he or she is expected to recall. These
modifications are very easy to try out with standardized test items on

which the student was unsuccessful. The performance differences between standard and nonstandard administrations shed light on exactly what the processing capacity of a youngster is if given sufficient time to take it all in. It should be noted that other youngsters may require very rapid fire information presentation in order to grab and regrab attention. Again, this should be experimented with as part of the evaluation process.

3. *Matching task repetitions to students' practice needs.* For students with reading disabilities, practice does not always make perfect. Teachers may find it hard to understand why Tommy can't read the same word later in a paragraph, when he could read it on the first line. Why does his writing deteriorate as he gets to the bottom of a 100-word passage? One of our assessment goals must be to ascertain the number of task repetitions that will overwhelm and exhaust a student. If we are sensitive to the point at which deterioration is likely to set in after repeated memory searches, we will limit instruction accordingly and refrain from asking students to "do it just one more time." Guidelines regarding the amount of overlearning, at what intervals, and with what types of review are important to develop. A case in point is 13-year-old Rachael, who began her assignment with a good under-standing of many capitalization rules. However, after recording which of 21 capitalization rules was violated in 500 sentences, she became overwhelmed and confused about even those rules she had initially grasped.

4. *Matching tasks to students' stronger modalities.* While capi-talizing on students' stronger modalities in reading instruction makes intuitive sense, very little good research has been conducted on the efficacy of this practice. The research thus far indicates that matching by modality either helps or can't hurt. It may be useful to run a mini-experiment in which several methods are used to teach a child sight words (e.g., phonetic analysis, language experience approach, neuro-logical impress method). Testing the child at varying intervals for recall sheds light on the most efficacious methods to pursue.

5. *Matching tasks to cognitive style.* We have already explored the fact that, since many reading disabled students can not break away from their preferred way of perceiving their environment, we must alter our methods to be congruent with their styles. One might try telling impulsive students the word in order to match their global styles, and then ask them why the parts combine to sound as they do. One might see whether an impulsive student's comprehension will increase if

taught questioning techniques. This student might learn to attend better to details by correcting his or her own papers, underlining word endings, or outlining stories. The overly reflective student, on the other hand, may require attention drawn to subheadings in order to "see the forest from the trees." Likewise, low conceptual level learners need to be given the conclusions before doing experiments, in order to know what to be looking for; they need to be given the actual mnemonics that will aid recall because they have difficulty generating these independently. If discovery is not left to chance and learning strategies are built into tasks, these students will demonstrate much greater conceptual flexibility.

6. *Matching incentives to cognitive style.*   Children differ in what they find rewarding when putting energy into their studies. For some, high interest materials are sufficient. For others, teacher and parent praise is sufficient. For others, concrete rewards, privileges, contracting, charting, and following less favored with more favored activities are important ways of building motivation. An ecological assessment surveys the child's environment, determines "what turns him or her on," and builds these motivators into the academic setting. In doing so, we remain sensitive to those children who are trying as hard as they can, and who are already working at peak capacity. Adding more incentives may only frustrate these youngsters further and lead them to feel that their efforts are never good enough. For all children, acknowledgement of effort is far more important than the accuracy itself.

7. *Building generalization into tasks.*   Due to the myriad factors that impinge on performance, we can't expect our students to automatically transfer information or learning sets to appropriate situations. Having learned 10 sight words in the resource room, the child may not recognize them in his or her reading book when back in the classroom. We must get a sense of how much a student will generalize on his or her own, and then plan for generalization by building it into our tasks: e.g., use many examples to deepen application, instruct the same content in several settings, remind students to remember to generalize.

8. *Matching teaching instructions to students' learning strategies.*   The teacher/student match is critical to consider in class placement, because the impulsive teacher may overwhelm the reflective student with a constant barrage of information and tangents. On the other hand, the reflective teacher's slow-paced, detailed approach may bore the impulsive student. In some cases, teacher directions do not match those in the text, and the lack of a consistent strategy only increases student confusion. Most importantly, we must remember

what powerful models teachers are. Since children at the end of the year will tend to reason about the curriculum in a manner modeled by their teachers, the human match with the child's needs cannot be overlooked.

Family-Based Contributors

No assessment can be complete without dealing with the role that families play in fostering or inhibiting their children's ability to learn to full potential. Parents constitute children's first and most important school, their most powerful models, and their greatest advocates. They deserve as much attention in the assessment process as do children, curricula, teachers, and schools. The parent, as well as the student, needs to become a partner in the evaluation process.

Home visits are very helpful in gaining insight into family factors that may be contributing to or ameliorating learning difficulties. Whenever possible, parents should be encouraged to observe evaluations through a one-way mirror, accompanied by a team member who can explain what they are seeing. Such observation helps parents come to understand their children's needs, the role they play as parents, and how they might change. Parents are in the best position to inform us whether we are seeing a true picture of their child. They are in the best position to suggest techniques that they've found helpful; and they are often the only ones that can shed light on the family's part in the child's learning difficulties. Such intensive involvement in the evaluation process is a powerful teacher and helps with difficult decision making. Max's father, for example, shed tears for the first time publicly when observing his 10-year-olds' reading struggle and self-deprecating comments. After the session, he took his son in his arms and shared with him the pain of his own reading disability which, as a painter, he had kept well hidden. It was as though years of burdens had been lifted from Max's shoulders. He was relieved; his dad was great, and he too would be all right. Another time, Liza's father was observing his 14-year-old's assessment in the company of five other female clinicians. When questioned about his daughter's early language development, he responded, "What do I know of her language development; no one talks in this house; we're in constant chaos, everyone's screaming, that's why I . . ." and he continued to tell us about his many extra marital escapades. In each case, the family information was critical to a better understanding of the child's needs, and the partnership of the parent facilitated decision-making and follow through. The many ways in which families impact on children's learning are essential considerations in an ecological assessment: quality of nutrition and stimulation, sociocultural differences, emotional climate, environmental toxins, and parents as advocates, models, and teachers.

Quality of Nutrition and Stimulation

The most severe, long-lasting effects of malnutrition and sensory deprivation on brain maturation occur in the first 2 years of life, long before the child comes to our attention with a reading disability. Nevertheless, a hungry child is not likely to be highly motivated to attend to classwork. Similarly, a child whose home background does not provide the necessary foundation on which school goals can build is at high risk for learning failure. Cheryl, for example, came from a very loving yet insular Italian speaking home, devoid of newspapers and friendships in the community. Cheryl knew very little English when she entered school, had never been allowed to cut with scissors for fear of hurting herself, had little experience with American preschool learning toys, had never used crayons, and had no knowledge of such "Americana" as Sesame Street, Little Red Riding Hood, the Gingerbread Man, and Goldilocks. Although by third grade her English sounded like a native's, remaining voids in vocabulary and experiential background led to confusion, difficulty dealing with English phonemes, and at times an inability to relate to the topics being discussed in her text (e.g., zoo, outerspace). Cheryl's parents recognized their role in her problems and tried very hard to modify their situation.

Sociocultural Differences

Sociocultural minorities are overrepresented in disabled populations due to greater complications of pregnancy and birth, malnutrition, contact with toxins, accidents, and poorer medical care, all of which can compromise brain development. Because learning experiences are neurochemically represented in the brain, these children enter school with a set of cognitive structures and learning experiences that are mismatched with the middle-class school curriculum. The greatest mismatch is in language differences. We need to be sensitive to these factors so that participation in parent education programs can be encouraged and so that programs that better match students' experiential backgrounds can be developed.

Emotional Climate

School failure is correlated with family disorganization, divorce, emotional instability, maternal stress during pregnancy, poor parental temperament, and home reinforcement of behaviors incompatible with school success. Since any type of stress, pain, or effort activates the brain through increased blood flow, it makes sense that emotional states can cause neurological diseases (e.g., tension headaches), intensify a disease process (e.g., bring on seizures), or simulate a neurological disorder (e.g., hysterical paralysis of a limb). If environmental stress can trigger emotional states that become unique brain states, then these altered brain states can contribute to learning problems. Consequently, it is very important if a child is troubled that we learn the source of these troubles, and intervene to create an emotional state more capable of tackling learning.

Environmental Toxins

There is a good deal of evidence that, because the fetus has no placental barrier against toxic substances, maternal cigarette smoking and alcohol can result in later hyperactivity and learning problems. Although it is too late to do anything about this by the time we are studying a child's reading disabilities, it is not too late to investigate the current influence of toxins such as environmental lead, mercury, marijuana, carbon monoxide, and toxins brought home by parents from the workplace. These may impact in subtle ways to decrease attention and school achievement. While the toxic effects of food additives, preservatives, and artificial colors have received much attention in recent years, it seems that these impact on attention and activity level for only a small number of young preschoolers.

Parents as Advocates, Models, and Teachers

It is our role to suggest ways in which parents can help ameliorate learning difficulties by becoming better advocates, models, and teachers for their children. Research clearly indicates that intelligence and school achievement are more highly related to the quality of the parent child interaction than to socioeconomic status or perinatal stress. Therefore, the family can do much to make up for a poor start in life. Unfortunately, we find that at times parents express less affection for their reading disabled offspring than for other siblings, and they may expect even less of them than the students expect of themselves. These children's successes may be viewed less positively, and their failures more negatively, than those of nondisabled children. Clearly, parental interactions with their offspring play a key role in helping to overcome learning difficulties, and we have a responsibility to come to grips with these in our evaluation process.

School-Based Contributors

Several school factors contribute to a student's academic and social-emotional development: quality of teaching, physical characteristics, organizational characteristics, and human characteristics. Observation within the students' classrooms and discussion with their teachers are important in ascertaining which school features may be used to overcome difficulties, and which may be aggravating the problems.

Quality of Teaching

The intensity and quality of past teaching attempts often are reflected in the gaps shown by reading disabled children. Before we hasten to "blame the child" for his or her learning weaknesses, we must be certain that the child has had every opportunity to profit from good instruction. An understanding of the child's past learning experiences sheds light on the current situation and sets a direction for change.

Physical Characteristics

Background noise, meaningful noise, and visual distractions deter attention equally for both typical and disabled learners. However, students with reading disabilities can least afford any more lost opportunities for learning. Consequently, their classroom settings need to be evaluated, so that these distractions are minimized and factors that can enhance effort and attention are maximized: pleasant surroundings, sitting in clusters of two or three desks rather than in rows, having the teacher circulate during instruction, sitting front and center near the teacher, smaller class size, and smaller schools. While open-space settings do not seem to influence academic achievement, they do lend themselves to greater interaction with peers and more favorable attitudes toward school.

Organizational Characteristics

Placement decisions can be made only after sorting out the academic, emotional, and social pros and cons of labelling and participation in special programs. It has been found that academic gains are greater in structured than open-education programs, due to greater time spent on task. Certainly, placement should be guided by that environment in which the child will have most opportunity to practice his or her skills, model age appropriate social behaviors, and maintain a positive sense of self.

Human Characteristics

Recognizing that teacher–student interactions tend to be more numerous, positive, and of higher quality in special classes, it is important that we work toward developing these same interaction patterns in the mainstream. Unfortunately, studies find that the interactions of many reading-disabled children with their regular class teachers may be deterred by more-negative teacher attitudes toward boys, children of low socioeconomic status, racial minorities, low achievers, and those with less positive nonverbal behavior. Of course, these attributes are all characteristic of children with learning difficulties. Research indicates that many of these children are less popular and accepted than their normal achieving classmates. They often are ignored by teachers and peers when initiating verbal interactions, they are judged more negatively by teachers, they are often objects of negative statements, and they frequently receive criticism and warnings from teachers. It seems that, as their appearance and athletic abilities improve, so does their social status. Knowing this, we educators must keep our eyes open for how life in the classroom might be different for students with reading disabilities than for their peers. We must then work toward modifying the setting in order to promote the child's success and integration.

Conclusions

Assessment is critical to planning meaningful interventions for students with reading difficulties. An ecological approach to reading assessment responds to the insufficiency of traditional methods in specifying precisely what students are ready to learn and how they might learn best. Traditional methods do not comprehensively address the learner, task, and setting factors that interact to make each student's needs unique.

By now it should be evident that assessment is not the same as testing. There are many other sources of information: records, observations in natural settings, interviews, trial teaching, behavior and academic checklists, asking the child. Assessment conclusions become more valid and generalizable the more closely the evaluation criteria coincide with classroom behavioral and academic objectives. The more measurement can take place right in the classroom and right on the actual curriculum, the better.

A significant problem with our standardized testing tools is that they hold the environment constant in order to specify how children compare with typical peers in the products of their learning. These tools contradict our sensitivity to the fact that children live and learn within an ecological system that impacts on their successes and failures. While the results of standardized measures are useful to our understanding of a student, they do not tell us how tasks and environments can be altered to maximize success.

In contrast, a process approach in reading assessment holds the child constant and changes the tasks and settings, just as intervention will do. While our standard tools tend to tell us what the child with reading disabilities "can't" do, process assessment helps discover under what conditions a child "can." We have seen that we do this by hypothesizing about what the interference with performance might be, modifying the task or setting accordingly, having the student attempt the task again, and then observing whether or not there are any gains (e.g., increased time to process information, guiding attention to salient features, heightening motivation, teaching learning strategies). If gains are apparent, then we've identified a "performance difficulty" when specific task attributes are incongruent with the child's way of knowing. These task modifications become an important part of the recommended classroom techniques. In process assessment, deficits at first only mean that the child *didn't*, not *couldn't*. While test manuals will admonish against altering instructions or environments, it is the very discrepancy between initial performance and performance after alterations that tells us what competencies a child does have if the task is matched to his or her preferred strategies. We put our hypotheses to the ultimate test when we implement them in the classroom and measure their impact.

What if the child is still unsuccessful after these alterations? Then we assume that there is an ability deficit. The objective, in any form, is too hard for the child. We then use task analysis to break the objective into easier components, until we identify the portion of the task the child has actually mastered, the hierarchy for teaching, and the child's unique ways of going about learning.

Clearly, there is no easy way to understand reading disabilitiies. The complexities that go into each individual's manifestations of reading disabilities are nearly impossible to grasp. Since we as educators must take responsibility for analyzing how the nature of our tasks and settings can be matched to each child's unique abilities and learning styles, we are responsible for taking a broad view of children. Children will change only as a result of what we do with and expect of them, how we do it and expect it, who does it and expects it, and where it's done and expected. Therefore, in taking an ecological approach to reading assessment, we look inward as well as outward, for no one facet of the puzzle can be understood without the others.

Suggested Readings
Physiological Learner-Based Contributors

Organic Factors

Duffy, F. H., & Geschwind, N. (1985). *Dyslexia: Current status and future directions.* Boston: Little, Brown & Company College-Hill Press.

Gaddes, W. H. (1985). *Learning disabilities and brain function: A neuropsychological approach* (2nd ed.). New York: Springer Verlag.

Rourke, B. P., Fisk, J. L., & Strang, J.D. (1986). *Neuropsychological assessment of children: A treatment-oriented approach.* New York: Guilford Press.

Hereditary Factors

Smith, S. D. (1985). *Genetics and learning disabilities.* Boston: Little, Brown & Company College-Hill Press.

Biochemical Factors

Denckla, M. B. (1979). Childhood learning disabilities. In K. M. Heilman & E. Valenstein (Eds.), *Clinical neuropsychology.* New York: Oxford University Press.

Gadow, K. D. (1985). *Children on medication: Vol. 1. Hyperactivity, learning disabilities, and mental retardation.* Boston: Little, Brown & Company College-Hill Press.

Ross, D. M., & Ross, S. A. (1982). *Hyperactivity: Current issues, research, and theory* (2nd ed.). New York: John Wiley & Sons.

Swanson, J. M., & Kinsbourne, M. (1976). Stimulant-related state-dependent learning in hyperactive children. *Science, 192,* 1354–1357.

Individual Characteristics

Cognitive Abilities

Haywood, H. C., & Switzky, H. N. (1986). The malleability of intelligence: Cognitive processes as a function of polygenic-experiential interaction. School Psychology Review, 15, 245–255.

Smith, C. R. (1980). Assessment alternatives: Non-standard procedures. *School Psychology Review, 9,* 46–57.

Cognitive Styles

Coop, R. H., & Sigel, I. E. (1971). Cognitive style: Implications for learning and instruction. *Psychology in the Schools, 8,* 152–161.

Gersten, R., Woodward, J., & Darch, C. (1986). Direct instruction: A research-based approach to curriculum design and teaching. *Exceptional Children, 53,* 17–31.

Hunt, D. E. (1974). Learning styles and teaching strategies. *High School Behavioral Science, 2,* 22–34.

Hunt, D. E., Joyce, B. R., Greenwood, J., Noy, J. E., Reid, R., & Weil, M. (1974). Student conceptual level and models of teaching: Theoretical and empirical coordination of two models. *Interchange, 5,* 19–30.

Keogh, B. K. (1973). Perceptual and cognitive styles: Implications for special education. In L. Mann & D. A. Sabatino (Eds.), *The first review of special education.* Philadelphia: JSE Press.

McLachlan, J. F. C., & Hunt, D. E. (1973). Differential effects of discovery learning as a function of conceptual level. *Canadian Journal of Behavioral Science, 5,* 152–160.

Motivation

Adelman, H. S., & Chaney, L. A. (1982). Impact of motivation on task performance of children with and without psychoeducational problems. *Journal of Learning Disabilities, 15,* 242–244.

Adelman, H. S., & Taylor, L. (1983). Classifying students by inferred motivation to learn. *Learning Disability Quarterly, 6,* 201–206.

Diener, C., & Dweck, C. (1978). An analysis of learned helplessness: Continuous changes in performance, strategy, and achievement cognitions following failure. *Journal of Personality and Social Psychology, 35,* 451–462.

Grimes, L. (1981). Learned helplessness and attribution theory: Redefining children's learning problems. *Learning Disability Quarterly, 4,* 91–100.

Malouf, D. (1983). Do rewards reduce student motivation? *School Psychology Review, 12,* 1–11.

Wiener, B. (1980). *Human motivation.* New York: Holt, Rinehart, & Winston.

Personality-Temperament

Chess, S., & Thomas, A. (1986). *Temperament in clinical practice.* New York: Guilford Press.

Minskoff, E. (1980). Teaching approach for developing nonverbal communication skills in students with social perception deficits. Part I. The basic approach and body language cues. *Journal of Learning Disabilities, 13,* 118–124.

Pullis, M. (1985). LD students' temperament characteristics and their impact on decisions by resource and mainstream teachers. *Learning Disability Quarterly, 8,* 109–122.

Valenstein, E., & Heilman, K. M. (1979). Emotional disorders resulting from lesion of the central nervous system. In K. M. Heilman & E. Valenstein (Eds.), *Clinical neuropsychology.* Oxford, England: Oxford University Press.

Information Processing

Brown, A. L. (1975). The development of memory: Knowing, knowing about knowing, and knowing how to know. In H. W. Reese (Ed.), *Advances in child development and behavior* (Vol. 10). New York: Academic Press.

Brown, A. L. (1978). Knowing when, where, and how to remember: A problem of metacognition. In R. Glaser (Ed.), *Advances in instructional psychology.* Hillsdale, NJ; Erlbaum.

Butler, K. G., & Wallach, G. P. (1982). *Language disorders and learning disabilities.* Rockville, MD: Aspen Pub.

Ceci, S. J. (1983). Automatic and purposive semantic processing characteristics of normal and language/learning-disabled children. *Developmental Psychology, 19,* 427–439.

Ceci, S. J. (Ed.). (1986). *Handbook of cognitive, social, and neuropsychological aspects of learning disabilities* (Vols. 1 & 2). Hillsdale, NJ: Erlbaum.

Flavell, J. H. (1976). Metacognitive aspects of problem solving. In L. B. Resnick (Ed.), *The nature of intelligence.* Hillsdale, NJ: Erlbaum.

Hagen, J. W., Jongeward, R. H., & Kail, R. V. (1975). Cognitive perspectives on the development of memory. In H. W. Reese (Ed.), *Advances in child development and behavior* (Vol. 10). New York: Academic Press.

John, E. R., Karmel, B. Z., Corning, W. C., Easton, P., Brown, D., Ann, H., John, M., Harmony, T., Prichep, L., Toro, A., Gerson, I., Bartlett, F., Thatcher, R., Kay, H., Valdes, P., & Schwartz, E. (1977). Neurometrics. *Science 196,* 1393–1410.

John, E. R., Thatcher, R., Smith, C., & Kaye, H. (1977, March). *Neurometrics.* Symposium presented at the Association for Children with Learning Disabilities, 14th International Conference, Washington, DC.

Kavale, K. A. (1981). The relationship between auditory perceptual skills and reading ability: A meta-analysis. *Journal of Learning Disabilities, 14,* 539–546.

Kavale, K. A. (1982). Meta-analysis of the relationship between visual perceptual skills and reading achievement. *Journal of Learning Disabilities, 15,* 42–51.

Kinsbourne, M., & Caplan, P. (1979). *Children's learning and attention problems.* Boston: Little, Brown, & Company.

Lassen, N. A., Ingvar, D. H., & Skinhøj, E. (1978). Brain function and blood flow. *Scientific American, 239,* 62–71.

Pelham, W. E. (1981). Attention deficits in hyperactive and learning disabled children. *Exceptional Education Quarterly, 2*(3), 13–23.

8 SMITH

8 SMITH

Wallach, G. P., & Butler, K. G. (1984). *Language learning disabilities in school-age children.* Baltimore, MD: Williams & Wilkins.

Task-Based Contributors

Match of Tasks to Maturational Levels

Ames, L. B. (1977). Learning disabilities: Time to check our roadmaps? *Journal of Learning Disabilities, 10,* 328–330.
Fuchs, L. S., & Fuchs, D. (Eds.). (1986). Mini-series on linking assessment to instructional interventions. *School Psychology Review, 15,* 317–374.
Smith, C. R. (1986). The future of the LD field: Intervention approaches. *Journal of Learning Disabilities, 19,* 461–472.
Sperry, V. B. (1974). *A language approach to learning disabilities.* Palo Alto, CA: Consulting Psychologists Press.
Tucker, J. A. (1985). Curriculum-based assessment. *Exceptional Children, 52,* entire issue.
Zigmond, N., & Miller, S. E. (1986). Assessment for instructional planning. *Exceptional Children, 52,* 501–509

Match of Tasks to Cognitive Style

Deshler, D. D., & Schumaker, J. B. (1986). Learning strategies: An instructional alternative for low-achieving adolescents. *Exceptional Children, 52,* 583–590.
Graham, S., & Freeman, S. (1985). Strategy training and teacher- vs. student-controlled study condition: Effects on LD students' spelling performance. *Learning Disability Quarterly, 8,* 267–274.
Pearl, R. (1982). LD children's attributions for success and failure: A replication with a labeled LD sample. *Learning Disability Quarterly, 5,* 173–176.
McLeskey, J., Reith, H. J., & Polsgrove, L. (1980). The implications of response generalization for improving the effectiveness of programs for learning disabled children. *Journal of Learning Disabilities, 13,* 287–290.
Miller, M., & Rohr, M. E. (1980). Verbal mediation for perceptual deficits in learning disabilities: A review and suggestions. *Journal of Learning Disabilities, 13,* 319–321.
Smith, C. R. (1985). Learning disabilities: Past and present. *Journal of Learning Disabilities, 18,* 513–517.
Stokes, T. F., & Baer, D. M. (1977). An implicit technology of generalization. *Journal of Applied Behavior Analysis, 10,* 349–367.
Torgeson, J. K. (1980). Conceptual and educational implications of the use of efficient task strategies by learning disabled children. *Journal of Learning Disabilities, 13,* 364–371.

Torgesen, J., & Goldman, T. (1977). Verbal rehearsal and short-term memory in reading disabled children. *Child Development, 48,* 56–60.

Family-Based Contributors

Quality of Nutrition and Stimulation

Greenough, W. T. (1976). Enduring brain effects of differential experience and training. In M. R. Rosenzweig & E. L. Bennet (Eds.), *Neural mechanisms of learning and memory.* Cambridge, MA: MIT Press.

Krech, D., Rosenzweig, M. R., & Bennett, E. L. (1966). Environmental impoverishment, social isolation, and changes in brain chemistry and anatomy. *Physiology and Behavior, 1,* 99–104.

Rosenzweig, M. R. (1966). Environmental complexity, cerebral change, and behavior. *American Psychologist, 21,* 321–332.

Sociocultural Differences

Bakker, D. J. (1984). The brain as a dependent variable. *Journal of Clinical Neuropsychology, 6,* 1–6.

Lerner, B. (1981). The minimum competence testing movement: Social scientific, and legal implications. American Psychologist, 36, 1057–1066.

Emotional Climate

Abramson, M., Willson, V., Yoshida, R. K., & Hagerty, G. (1983). Parent's perceptions of their learning disabled child's educational performance. *Learning Disability Quarterly, 6,* 184–194.

Forness, S. R. (1981). Concepts of learning and behavior disorders: Implications for research and practice. Exceptional Children, 48, 56–64.

Environmental Toxins

Swanson, J. M., & Kinsbourne, M. (1980). Food dyes impair performance of hyperactive children on a laboratory learning test. *Science, 207,* 1485–1487.

Thatcher, R. W., & Lester, M. L. (1985). Nutrition environmental toxins and computerized EEG: A mini-max approach to learning disabilities. *Journal of Learning Disabilities, 18,* 287–297.

Weiss, B., Williams, J. H., Margen, S., Abrams, B., Caan, B., Citron, L. J., Cox, C., McKibben, J., Ogar, D., and Shultz, S. (1980). Behavioral responses to artificial food colors. *Science, 207,* 1487–1489.

Parents as Advocates, Models, and Teachers

Werner, E. E. (1980).Environmental interaction in minimal brain dysfunction. In H. E. Rie & E. D. Rie (Eds.), *Handbook of minimal brain dysfunction*. New York: John Wiley & Sons.

Werner, E. E., & Smith, R. (1977). *Kauai's children come of age*. Honolulu, HI: University of Hawaii Press.

Williams, E. (1983). The family. In C. R. Smith, *Learning disabilities: The interaction of learner, task, and setting*. Boston: Little, Brown, & Company.

School-Based Contributors

Quality of Teaching

Hiltonsmith, R. (1983). The school. In C. R. Smith, *Learning disabilities: The interaction of learner, task and setting*. Boston: Little, Brown, & Company.

Smith, C. R. (1983). *Learning disabilities: The interaction of learner, task, and setting*. Boston: Little, Brown, & Company.

Wolff, R. M. (1977). *Achievement in America: National report of the United States for the International Educational Achievement Project*. New York: Teachers College Press.

Physical Characteristics

Good, T., & Brophy, J. (1978), *Looking in classrooms*. New York: Harper & Row.

Organizational Characteristics

Johnson, D. W., Johnson, R. T., Warring, D., & Maruyama, G. (1986). Different cooperative learning procedures and cross-handicap relationships. *Exceptional Children, 53,* 247–252.

Lieberman, L. MN. (1986). *Special Educator's guide to regular education*. Newtonville, MA: Glo Worm Pub.

Meisel, C. J. (1985). *Mainstreaming handicapped children: Outcomes, controversies, and new directions*. Hillsdale, NJ: Lawrence Erlbaum Association.

Morsink, C. V. (1984). *Teaching special needs students in regular classrooms*. Boston: Little, Brown, & Company.

Reynolds, M. C., Wang, M. C., & Walberg, H. J. (1987). The necessary restructuring of special and regular education. *Exceptional Children, 53,* 391–398.

Zigmond, N., Villecorsa, A., & Leinhardt, G. (1982). Reading instruction for students with learning disabilities. In K.B. Butler & G. P. Wallach (Eds.), *Language disorders and learning disabilities*. Rockville, MD: Aspen Publishers.

Human Characteristics

Brophy, J., & Good, T. (1974). *Teacher–student relationships.* New York: Holt, Reinhart, & Winston.

Garrett, M. K., & Crump, W. D. (1980). Peer acceptance, teacher preference, and self-appraisal of social status among learning disabled students. Learning Disability Quarterly, 3(3), 42–48.

Jones, V. F., & Jones, L. S. (1986). *Comprehensive classroom management: Creating positive learning environments* (2nd ed.). Rockleigh, NJ: Allyn & Bacon.

LaGreca, A. M., & Mesibov, G. B. (1981). Facilitating interpersonal functioning with peers in learning disabled children. *Journal of Learning Disabilities, 14,* 197–199.

Washington, V. (1979). Noncognitive effects of instruction: A look at teacher behavior and effectiveness. *Educational Horizons, 57,* 209–213.

Chapter 4

Prevention of Reading Problems

Rosa A. Hagin

Fordham University

Most people would agree that, compared with intervention after a problem has occurred, prevention is not only easier, it is probably cheaper and better for one's mental health. This chapter will consider the validity of this piece of folk wisdom with regard to reading problems. It will deal with the prevention of reading problems first, through some general preventive principles as they relate to the teaching of reading, and second through an illustration of a specific preventive approach that has continued in public schools in New York City for the past dozen years.

General Principles of Prevention

Early events in a child's life are reflected in later outcomes. Studies of school dropouts and poorly performing high school graduates testify to the significant role of reading with these educational failures. For example, Fitzsimmons S. J., Cheever J., Leonard E. and Macunovich D. (1969) found, in a retrospective review of school records, that signs of learning problems were apparent early in the school lives of these pupils: 50% of the dropouts or low achieving graduates were identifiable by second grade, 75% by fourth grade, and 90% by seventh grade. These investigators noticed signs of "spreading failure" first in the areas of reading, then with mathematics, and, later, in the content subjects as well. They concluded that communication skills like reading are vital to school success.

Prevention of reading problems also makes sense financially. Special remedial provisions add considerably to educational costs. The various pull-out or resource room services double the per-pupil costs, because the budget must provide both the per-pupil cost for the regular classroom seat as well as a proportion of the resource room costs, 1/20th to 1/30th depending upon the number of children assigned to the remedial program. The self-contained special class programs are even more costly because of limitations in enrollments resulting in higher individual costs per pupil, as well as the provision of auxiliary services such as salaries for educational assistants, transportation, and diagnostic and support services. Tuition costs for special schools for learning disabled children may range even higher than self-contained classes. The costs of these remedial services contrast with the per-pupil costs of a preventive program operated with the services of a teacher and an educational assistant: $636 per year for a 2-year period in the early grades.

When one considers that 1,800,000 children in the United States have been identified as learning disabled, the costs for remediation *after* failure has occurred represent a significant investment of education funds. While a variety of educational provisions are necessary for the appropriate education of all children in our schools, prudent planning would lead to the consideration of prevention as a part of the cascade of educational services to children at risk for reading failure.

Apart from financial considerations, the mental health effects of learning failure recommend consideration of preventive approaches. In a report of the President's Commission on Mental Health, Bryant (1978) stated that early identification and intervention are critical if children are to avoid the self-devaluation resulting from reading failure. He further stated that providing every child the opportunity for success in learning should be designated as an area of highest priority in the mental health movement in our country.

Definitions of Prevention

Youngsters to whom I give the Wechsler Intelligence Scale for Children often define the word *prevention* as "making something not happen." Dictionary definitions of prevention describe it as action to avoid occurrence of a disease or disability in large populations. The classical public health definition of prevention (Goldston, 1977) is a three-part one with special relevance to preventive approaches in education:

> *primary prevention:* actions taken prior to the onset of a disease to intercept its causation or to modify its course.
> *secondary prevention:* early diagnosis and treatment.
> *tertiary prevention:* rehabilitation efforts to reduce the residual effects of an illness or a disorder (p. 19).

Primary prevention characterizes many of the medical efforts that have resulted in an increase in the number of preventable diseases. In our lifetimes, these efforts have resulted in the virtual disappearance of polio, measles, and typhoid fever. Prenatal detection and monitoring of pregnancies have made it possible to prevent the occurrence of many neural tube defects and effects of teratogenic agents. Screening of newborns has guarded them from effects of inborn errors of metabolism, such as phenylketonuria.

Unfortunately, it is not possible to apply primary prevention to the problems of education, where simple linear cause-and-effect relationships between toxic agents and the conditions one is attempting to prevent do not exist. Educational problems are usually multi-determined. In making educational predictions, one must take into account, not only the children's individual patterns of development, but also the environmental stresses and supports and the match between individual children and the setting in which their schooling occurs. It is not just a matter of discovering and correcting what is wrong within the child, but in understanding and dealing with the forces and the feedback loops that influence the quality of the children's lives. This diversity should give pause to even the most courageous investigator.

Barriers to Prevention

Yet prevention is an appealing concept. Few people would admit to being opposed to it and most people believe that they really are working at it. Albee and Joffe (1977) have said that practically any "effort aimed at improving child rearing, increasing communication among family members, building inner controls and self esteem, reducing stress or pollution, in short everything aimed at improving the human condition and at making life more fulfilling and meaningful may be considered to be part of prevention." (p. 19) This somewhat over-encompassing definition of prevention sounds like a promise soon to be realized. However, it contrasts markedly with the body of research evidence that does not support the belief that nonspecific global approaches are effective. Erlenmeyer-Kimling (1977) has shown that real, lasting results come from *specific* programs, based on *specific* formulations of the conditions we attempt to prevent.

Other barriers to large scale prevention efforts exist. There is a lack of a vocal constituency to lobby for preventive measures. Indeed, current legislation for special education gives strong legal and financial encouragement to local school district programs for children only *after* they have failed.

There is also difficulty in documenting results of preventive programs. Traditional research methods may be inadequate for demonstrating the results of prevention. The need for control groups in a typical research paradigm raises ethical issues because such control conditions imply the withholding of services or the manipulation of individuals. Finally, the need for time to demonstrate results adds to the difficulties researchers face in documenting that one has "made things not happen" in a preventive program.

Background of Our Preventive Approach

When we started work in the prevention of reading problems, we already had some experience with learning problems. Our surveys described the variety of children with learning problems who came for clinical services to the Mental Hygiene Clinic of Bellevue Psychiatric Hospital (Silver & Hagin, 1960, 1965). Our follow-up studies had shown us the power and vicissitudes of educational intervention (Silver & Hagin, 1964; Silver & Hagin, 1966). These studies documented the tenacious quality of the neuropsychological deficits associated with specific language disability. They also documented the poorer prognosis in remediation for the children with central nervous system findings on neurological examination, and the strong relationship between improvement in neuropsychological measures and improvement in oral reading and reading comprehension (Silver & Hagin, 1972a).

This work implied a theoretical position that accurate spatial orientation and temporal organization is basic to the acquisition of skill in reading. Conversely, this position implied that children with difficulties in organizing symbols in space and sounds in time were likely to experience difficulties in learning to read, thus providing a set of marker variables for locating children in need of preventive serivces. These marker variables were applied to intact groups of first graders in a local public school. Predictions made in first grade and compared with outcomes in third grade were reported for a sample of 168 children

(Silver & Hagin, 1972b). These predictions were accurate for 94% of the group, with one false positive (a child for whom we predicted reading failure who achieved adequately in third grade) and nine false negatives (children for whom we predicted adequate achievement but who were achieving below expectancy in third grade). Within the false negative group, there were two children with emotional problems that interfered with school learning and seven children with limited English proficiency whose abstract language abilities were not adequate for the conceptual demands of reading comprehension.

Having surveyed the incidence and variety of learning problems in school-based samples, we began a long-term commitment to prevention of learning problems through early identification, clinical diagnosis, and school-based intervention. With wider dissemination of our preventive approach, we found we could not continue the luxury of individual clinical studies of each child. To reduce the costs of clinical studies while preserving the cues for individual intervention, we developed a three-part approach: (a) scanning intact groups to locate vulnerable children with the SEARCH test, (b) clinical studies of only those children found to be vulnerable during scanning, and (c) intervention based on the methods described in TEACH.

Development of SEARCH

The basic data for SEARCH (Silver & Hagin, 1976) were drawn from individual clinical studies of intact groups of first graders. Factor analysis of the 20 variables elicited in these examinations produced five factors: an auditory verbal factor, a visual-spatial-neurological factor, chronological age, psychiatric rating, and intellectual functioning. Neuropsychological measures made their strongest contribution to the first two factors, with most of the auditory tests clustering on Factor I and with visual and visual-motor tests appearing on Factor II. The equal weight of these factors within the total variance underlined the importance of treating the two modalities separately in the scanning test. What was also striking was the relative independence of the neuropsychological factors from general cognitive abilities as seen in Factor V, from general maturation as represented by Factor III (chronological age), and from psychiatric rating (Factor IV).

The factor analysis helped define the components that should be tapped in the planned modification of the clinical battery for screening purposes. Loadings within factors helped us to locate those measures that most clearly defined each component. The brief scanning measure, SEARCH, that emerged from these beginnings consisted of 10 components: three tests of visual perception (discrimination, recall, and visual motor control), two auditory tests (discrimination and rote sequencing), two intermodal tests (articulation and initials), and three body image tests (directionality, finger schema, and pencil grip). The test yields a total SEARCH score (with values expressed on a 10-point scale) as a measure of vulnerability and a profile of individual components to describe individual patterns of functioning.

In our preventive approach, SEARCH is used to scan an entire grade of children in kindergarten or early in first grade. Age and demographic norms are available in the manual, but, when the size of the sample permits, local norms are also recommended. While statistical character-istics of SEARCH are described in detail in the manual (Silver & Hagin, 1981), some information is relevant to this discussion. Total SEARCH scores yield a multiple correlation of .89 with reading achievement at the end of first and second grade. Test-retest reliability is .81, and the standard error of the measure is .89 of a total SEARCH score unit. Follow-up studies of subgroups at the end of second grade were conducted to assess validity of predictions. Prediction–performance ratios, which take into account both false negatives and false positives, range from 83% in one sample (N = 153) to 87% in a second sample (N = 40).

Comparisons with Educational and Clinical Criteria

The predictive utility of SEARCH was first studied in terms of educa-tional criteria, outcomes in reading at the end of first and second grade. Reading achievement, as measured by the Wide Range Achievement Test and by teacher ratings of progress, was secured in a group of 52 children for whom no intervention services were provided. When the group was dichotomized at the median Oral Reading Score, it was found that no child who earned a SEARCH score of 0 through 5 placed above the median in oral reading, that 38% of those earning SEARCH scores of 6 and 7 placed above the median, and that 87% of those earning SEARCH scores of 8 through 10 placed above the median. The median test yielded a Chi Square value of 21.39 ($p < .001$).

SEARCH scores obtained during kindergarten showed a similar relationship to teacher ratings of progress during first and second grade reading instruction. When asked to rate the children's progress on a four-point scale (1: well below average, 2: low average, 3: high average, 4: well above average), the teachers assigned high ratings to only one child of the seven who earned SEARCH scores of 0 through 3, to three of the nine earning scores of 4 and 5, to nine of the 14 earning scores of

6 and 7, and to 22 of the 23 children who earned scores of 8 through 10. Chi square value for the median test for these ratings was 17.22 ($p <$ .001). Thus children who earned SEARCH scores of 8 through 10 tended to fall within the group of successful readers, and children with SEARCH scores below 6 tended to fall within the group of unsuccessful readers, both by specific test scores and more general teacher rating criteria.

This analysis also highlighted another group, the children earning borderline SEARCH scores of 6 and 7, whose chances for success in learning to read appeared somewhat uncertain. Clues for understanding these children were obtained when SEARCH scores were related to clinical diagnosis which was available for a sample of 171 children.

While SEARCH is used to locate children who are vulnerable to learning problems, it is the diagnostic phase that helps us to understand *why* they are vulnerable. These services are interdisciplinary in character, involving psychological, educational, developmental, and neurological studies of the children whom SEARCH has identified as vulnerable. These studies provide information which points directions and sets priorities for intervention choices.

The predictive validity for SEARCH was also studied in relation to clinical criteria. Just how varied diagnostic findings can be within an intact sample of first graders is illustrated in Table 1. This table reports the clinical diagnoses for all first grade children enrolled in two schools (N = 171).

Based on the findings of clinical examinations, groupings could be

Table 1. SEARCH Scores and Clinical Diagnosis First Grade Kips Bay School and Soho School 1973–74

Total SEARCH Score	Chr. III	Gen. Ret.	Organ.	SLD	Emot. Fam. Prob.	No Dev.	Cult. Diff.	Total
8–10			1	1	5	61	1	69
6–7			2*	7	17	16	1	43
4–5	1		6	23	3	2	2	37
0–3	1	2	19	22				
Total	2	2	28	31	25	79	4	171

*One child was in our nursery program and so had the benefit of intervention.

Key to Abbreviations
Chr. III = Chronically Ill
Gen. Ret. = General Retardation
Organ. = Deviation on Neurological Examination
SLD = Specific Language Disability
Emot. Fam. Prob. = Emotional and/or Family Problems
No Dev. = No Deviation
Cult. Diff. = Cultural Difference

made on the basis of primary diagnoses. While findings for a substantial portion of the group were within normal limits on clinical examinations, a variety of problems were seen in some of the children. Some children were found to have chronic physical illnesses (asthma, congenital cardiac anomalies) that interfered with regular attendance at school. Some children showed, on neurological examination, signs suggesting defects of the central nervous system. A few children were found to be immature in all parameters of development; the cause of this retardation was, however, obscure. Some children had specific language disabilities. Psychiatric examination with a few children revealed emotional problems severe enough to impair learning at school.

Table 1 also shows how these clinical diagnoses relate to SEARCH score groupings. Children who earned SEARCH scores of 8 through 10 (i.e., scores predicting success in learning to read in the early grades) tended to fall into the group whose clinical examinations were described as being within normal limits. In contrast, the children who earned SEARCH scores within the vulnerable ranges educationally (i.e., scores below 6) tended to have positive findings on clinical examination. For those with SEARCH scores of 4 and 5, the characteristic diagnosis tended to be that of specific language disability. For those with SEARCH scores in the 0 to 3 range, the characteristic diagnosis was some pervasive physiological condition involving lowered physical vitality or deviations in central nervous system functioning. This analysis helped to clarify the composition of the borderline SEARCH score group (scores 6 and 7) in which there is a cluster of children who probably will make normal progress in reading, as well as a definite cluster of children with emotional or environmental problems severe enough to interfere with learning.

Thus, while SEARCH was found to be helpful in locating children vulnerable to failure in beginning reading, it is also useful in allocating intervention services appropriately. For children who earn SEARCH scores within the vulnerable ranges, educational intervention is appropriate. For the group earning SEARCH scores of 4 and 5, such intervention may be adequate, without the need for further diagnostic services, because this group tends to be clearly the specific language disabilities. The SEARCH score group earning the lowest score ranges, while in need of educational intervention, may have more pervasive problems and should, therefore, have the benefit of clinical diagnosis as well. Children earning SEARCH scores of 6 and 7 may have a chance for normal achievement. Therefore, they should not be rushed into educational intervention services. If they experience trouble with beginning reading, this may reflect the need for other kinds of services (e.g., counseling, social work services to the families), rather than the need for educational intervention.

To summarize the implications of the clinical data from Table 1 for planning intervention:

- for children earning SEARCH scores of 4 and 5, educational intervention may be appropriate and adequate for the prevention of learning problems;
- for the children earning SEARCH scores of 0 to 3, educational intervention may be appropriate, but it may be insufficient in terms of their need for additional services;
- for children earning SEARCH scores of 6 and 7, educational intervention may be inappropriate.

Thus, while SEARCH is helpful in locating children vulnerable to learning failure, it may also be useful in offering clues for planning intervention priorities.

Educational Intervention

The educational intervention approach used in our preventive projects is described in the manual *TEACH: Learning Tasks for the Prevention of Learning Disability* (Hagin, Silver, & Kreeger, 1976). This approach utilizes directed activities to develop skills basic to learning to read, write, and spell. We believe that a well-rounded intervention program should include teaching at three levels: (a) tasks directed toward accuracy of perception within single modalities relevant to reading, (b) intermodal tasks to relate percepts from different modalities to each other, and (c) verbal tasks to insure transfer to school learning. Initially, this approach uses activities that are, insofar as possible, directed toward stimulation of a single perceptual modality at a time. We chose to work with perceptual input in this way in order to bring all modalities to a level of readiness for reading instruction. It has been our experience that reading draws upon a complex of perceptual skills; if one modality is deficient, learning cannot be expected to proceed easily.

The learning tasks of TEACH proceed through three stages of increasing complexity:

- the recognition stage, which requires children to make simple discrimination responses by determining whether two stimuli are the similar or different.

- the copying stage, which requires that children initiate a motor response while the teacher continues to provide structure which guides their responses.
- the recall stage, which requires children to build their own structures for responding with minimal cues from the teacher.

Mastery of each learning stage is demonstrated by the application of our "three by three rule." By this rule, children are considered to have mastered a task when they have responded correctly three times during three separate lessons.

This preventive approach implies carefully sequenced and controlled presentation of tasks. Work with children is individual or in very small groups. The processes by which tasks are accomplished are as important as the successful completion of the task. Trial and error solutions are discouraged, not only because they permit the child to practice ineffi-cient solutions, but also because the task may be solved eventually but the learner may be unaware of the process by which it was accom-plished.

When an error occurs the teacher gives immediate feedback. Prompts to learning are given in the same modality as the task itself. For example, the teacher is told to use color cues when the child is working on a task requiring the matching of basic forms because it is a visual task. Visual perception skills would not be enhanced if, for example, auditory-verbal cues such as naming the figures were used. Studies of human inform-ation processing have shown that loss of information occurs when the subject is required to shift between input channels (Mowbray, 1964). Before presenting a task, the teacher is advised to consider the task carefully in order to give proper modality-based feedback.

The processes, as well as the products of learning, are important in use of the TEACH tasks if the skills are to become automatically accessible for transfer into classroom work in reading and the language arts. It follows that teachers must monitor the *way* children solve the tasks presented. Children should not be encouraged to substitute a modality in which they are competent for one in which they are weaker in order to complete a task, for readiness for reading and the language arts requires a complex of perceptual skills. If one modality is deficient, learning cannot be expected to proceed easily.

The TEACH program provides 55 learning activities, called teaching tasks, organized into five clusters that mesh with the components of SEARCH. Tasks can be accessed through a Skills Index that insures ease of matching activities to learners' needs. An individual teaching plan is developed for each child according to the following guiding questions:

- *Is this child vulnerable?*
  This question is answered with reference to the total SEARCH score and to the qualitative aspects of the scanning test results.
- *Is further diagnosis necessary?*
  This question is answered with reference to the total SEARCH score group and the qualitative aspects of the child's response to scanning. Where diagnostic services are limited, particular priority is given to children earning scores within the 0 to 3 range.
- *What are the strengths and needs?*
  Answers to this question are based on the child's profile of SEARCH components and the qualitative aspects of the scanning and diagnostic data.
- *What are the teaching priorities?*
  The teacher is referred to the Skills Index in TEACH in order to locate specific tasks appropriate to the child's needs and to the cluster organization to sequence these tasks in keeping with the child's level of development.

Teachers are encouraged to use "recap" at the end of each session to record the work accomplished in a daily log, and to keep the children informed on their progress in mastering the tasks.

Results of Intervention

In addition to various studies of the identification and intervention program (Silver, Hagin, & Beecher, 1978; Silver & Hagin, 1972) and a cross-validation study reported by Arnold, L. E., Barneby, N., McManus, J., & Smeltzer, D. (1977), our preventive program was evaluated in a submission to the Joint Dissemination Review Panel of the U.S. Department of Education and the National Institute of Education. This panel, known as JDRP, invites innovative programs to submit data concerning their educational impact, cost effectiveness, and replicability. Programs that meet the JDRP criteria are accepted for dissemination through the National Diffusion Network and appear in the Department of Education's publication *Educational Programs that Work*. Our preventive program was approved for such dissemination on the basis of two evaluation studies described below.

In the first study, all children in kindergarten in seven participating schools were scanned with SEARCH. Those found to be vulnerable were placed randomly in intervention and control groups and were evaluated (a) at the end of first and second grades, during which intervention with TEACH was provided to the intervention group; and (b) at the end of third grade, 1 year after intervention had been completed.

At the end of first grade, the sample consisted of 87 children in intervention and 39 in the control condition. At the end of third grade, pupil mobility had reduced the intervention group to 47 children and the control group to 14. At the beginning of the study, preintervention, there were no statistically significant differences between intervention and control groups on relevant variables (SEARCH, Wechsler Pre-school, and Primary Scale IQ scores). At the end of third grade, with the size of groups reduced by pupil mobility, preintervention scores were again examined and found not to be significantly different between the two groups.

Evaluation assessed perception at the end of first grade with a retest of SEARCH, and oral reading and word attack skills at the end of first, second, and third grades with the Wide Range Achievement Test and the Word Identification and Word Attack Sections of the Woodcock-Johnson Reading Mastery Test. Reading comprehension was assessed at the end of second grade with the Mastery Tests, Levels A-F, of the SRA Basic Reading Series.

At the end of first grade the intervention group earned higher scores on SEARCH retest than the equally vulnerable controls ($F = 31.52$, $p < .0001$). More important practically, the intervention group also earned significantly higher scores in oral reading ($F = 10.31$, $p < .002$), in word identification ($F = 7.58$, $p < .01$), and in word attack ($F = 5.51$, $p\ .02$).

At the end of second grade the differences between intervention and control groups were more striking, with the measures of oral reading, word identification, and word attack (respectively, $F = 11.71$, $p < 110$; $F = 9.74$, $p < .003$; $F = 20.64$, $p < .0001$). These gains in decoding skills were reflected in more accurate reading comprehension in the intervention than in the control group ($F = 25.18$, $p < .0001$). With retests using the same measures at the end of third grade, differences between the intervention and control groups remained as sharp as the differences at the end of second grade. These data are especially important because intervention services were structured as a 2-year program. Thus, although direct services were terminated at the end of second grade, impact upon reading achievement in the intervention group children continued to be discernible a year later.

In order to avoid withholding services from a no-treatment control group, our second study contrasted two cohorts which were given varying amounts of intervention services. The 91 children in the second study were randomly assigned to one of two cohorts: Cohort I, which began intervention in the September, and Cohort II, which began intervention in February, of the first grade year. This study, therefore, contrasted the effects of a full year versus a half year of intervention upon perception and educational progress. At the end of first grade, scores for children in Cohort I exceeded those for children in Cohort II in perception, oral reading, word identification, and word attack at a statistically significant level (respectively, $F = 12.39$ $p < .05$; $F = 15.54$, $p < .02$; $F = 4.70$, $p < .04$; $F = 3.96$, $p < .05$). In second grade the same kind of contrasts persisted with measures of oral reading, word identification, word attack, and reading comprehension (respectively, $F = 10.12$, $p < .0025$; $F = 8.06$, $p < .006$; $F = 6.81$, $p < .01$; $F = 4.51$,[2] $p < .03$). As can be seen, the contrasts between the groups with more/less intervention in our study are not as sharp as those in the first study, which compared intervention/no-intervention effects, although they all occurred in the expected direction, thus confirming the educational impact of our preventive program.

We also studied the effects of early intervention on the mental health of children 3 years after intervention was completed. Thirty-five children who had been scanned with SEARCH during kindergarten were located in fifth grade. Of this group, 19 children had earned scores within the normal progress range and 16 had earned vulnerable scores and had received educational intervention with TEACH. We collected data in the form of human figure drawings and report card ratings to determine how the children who had been identified as vulnerable differed from their normal progress classmates as fifth graders.

Report card ratings of individual pupil characteristics concerning motivation for school learning, estimates of school achievement, and interpersonal adjustment were obtained from the schools' permanent record cards for the period from third to fifth grade. These data were averaged for each child and examined in terms of the Chi square statistic to assess differences in the teachers' ratings of these characteristics between children in the intervention and the normal progress groups. Significant differences ($p < .05$) were found in two areas: responsibility and teachers' estimates of reading vocabulary. No significant differences were found between the groups in the ratings of eight other areas: work-study habits, classroom participation, teachers' estimates of reading comprehension, teachers' estimates of mathematics achievement, social behavior, gets along well with others, observes school rules, satisfied with a reasonable amount of attention. Thus, in most areas of academic achievement and social adjustment, the vulnerable children who had had educational intervention were not distinguishable from their classmates for whom normal progress had been predicted by SEARCH.

Findings with human-figures drawings were similar in character.

Such drawings have long been regarded as an important clinical tool, providing a measure of the child's concept of self and mirroring biologically determined laws of growth and development, modified in the light of sensory and social experiences. Two sets of drawings were available: drawings done in kindergarten, and drawings done in fifth grade. A judge, a clinical psychologist who was unaware of the group membership of the children, was asked to sort the drawings on the basis of signs of vulnerability. The judge easily identified the drawings of the vulnerable group at kindergarten (Chi square = 7.67, p < .01), but produced a totally random sorting of the drawings done at fifth grade (Chi square = 0.17).

Data from these studies have convinced us that secondary prevention of reading disability and its emotional consequences is possible. Early identification of children vulnerable to learning failure, diagnostic evaluation, and specific educational intervention yielded statistically significant improvement in oral reading, word attack skills, and reading comprehension. By the end of fifth grade, children originally considered vulnerable were not distinguishable from their nonvulnerable peers on a variety of behavior measures.

Summary

Some general principles and specific procedures for a program for the prevention of reading failure have been described. The use of marker variables to locate target children, to assess their strengths and needs, and to plan and implement an individualized intervention program has been illustrated. The long-term effects of the program have been assessed through measures of reading achievement, motivation, and interpersonal adjustment. These data provide persuasive evidence, not only that prevention of reading problems is possible, but that it is indeed prudent in terms of the educational impact and emotional adjustment of the children served.

References

Albee, G. W., & Joffe, J. M. (1977). *Primary prevention of psychopathology.* Hanover, NH: University of Vermont Press, pg. 19.

Arnold, L. E., Barneby, N., McManus, J., & Smeltzer, D. (1977). Prevention by specific perceptual remediation for vulnerable first graders. *Archives of General psychiatry, 34,* 1279–1294.

Bryant, T. E. (1978). The effect of student failure on the quality of family life and community mental health. *Bulletin of the Orton Society, 28,* 8–14.

Erlenmeyer-Kimling, L. (1977). Issues pertaining to prevention and intervention of genetic disorders affecting human behavior. In G. W. Albee & J. M. Joffe (Eds.), *Primary prevention of psychopathology*. Hanover, NH: University of Vermont Press.

Fitzsimmons, S. J., Cheever, J., Leonard, E., & Macunovich, D. (1969). School failures: Now and tomorrow. *Developmental Psychology, 1,* 134–147.

Goldston, S. E. (1977). Defining primary prevention. In G. W. Albee & J. W. Joffee, (Eds.), *Primary Prevention of Psychopathology* (pg. 19). Hanover, NH: University of Vermont Press.

Hagin, R. A., Silver, A. A., & Kreeger, H. (1976). *TEACH: Learning tasks for the prevention of learning disability.* New York: Walker Educational Book Corporation.

Mowbray, G. H. (1964). Perception and retention of verbal information presented during auditory shadowing. *Journal of the Acoustical Society of America, 36,* 1459–64.

Silver, A. A., & Hagin, R. A. (1960). Specific reading disability: Delineation of the syndrome and relationship to cerebral dominance. *Comprehensive Psychiatry, 1,* 126–34.

Silver, A. A., & Hagin, R. A. (1964). Specific reading disability: Follow-up studies. *American Journal of Orthopsychiatry, 34,* 744–752.

Silver, A. A., & Hagin, R. A. (1965). Developmental language disability simulating mental retardation. *Journal of the American Academy of Child Psychiatry, 4,* 485–493.

Silver, A. A., & Hagin, R. A. (1966). Maturation of perceptual functions in children with specific reading disability. *The Reading Teacher, 19,* 253–59.

Silver, A. A., & Hagin, R. A. (1972a). *Effects of perceptual stimulation on perception, on reading ability, and of the establishment of cerebral dominance for language: an experimental study.* Final report to the Carnegie Corporation of New York.

Silver, A. A., & Hagin, R. A., (1972b). Profile of a first grade: A basis for preventive psychiatry. *Journal of the American Academy of Child Psychiatry, 11,* 645–674.

Silver, A. A., & Hagin, R. A. (1976). *SEARCH: A scanning instrument for identification of potential learning disability,* New York: Walker Educational Book Corporation.

Silver, A. A., Hagin, R. A., & Beecher, R. (1978). Scanning, diagnosis, and intervention in the prevention of reading disabilities. *Journal of Learning Disabilities, 11,* 437–449.

PART II

THE SPECIAL LEARNER AND THE READING TASK

Chapter 5

The Development of Oral Language and Reading

Sharon L. James

University of Wisconsin-Madison

Reading is a crucial ability for success in many areas of life. It is a necessary skill for achievement in school and in many jobs. It is a basic tool for learning throughout our lives. And yet there are youngsters who finish school without attaining full literacy. Downing and Leong (1982) have estimated that between 10% and 15% of monolingual English speaking school children with no apparent visual, hearing, or mental deficits encounter some difficulty in learning to read. Of these children, a significant number will never become competent readers.

The importance of reading for lifelong learning and success, and the fact that a substantial number of children fail to obtain full literacy, has led experts to ask what kinds of abilities are critical to learning to read. It generally is agreed that reading is a skill involving complex integration of a variety of cognitive, linguistic, and perceptual behaviors. The important question is which behaviors are crucial to reading development and performance.

Until fairly recently, reading was considered primarily a visual-perceptual process, and reading problems were explained as deficits in visual perception and perceptual-motor skills. This viewpoint resulted in assessment batteries focusing on perceptual-motor tasks and on training programs to teach perceptual skills. However, there is now considerable evidence that deficits in visual perception do not account for most reading disabilities and that perceptual-motor training does not improve skills (Calfee, 1975, 1977; Hammill, 1972; Larsen & Hammill, 1975; Shankweiler & Liberman, 1972; Velluntino, 1977, 1979). These findings have led researchers to look for other abilities that may be closely related to reading.

Most recently, several investigators have focused on oral language abilities and their relationship to reading (Blachman, 1984a,b; Blachman & James, 1985; Gleitman & Rozin, 1977; Liberman, Shankweiler, Liberman, Fowler, & Fischer, 1977; Perfetti & Lesgold, 1977, 1979; Tunmer, Pratt, & Herriman, 1984; Velluntino, 1977, 1979). Although most people assume oral language knowledge is the basis for learning to read and write, we have not known very much about the types of oral language skills that are most closely related to understanding and producing written language. Discovering the nature of this relationship has been the most recent thrust in reading research. Much of the current research grew out of *Language by Ear and by Eye* by Kavanagh and Mattingly (1972). In this book, Mattingly suggested that the proficient reader must have two types of linguistic ability, which he referred to as *primary linguistic activity* and *secondary linguistic activity*. Primary linguistic activity refers to the use of an internalized set of rules to produce and understand language. Secondary linguistic activity refers to the language user's ability to reflect upon and manipulate the units and rules of spoken language. It involves treating language as an object of thought, as opposed to using language to comprehend and produce sentences. This conscious awareness of language also is called *metalinguistics.* Assuming that Mattingly's suggestion is correct, then reading development is related, not only to the child's primary linguistic knowledge – to knowledge of linguistic units and rules – but also to his or her ability to reflect on and consciously manipulate those units and rules.

Much of the most recent research on the relationship between oral language abilities and reading development has focused on metalinguistic abilities rather than primary linguistic abilities. The major reason for this focus is that normally developing children have acquired most of their primary linguistic knowledge before they begin the reading acquisition process. Although they continue to acquire some primary linguistic knowledge throughout the school years, they have mastered the basic rules for phonology, syntax, semantics, and pragmatics by the time they reach school. On the other hand, metalinguistic abilities are just beginning to emerge in the early elementary school grades, between about 5 and 8 years of age (Hakes, 1980; Tunmer & Herriman, 1984). Children also are beginning to learn to read during this period, which has led some investigators to hypothesize that metalinguistic abilities may be the oral language abilities most closely related to reading development. It has been argued that the child's fundamental task in reading is to "map the printed text onto his existing language" (Tunmer & Bowey, 1984, p. 160), and that this process requires conscious awareness of linguistic units and rules. There are at least three major hypotheses about the relationship between metalinguistic awareness and reading. One hypothesis is that some aspects of metalinguistic awareness are prerequisite for learning to read (Mattingly, 1972, 1984). A second hypothesis is that the process of learning to read is in itself responsible for children's conscious awareness of language (Donaldson, 1978; Vygotsky, 1962). A third hypothesis, presented by Downing (1984), Francis (1973), and Ehri (1979), among others, is that there is an interaction between metalinguistic abilities and reading. According to this hypothesis, a certain amount of metalinguistic awareness is required before the child learns to read, but learning to read in turn increases the child's awareness of language. At this point in time, we do not have the kind of evidence which would allow us to accept one of these hypotheses. We do have evidence, which will be discussed later in this chapter, that certain types of metalinguistic abilities are related to reading achievement; however, we cannot yet make definitive statements about the causal relationship between the two.

Metalinguistic Abilities Related to Reading

Tunmer and Bowey (1984) reviewed the literature in metalinguistic development and hypothesized that there are four categories of metalinguistic abilities which are related to the child's progress from beginning to skilled reading. These four categories of abilities, which emerge between 5 and 8 years of age, are word awareness, phonological awareness, syntactic awareness, and pragmatic awareness. Tunmer and Bowey suggest that the relative importance of these different metalinguistic abilities to reading depends on the child's stage of reading development. For example, they argue that, in the early stages of reading acquisition when the child is learning to decode, the child's word and phonological awareness will be closely related to reading performance. Later, when the child is learning to read and understand connected text, metalinguistic knowledge of syntax and pragmatics may be more important. Each type of metalinguistic ability and its hypothesized relationship to reading development will be discussed.

Word Awareness

Word awareness refers to the ability to treat words as objects of thought. It involves recognizing that utterances are made up of and can be broken down into individual words. This ability often is tested by having a child "tap out" the number of words in a spoken sentence. Word awareness also involves knowing that words are arbitrary units which are separate from the object, person, or event to which they refer. This knowledge often is tested by asking the child to explain what a word is and to judge words as long, short, easy, and difficult. For example, a child might be asked to judge the word *hose* (a short word with a long referent) as long or short, and then to explain his judgment. Tunmer and Bowey (1984) suggest that word awareness is related to the recognition that written words correspond to spoken words, which is the first step in the reading acquisition process. The child seems to begin the process of mapping printed text onto spoken language at the word level. Thus, word awareness would be expected to be very important for the beginning reader.

Phonological Awareness

Phonological awareness refers to the ability to understand that words can be segmented into individual sounds or phonemes. In order to measure a child's phonological awareness, investigators have had the child tap out the number of phonemes in different words or say only a little bit of word (e.g., say *belt* without the /t/ sound). This type of metalinguistic awareness is related to the beginning reader's ability to recognize the correspondences between letters (graphemes) and sounds (phonemes). Recognizing grapheme/phoneme correspondences also is very important in the early stages of reading when the child is developing basic decoding skills.

Grammatical Awareness

Grammatical awareness refers to the ability to reflect upon the syntactic/semantic properties of sentences. This kind of metalinguistic awareness has most commonly been measured by asking children to judge the acceptability of normal and grammatically deviant sentences (e.g., "Julie riding is a horse") and to correct those sentences judged as ungrammatical. Grammatical awareness also has been assessed by asking children to detect the ambiguity in sentences, jokes, or riddles (e.g., "What happened to the man who fell from a 10-story building? Nothing; he was wearing a light fall suit"). The ability to judge/correct grammatical and ungrammatical sentences and to detect ambiguity requires the child to consciously think about the grammatical rules governing sentences. Grammatical awareness is believed to be related to more skilled reading involving comprehension (Ryan & Ledger, 1984;

Tunmer & Bowey, 1984). "Skilled reading is primarily an activity of exploiting the syntactic and semantic redundancies of language to generate hypotheses or guesses about the text yet to be encountered" (Tunmer & Bowey, 1984, p. 161).

Pragmatic Awareness

Pragmatic awareness refers to the knowledge one has about the rules governing language use in context. In relation to reading, the most important aspects of pragmatic awareness would seem to be knowledge about the relationships among sentences in discourse and the ability to relate new information to previously given or old information. Although there are few studies of this aspect of metalinguistics, investigators have looked at children's ability to recognize and evaluate the adequacy and consistency of the information presented in oral discourse (Bearison & Levey, 1977; Cogsgrove & Patterson, 1977, 1978; Flavell, Speer, Green, & August, 1981; Markman, 1977, 1979; Robinson & Robinson, 1978, 1980; Tunmer, Nesdale, & Pratt, 1983). The awareness of the rules governing oral discourse would seem to be related to the ability to read and comprehend connected text. As Tunmer and Bowey (1984) point out, "children must also notice relationships that obtain *among* groups of sentences and the context in which they are embedded to fully understand what they read" (p. 165).

Figure 1, adapted from Tunmer and Bowey (1984), summarizes the hypothesized relationship between the four types of metalinguistic abilities and the child's stage of reading development. When the child is learning to recognize printed whole words, *word awareness* is of primary importance. As the child begins to learn about grapheme–phoneme correspondence, *phonological awareness* is dominant. More skilled reading involving reading and understanding sentences and connected text requires greater *grammatical* and *pragmatic awareness.* This is not to suggest that children lose their word and phonological awareness as their reading skills develop, but rather that the relationship between metalinguistic abilities and reading varies, depending on the child's level of reading skills. Just as children continue to use their word recognition and decoding skills as they become more skilled readers, so they also continue to use word and phonological awareness in addition to grammatical and pragmatic awareness.

Studies of the Relation Between Metalinguistics and Reading

The metalinguistic ability which has been investigated most frequently in its relationship to reading is phonological awareness. Results from

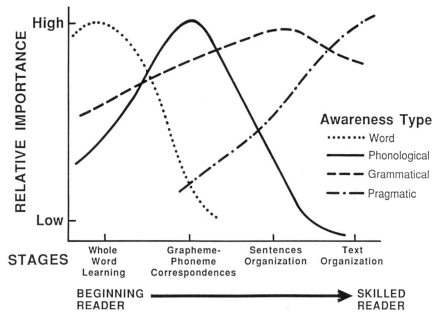

Figure 1.   Relative Importance of Awareness Types at Different Hypothesized Stages of Reading Development.
   SOURCE: Adapted from Tunmer, W., & Bowey, J. Metalinguistic awareness and reading development. In W. Tunmer, C. Pratt, & M. Herriman (Eds.), *Metalinguistic awareness in children.* New York: Springer-Verlag, 1984.

several studies (Blachman, 1984a,b; Blachman & James, 1985; Calfee, Lindamood, & Lindamood, 1973; Fox and Routh, 1975; Liberman, Shankweiler, Fischer, & Carter, 1974; Rosner & Simon, 1971; Zifcak, 1981) indicate that the ability to segment words into phonemes is related to success in beginning reading. As Valtin (1984) points out, "In order to understand the alphabetic principle found in most written languages and to be able to profit from this principle in reading and writing, the child needs the apprehension that spoken language can be segmented into smaller units that are represented by letters" (p. 227).
   Another metalinguistic ability which has received some attention in relation to reading development is word awareness. There is evidence that young children have difficulty segmenting sentences into words (Ehri, 1975; Holden & McGinitie, 1972; Karpova, 1966) and in separating words from their referents (Berthoud-Papandropoulou, 1978; Ianco-Worrall, 1972; Markman, 1976; Osherson & Markman, 1975), although children's word awareness improves greatly once they are in school and have begun reading instruction (Francis, 1973; Papandropoulou & Sinclair, 1974). Further, some investigators have reported that aware-

ness of word boundaries in beginning readers is a significant predictor of reading achievement (Evans, Taylor, & Blum, 1979; McNinch, 1974).

Although grammatical awareness has received much less attention than phonological and word awareness, there is some evidence that this metalinguistic ability also is related to reading performance. Studies with children in the early elementary grades have revealed that the ability to judge and correct the grammaticality of sentences is significantly correlated with reading scores (Ryan & Ledger, 1979; Willows & Ryan, 1983). Grammatical awareness also appears to discriminate between skilled and less skilled or good and poor readers in the middle and upper grades (Bowey, 1983; Forrest-Pressley, 1983; Menyuk & Flood, 1981).

One recent study has been concerned with the relationship between reading and a number of different metalinguistic abilities over time. Blachman and James (1985, 1986) have investigated reading and metalinguistic development in a group of children during the first, second, and third grades. Their subjects included 53 normally developing children who were given a set of oral language tasks and a set of reading achievement measures. Four of the oral language tasks were designed to assess metalinguistic abilities:

1. Phoneme segmentation task (Liberman et al., 1974), which required the children to tap out the number of phonemes in 42 different words.

2. Word referent tasks (adapted from van Kleeck, 1984), in which the children were asked a variety of questions to determine if they could separate a word from its referent. The children were asked to define the term *word*, to generate long and short words, and to judge words as long or short and give reasons for their judgments (e.g., to judge *spaghetti* and *hose* and explain what makes them long or short).

3. Syntactic judgments and corrections task which required the children to judge the grammaticality of 10 well-formed and 10 ungrammatical sentences, and to correct those sentences judged as ungrammatical. The ungrammatical sentences contained either word order (e.g., "His dad has a car blue") or grammatical morpheme violations (e.g., "Lassie is one of his dog").

4. Riddle task, in which the children were asked to explain what was funny about various riddles, some of which involved lexical ambiguity (e.g., "What dog keeps the best time? A watch dog") and some involving structural ambiguity (e.g., "How do you keep fish from smelling? Cut off their noses"). This task appears to tap both the child's word awareness in the lexically ambiguous riddles and his or her grammatical awareness in the structurally ambiguous riddles.

The children also were given three standardized reading achievement measures:

1. Word identification subtest of the *Woodcock Reading Mastery Tests* (Form A), which required children to read single words on a graded word list.

2. Word attack subtest of the *Woodcock Reading Mastery Tests* (Form A), in which the children had to read a list of phonetically regular nonsense words (e.g., *ift, weet*).

3. Paragraph reading subtest of the *Spache Diagnostic Reading Scales* (1981) requiring the children to read increasingly difficult connected text and to answer questions about the content of the material. At the first grade level, the children did not answer the comprehension questions; therefore, the subtest was used only as a measure of word recognition in context. At the second grade level, the children responded to the questions giving us a measure of reading comprehension also.

Results from the first and second grades are presented in Table 1. These results can be summarized as follows:

1. The ability to segment words into phonemes was related to all of the reading achievement measures in both grades. Correcting ungrammatical sentences also was related to all but one of the reading measures in both grades. It is interesting to note that the syntactic corrections measure was more highly correlated with the reading measures than was the syntactic judgments task.

2. The ability to separate words from their referents was not strongly related to these measures of reading achievement. It was significantly correlated only with the ability to read lists of words (word identification) in the second grade.

3. Performance on the Riddles task was not related to any reading achievement measures in the first grade, but was related to all three reading measures in the second grade. It was most strongly correlated to the more skilled reading required on the Spache Paragraph Reading subtest.

In order to determine which metalinguistic tasks administered in the first grade best predicted reading achievement performance in the second grade, a stepwise multiple regression analysis was performed. This analysis revealed that the best predictors for both Word Identification and Word Attack subtests were Phoneme Segmentation and Syntactic Corrections. The best predictor for second grade performance on the Paragraph Reading Comprehension measure was first grade performance on the Phoneme Segmentation, Syntactic Corrections, and Riddles tasks.

These results indicate that *phonological awareness*, as measured by the Phoneme Segmentation task, and *grammatical awareness*, as measured by the Syntactic Corrections task, *are significantly related to reading achievement in beginning readers and are significant predictors of reading performance.*

Table 1. Pearson Product-Moment Correlations Between the Metalinguistic Tasks and Measures of Reading Achievement in the First and Second Grades

Variable	Woodcock Word Identification		Woodcock Word Attack		Spache Paragraphs	
	First	Second	First	Second	First[a]	Second[b]
Phoneme Segmentation	.51**	.44**	.41*	.54**	.43*	.46**
Word Referent	.29	.46**	.10	.34	.26	.22
Syntactic Judgments	.37**	.368	.21	.27	.40*	.43*
Syntactic Corrections	.40*	.41*	.32	.45**	.45**	.54**
Riddles	.22	.36*	.32	.37*	.19	.52**

*p < .01   **p < .001   [a]without comprehension questions   [b]with comprehension questions

Sources: Blackman, B. & James, S. (Dec., 1986) A longitudinal study of metalinguistic abilities and reading achievement in primary grade children. Paper presented at the National Reading Conference, Austin, TX.

Word awareness, as measured by the ability to separate words from their referents, *is related only to the ability to read lists of words and does not seem to be an important predictor of reading achievement.* This finding seems to support Tunmer and Bowey's (1984) hypothesis about the relationship between word awareness and early whole word recognition in beginning readers. *The ability to explain linguistic ambiguity in riddles, which reflects both grammatical and word awareness, seems to be related to more skilled reading involving text comprehension.* As Tunmer and Bowey (1984) have suggested, grammatical awareness, which was measured in both the Syntactic Corrections and the Riddles tasks, may be related to more skilled aspects of reading. Results from the third year of this longitudinal study will provide further information about the differential relationship among specific metalinguistic abilities and specific reading skills.

Implications for Children with Language and Reading Diabilities

There is considerable evidence that children with a history of oral language disabilities have difficulty in learning to read (Maxwell & Wallach, 1984; Weiner, 1985). Furthermore, many children with reading disabilities have been found to have deficits in their primary linguistic abilities, including vocabulary, morphology, and syntax (Byrne, 1981; Fletcher, Satz, & Scholes, 1981; Hook & Johnson, 1978; Vogel, 1974, 1977). Children who have delays or deficits in their basic knowledge of semantics, morphology, and syntax are likely to have some difficulty in learning to read. As Gough (1975) argues, "knowledge of the language being read is at the heart of the reading process, and without that knowledge reading simply could not take place" (p. 15).

The research reviewed in this chapter suggests that secondary linguistic or metalinguistic abilities also are related to reading performance, and, therefore, that deficits in metalinguistic abilities may be associated with reading impairment. There is evidence that some reading-disabled children with seemingly normal primary linguistic knowledge have deficits in their metalinguistic abilities. Kamhi and Catts (1986) studied a group of primary school children identified as reading disabled who scored within normal age limits on a test of vocabulary and syntactic knowledge (Test of Language Development-Primary, by Newcomer & Hammill, 1982). They found that these reading-disabled children scored lower than their normal age peers on metalinguistic tasks requiring word awareness, phonological awareness, and grammatical awareness. Thus, even though the reading disabled subjects appeared to have no deficits in their primary linguistic abilities, they still had difficulties on metalinguistic tasks. A note of caution should be included here. The fact that reading disabled children have metalinguistic deficits does not mean that the reading disability is "caused" by the difficulty with metalinguistics. We do not have the kind of evidence that would allow us to predicate causality. All we can say at this point is that metalinguistic abilities and reading skills are related.

Early Identification of Reading Problems

One important implication of the relationship between metalinguistic and reading development is in the area of early identification. Experts agree that it is crucial to begin intervention as early as possible with children who are at risk for reading disabilities. The first step in this process is to identify those children in the early elementary school years. As Blachman (1983) has argued, our screening instruments need to include language tasks which are more directly related to reading. The results of the research reviewed in this chapter indicate that tasks assessing phonological, word, and grammatical awareness might be included. A number of metalinguistic tasks have been used quite successfully with children in the early elementary school years. For assessing the ability to segment words into phonemes, there are the tapping task developed by Liberman, et al. (1974), the word division task developed by Fox and Routh (1975), the elision task used by Rosner and Simon (1971), and the Lindamood Auditory Conceptualization Test (Lindamood and Lindamood, 1971). Some of these tasks, such as those used by Liberman, et al. and by Fox and Routh, also can be used to assess the child's ability to segment sentences into words. Van Kleeck (1984) has proposed an informal procedure for assessing word-referent differentiation in young children. Grammatical awareness can be assessed by having the child judge and correct the grammaticality of sentences (see Gleitman & Gleitman, 1979; Hakes, 1980; Pratt, Tunmer, & Bowey, 1984, for stimulus sentences) and by having the child explain the ambiguity in riddles or jokes (see Fowles & Glanz, 1977; Hirsch-Pasek, Gleitman, & Gleitman, 1978, for riddles). Children who demonstrate significant difficulty with these kinds of metalinguistic abilities should be assessed in more depth. It may be that such children are high risk for problems in reading acquisition.

Blachman (1983, 1984a,b) also has recommended that a rapid automatized naming (RAN) task be included on early screening instruments. She found that tasks requiring children to rapidly recall names of familiar objects, colors, and letters were significant predictors of measures of reading achievement in kindergarten and the first grade.

Instructional and Intervention Issues

The relationship between metalinguistic abilities and reading development raises some very important issues about reading instruction and
intervention programs. Several reading experts have argued that at least
one type of metalinguistic awareness, phonological awareness, should
be emphasized in beginning reading instruction (Blachman, 1984;
Elkonin, 1963; Liberman & Shankweiler, 1979; Williams, 1980) and in
remediation programs for language or reading disabled youngsters
(Blachman, 1984a,b; Catts & Kamhi, 1986). Although there have been
some reports of successful training of syllable and phonemic segmentation skills with normal 4- to 6-year-olds (Elkonin, 1963, 1973; Helfgott,
1976; Rosner, 1974), few researchers have investigated the effect of such
training on reading. In at least two studies where phonemic segmentation was part of a reading training program, reading performance
improved following training (Wallach & Wallach, 1976; Williams, 1980).
However, it is impossible from these studies to isolate the effect of
phonemic segmentation training, because other skills were taught also.
The viewpoint that metalinguistic abilities should be a focus of any
reading instruction program is not universal. Singer (1984) advocates
caution in instructional application until we have evidence that
metalinguistic abilities are causally related to reading acquisition. He
argues that, although we should not make metalinguistics a specific
instructional component at this time, we can add other useful linguistic
components to reading programs:

> We can help children identify morphemes in their orthography and teach
> them to relate their phonological, semantic, and syntactic processes to
> printed words. We can also provide them with linguistic information on
> printed words so that they can form hypotheses, test them, and corrobo-
> rate new entries in their lexicon. Also, we can help them relate these
> entries to morphemic and morphophonemic patterns in their orthography
> and even to parse sentences into phrase structures without trying to make
> them aware of their linguistic mechanisms and processes. (p. 206)

Although the kinds of activities Singer is suggesting are not designed to
teach metalinguistic awareness explicitly, it would seem that they might
facilitate development of metalinguistic awareness. In fact, many language arts, reading readiness and reading programs currently in use
seem to promote metalinguistic development (Byrne, 1981; Herriman &
Myhill, 1984). However, the issue of what kind and how much
metalinguistic training is needed is far from being answered. What we
need at this time are well-designed studies to determine how training in
metalinguistic awareness affects reading acquisition and how the spe-

cific types of metalinguistic knowledge (phonological, word, grammatical, and pragmatic) may be related to the different stages of reading development.

References

Bearison, D. J., & Levey, L. M. (1977). Children's comprehension of referential communication: Decoding ambiguous messages. *Child Development, 48,* 716–720.

Berthoud-Papandropoulou, I. (1978). An experimental study of children's ideas about language. In A. Sinclair, R. J. Jarvella, & W. J. M. Levelt (Eds.), *The child's conception of language.* New York: Springer-Verlag.

Blachman, B. A. (1983). Are we assessing the linguistic factors critical in early reading? *Annals of Dyslexia, 33,* 91–109.

Blachman, B. A. (1984a). Language analysis skills and early reading acquisition. In G. Wallach & K. Butler (Eds.), *Language learning disabilities in school-age children.* Baltimore, MD: Williams & Wilkens.

Blachman, B. A. (1984b). Relationship of rapid naming ability and language analysis skills to kingergarten and first-grade reading achievement. *Journal of Educational Psychology, 76,* 610–622.

Blachman, B. A., & James, S. L. (1985). Metalinguistic abilities and reading achievement in first-grade children. In J. Niles & R. Lalik (Eds.), *Issues in literacy: A research perspective.* Thirty-fourth Yearbook of the National Reading Conference.

Blachman, B. A., & James, S. L. (1986, December). *A longitudinal study of metalinguistic abilities and reading achievement in primary grade children.* Paper presented at the National Reading Conference, Austin, TX.

Bowey, J. A. (1983, September). *Syntactic control in relation to children's oral reading performance.* Paper presented at the Eighteenth Annual Australian Psychological Society Conference on Reading Acquisition, Sydney, Australia.

Byrne, B. (1981). Deficient syntactic control in poor readers: Is a weak phonetic memory code responsible? *Applied Psycholinguistics, 2,* 201–212.

Calfee, R. C. (1975). Memory and cognitive skills in reading acquisition. In D. Duane & M. Rawson (Eds.), *Reading perception and language.* Baltimore, MD: York Press.

Calfee, R. C. (1977). Assessment of independent reading skills: Basic research and practical applications. In A. S. Reber & D. L. Scarborough (Eds.), *Toward a psychology of reading.* Hillsdale, NJ: Erlbaum.

Calfee, R. C., Lindamood, P., & Lindamood, C. (1973). Acoustic-phonetic skills and reading—Kindergarten through twelfth grade. *Journal of Educational Psychology, 64,* 293–298.

Catts, H. W., & Kamhi, A. G. (1986). The linguistic basis of reading disorders: Implications for the speech-language pathologist. *Language, Speech, and Hearing Services in Schools, 17,* 329–341.

Cosgrove, J. M., & Patterson, C. J. (1977). Plans and the development of listener skills. *Developmental Psychology, 13,* 557–564.

Cosgrove, J. M., & Patterson, C. J. (1978). Generalization of training for children's listening skills. *Child's Development, 49,* 513–516.

Donaldson, M. (1978). *Children's minds.* London: Fontana.

Downing, J. (1984). Task awareness in the development of reading skill. In J. Downing & R. Valtin (Eds.), *Language awareness and learning to read.* New York: Springer-Verlag.

Downing, J., & Leong, C. K. (1982). *Psychology of reading.* New York: Macmillan.

Ehri, L. C. (1975). Word consciousness in readers and prereaders. *Journal of Educational Psychology, 67,* 204–212.

Ehri, L. C. (1979). Linguistic insight: Threshold of reading acquisition. In T. G. Waller & G. E. Mackinnon (Eds.), *Reading research: Advances in theory and practice.* New York: Academic Press.

Elkonin, D. B. (1963). The psychology of mastering the elements of reading. In B. Simon & J. Simon (Eds.), *Educational psychology in U.S.S.R.* London: Routledge & Kegan Paul.

Elkonin, D. B. (1973). U.S.S.R. In J. Downing (Ed.), *Comparative reading.* New York: Macmillan.

Evans, M., Taylor, N., & Blum, I. (1979). Children's written language awareness and its relation to reading acquisition. *Journal of Reading Behavior, 11,* 7–19.

Flavell, J. H., Speer, J. R., Green, F. L., & August, D. L. (1981). The development of comprehension monitoring and knowledge about communication. *Monographs of the Society for Research in Child Development, 46*(5, Serial No. 192).

Fletcher, J. M., Satz, P., & Scholes, R. (1981). Developmental changes in the linguistic performance correlates of reading achievements. *Brain and Language, 13,* 78–90.

Forrest-Pressley, D. L. (1983). *Cognitive and meta-cognitive aspects of reading.* New York: Springer-Verlag.

Fowles, B., & Glanz, M. E. (1977). Competence and talent in verbal riddle comprehension. *Journal of Child Language, 4,* 433–452.

Fox, B., & Routh, D. K. (1975). Analyzing spoken language into words, syllables, and phonemes: A developmental study. *Journal of Psycholinguistic Research, 4,* 331–342.

Francis, H. (1973). Children's experience of reading and notions of units in language. *British Journal of Educational Psychology, 43,* 17–23.

Gleitman, H., & Gleitman, L. R. (1979). Language use and language judgment. In C. Fillmore, D. Kempler, & W. S. Y. Wang (Eds.), *Individual differences in language ability and language behavior.* New York: Academic Press.

Gleitman, L. R., & Rozin, P. (1977). The structure and acquisition of reading, I: Relations between orthographies and the structure of language. In A. S. Reber & D. L. Scarborough (Eds.), *Toward a psychology of reading.* Hillsdale, NJ: Erlbaum.

Gough, P. B. (1975). The structure of language. In D. Duane & M. Rawson (Eds.), *Reading, perception and language.* Baltimore, MD: York Press.

Hakes, D. T. (1980). *The development of metalinguistic abilities in children.* New York: Springer-Verlag.

Hammill, D. (1972). Training visual perceptual processes. *Journal of Learning Disabilities, 5*, 552–559.

Helfgott, J. (1976). Phonemic segmentation and blending skills of kindergarten children: Implications for beginning reading acquisition. *Contemporary Educational Psychology, 1*, 157–169.

Herriman, M. L., & Myhill, M. E. (1984). Metalinguistic awareness and education. In W. E. Turner, C. Pratt, & M. L. Herriman (Eds.), *Metalinguistic awareness in children: Theory, research, and implications*. New York: Springer-Verlag.

Hirsch-Pasek, K., Gleitman, L. R., & Gleitman, H. (1978). What did the brain say to the mind? A study of the detection and report of ambiguity by young children. In A. Sinclair, R. J. Jarvella, & W. J. M. Levelt (Eds.), *The child's conception of language*. New York: Springer-Verlag.

Holden, W. H., & MacGinitie, W. H. (1972). Children's conceptions of word boundaries in speech and print. *Journal of Educational Psychology, 63*, 551–557.

Hook, P. E., & Johnson, D. J. (1978). Metalinguistic awareness and reading strategy. *Bulletin of the Orton Society, 28*, 62–78.

Ianco-Worrall, A. D. (1972). Bilingualism and cognitive development. *Child Development, 43*, 1390–1400.

Kahmi, A. G., & Catts, H. W. (1986). Toward an understanding of developmental language and reading disorders. *Journal of Speech and Hearing Disorders, 51*, 337–347.

Karpova, S. N. (1966). The preschooler's realization of the lexical structure of speech. In F. Smith & G. A. Miller (Eds.), *The genesis of language: A psycholinguistic approach*. Cambridge, MA: MIT Press.

Kavanagh, J. F., & Mattingly, I. G. (Eds.). (1972). *Language by ear and by eye*. Cambridge, MA: MIT Press.

Larsen, S. C., & Hammill, D. (1975). The relationship of selected visual perceptual abilities to school learning. *Journal of Special Education, 2*, 281–291.

Liberman, I. Y., & Shankweiler, D. (1979). Speech, the alphabet and teaching to read. In L. B. Resnick & P. A. Weaver (Eds.), *Theory and practice of early reading*. Hillsdale, NJ: Erlbaum.

Liberman, I. Y., Shankweiler, D., Fischer, F. W., & Carter, B. (1974). Explicit syllable and phoneme segmentation in the young child. *Journal of Experimental Child Psychology, 18*, 201–212.

Liberman, I. Y., Shankweiler, D., Liberman, A. M., Fowler, C., & Fischer, F. W. (1977). Phonetic segmentation and recoding in the beginning reader. In A. S. Reber & D. L. Scarborough (Eds.), *Toward a psychology of reading*. Hillsdale, NJ: Erlbaum.

Lindamood, C., & Lindamood, P. (1971). *L.A.C. Test: Lindamood Auditory Comprehension Test*. Boston: Teaching Resources.

Markman, E. M. (1976). Children's difficulty with word-referent differentiation. *Child Development, 47*, 742–749.

Markman, E. M. (1977). Realizing that you don't understand: A preliminary investigation. *Child Development, 28*, 986–992.

Markman, E. M. (1979). Realizing that you don't understand: Elementary school children's awareness of inconsistencies. *Child Development, 50*, 643–655.

Mattingly, I. G. (1972). Reading, the linguistic process, and linguistic awareness. In J. F. Kavanagh & I. G. Mattingly (Eds.), *Language by ear and by eye.* Cambridge, MA: MIT Press.

Mattingly, I. G. (1984). Reading, linguistic awareness, and language acquisition. In J. Downing & R. Valtin (Eds.), *Language awareness and learning to read.* New York: Springer-Verlag.

Maxwell, S., & Wallach, G. (1984). The language-learning disabilities connection: Symptoms of early language disability change over time. In G. Wallach & K. Butler (Eds.), *Language learning disabilities in school-age children.* Baltimore, MD: Williams & Wilkins.

McNinch, G. (1974). Awareness of aural and visual word boundary within a sample of first graders. *Perceptual and Motor Skills, 38,* 1127–1134.

Menyuk, P., & Flood, J. (1981). Linguistic competence, reading, writing problems, and remediation. *Bulletin of the Orton Society, 31,* 13–28.

Osherson, D., & Markman, E. M. (1975). Language and the ability to evaluate contradictions and tautologies. *Cognition, 3,* 213–226.

Papandropoulou, I., & Sinclair, H. (1974). What is a word? Experimental study of children's ideas on grammar. *Human Development, 17,* 241–258.

Perfetti, C. A., & Lesgold, A. M. (1977). Discourse comprehension and sources of individual differences. In M. A. Just & P. A. Carpenter (Eds.), *Cognitive processes in comprehension.* Hillsdale, NJ: Erlbaum.

Perfetti, C. A., & Lesgold, A. M. (1979). Coding and comprehension in skilled reading and implications for reading instruction. In L. B. Resnick & P. A. Weaver (Eds.), *Theory and practice of early reading* (Vol. 1). Hillsdale, NJ: Erlbaum.

Pratt, C., Tunmer, W. E., & Bowey, J. A. (1984). Children's capacity to correct grammatical violations in sentences. *Journal of Child Language, 11,* 129–141.

Robinson, E. J., & Robinson, W. P. (1978). Development of understanding about communication: Message inadequacy and its role in causing communication failure. *Genetic Psychological Monographs, 98,* 233–279.

Robinson, E. J., & Robinson, W. P. (1980). Egocentrism in verbal referential communication. In M. V. Cox (Ed.), *Are young children egocentric?* London: Batsford Academic and Educational, Ltd.

Rosner, J. (1974). Auditory analysis training with prereaders. *The Reading Teacher, 27,* 378–384.

Rosner, J., & Simon, D. (1971). The auditory analysis test: An initial report. *Journal of Learning Disabilities, 4,* 40–48.

Ryan, E. B., & Ledger, G. W. (1979). Grammaticality judgments, sentence repetitions, and sentence corrections of children learning to read. *International Journal of Psycholinguistics, 6,* 23–40.

Ryan, E. B., & Ledger, G. W. (1984). Learning to attend to sentence structure: Links between metalinguistic development and reading. In J. Downing & R. Valtin (Eds.), *Language awareness and learning to read.* New York: Springer-Verlag.

Shankweiler, D., & Liberman, I. Y. (1972). Misreading: A search for causes. In J. F. Kavanagh & I. G. Mattingly (Eds.), *Language by ear and by eye.* Cambridge, MA: MIT Press.

Singer, H. (1984). Learning to read and skilled reading: Multiple systems interacting within and between the reader and the text. In J. Downing & R. Valtin (Eds.), *Language awareness and learning to read*. New York: Springer-Verlag.

Tunmer, W. E., & Bowey, J. A. (1984). Metalinguistic awareness and reading acquisition. In W. E. Turner, C. Pratt, & M. L. Herriman (Eds.), *Metalinguistic awareness in children: Theory, research, and implications*. New York: Springer-Verlag.

Tunmer, W. E., & Herriman, M. L. (1984). The development of metalinguistic awareness: A conceptual overview. In W. E. Tunmer, C. Pratt, & M. L. Herriman (Eds.), *Metalinguistic awareness in children: Theory, research, and implications*. New York: Springer-Verlag.

Tunmer, W. E., Nesdale, A. R., & Pratt, C. (1983). The development of young children's logical inconsistencies. *Journal of Experimental Child Psychology, 36*, 97–108.

Tunmer, W. E., Pratt, C., & Herriman, M. L. (Eds.). (1984). *Metalinguistic awareness in children: Theory, research, and implications*. New York: Springer-Verlag.

Valtin, R. (1984). Awareness of features and functions of language. In J. Downing & R. Valtin (Eds.), *Language awareness and learning to read*. New York: Springer-Verlag.

Van Kleeck, A. (1984). Assessment and intervention: Does "meta" matter? In G. P. Wallach & K. G. Butler (Eds.), *Language learning disabilities in school-age children*. Baltimore, MD: Williams & Wilkens.

Velluntino, F. R. (1977). Alternative conceptualizations of dyslexia: Evidence in support of a verbal deficit hypothesis. *Harvard Educational Review, 47*, 334–354.

Velluntino, F. R. (1979). *Dyslexia: Theory and research*. Cambridge, MA: MIT Press.

Vogel, S. (1974). Syntactic abilities in normal and dyslexic children. *Journal of Learning Disabilities, 7*, 103–109.

Vogel, S. (1977). Morphological ability in normal and dyslexic children. *Journal of Learning Disabilities, 10*, 292–299.

Vygotsky, L. S. (1962). *Thought and language*. Cambridge, MA: MIT Press.

Wallach, M. A., & Wallach, L. (1976). *Teaching all children to read*. Chicago, IL: University of Chicago Press.

Weiner, P. (1985). The value of follow-up studies. *Topics in Language Disorders, 5*, 78–92.

Williams, J. P. (1980). Teaching decoding with an emphasis on phonemic analysis and phoneme blending. *Journal of Educational Psychology, 72*, 1–15.

Willows, D. M., & Ryan, E. B. (1983). *The role of a linguistic factor in the development of reading skill*. Paper presented at the American Educational Research Association, Montreal, Quebec.

Zifcak, M. (1981). Phonological awareness and reading acquisition. *Contemporary Educational Psychology, 6*, 117–126.

Chapter 6

Mediating: An Important Role for the Reading Teacher

Marilyn Cochran-Smith

University of Pennsylvania

In the 30 years since Sputnik, public and private monies have funded a tremendous amount of reading research. Despite the important findings of much of this research, we actually know very little about the precise ways in which individuals become literate. Indeed, in *Learning to Read*, Meek (1986) claims that "we are certain only that good readers pick their own way to literacy in the company of friends who encourage and sustain them and that . . . the enthusiasm of a trusted adult can make the difference" (p. 193). It is probable that we will never know precisely how individuals make the mental connections needed in order to read.

It is difficult for educators to settle for this kind of uncertainty and imprecision about the reading process. After all, our business as educators is intervention, and the 60 million American children who attend school every day will not wait for us to figure it out. For those who work everyday with children for whom learning to read does not come easily, there is a special urgency. We want desperately to know what we can do to help children become readers.

The good news is that we are beginning to know more and more about the kinds of activities and experiences that seem to support the connection-making process and help young children begin to pick their own ways. And we are beginning to understand more about the language learning environments in which readers and writers are made and the critical roles adults can play in these. This paper will address one of those roles.

Conceptual Framework

I will argue in this paper that one way we as teachers can sustain and encourage our young friends in their attempts to learn to read and write effectively is through a process called *mediation*. Simply put, mediation means that a more experienced language user (teacher, parent, or someone else) fills in some of the gaps that exist between children and the print they are attempting to read, write, or use in some way. As we will see in the pages that follow, through mediation, children extend the ways they can use and understand print beyond those ways that they can already perform by themselves. With the help of a teacher, who is more experienced with print than they are, children are able to participate in a wider range of literacy events. As time goes on, the teacher provides less and less help until children are able to make sense of and use print by themselves.

The idea of mediation is related to Bruner's (1978) notion of "scaffolding," introduced in his exploration of the role of dialogue in children's language acquisition. He describes scaffolding as the framework created by adults to help children in their attempts to use oral language successfully. The nature of the scaffolding changes as children develop and gain more competence with language. Old scaffolding "self-destructs" (to use Cazden's, 1980, phrase) as it is less and less needed, and new scaffolding appears. One way to think about the process of mediation that I will describe in this chapter is as a kind of scaffolding that temporarily enables children to deal with the written language of narrative texts and of environmental print until they are able to do without it. Mediation is a teaching strategy that can be especially important in dealing with young children and special learners who are apprentices in the literacy-learning process. But, as we shall see, it is not a teaching strategy that is limited to these groups.

Many of the examples I will present in the following pages are taken from an 18-month study of early reading and writing in a nursery school setting (Cochran-Smith, 1984). Examples of mediation with children from this age group make the mediation process and its instructional effects especially clear.[1] Examples of mediation with older children are

---

[1] The larger study focuses on adults and children observed over a period of 18 months at a private, cooperative nursery school in a residential section of Philadelphia. The study highlights both what these children seemed to know about print and some of the ways

based on less formal observations in a home setting.[2] These examples help to clarify the teacher's role in mediation and demonstrate that it is a teaching process that cuts across the age and ability levels of children.

The children in these examples at school and at home would not be labeled "special learners" according to the definitions commonly used in the field. But the strategy of mediation that these examples illustrate is appropriate for, and applicable to, all learners, because all learners acquire and develop competence in written language by using it and observing others using it in naturally occurring, authentic situations. These situations are interactive and social; they involve children, often with the help of adults, using written language to get things done in the world—to connect themselves with others, to organize their activities, to meet their own needs, and so on. Underlying this argument is a view of literacy as a communicative phenomenon aimed in any one instance at fulfilling a particular purpose in relation to a particular audience. Children's reading and writing development is a process of gradually getting better at communicating through print.

Two concepts will be useful as we look at the role of the teacher in mediating children's reading and writing development: the notion *literacy event*, and the distinction between *contextualized* and *decontextualized* print. A literacy event is generally defined as an event where written materials are integral to the interactions and interpretations of participants, or, as action sequences involving one or more persons where the production and/or comprehension of print plays a role (Anderson, Teale, & Estrada, 1980; Heath, 1978, 1982). Description and analysis of literacy events can help identify and clarify the contexts where print is used for and with children, the ways print is organized, the kinds of talk that accompany print uses, and the nature and extent of social participation and interaction that surround and support print experiences. This can help us understand both what children know about print and how they are coming to know it. All the vignettes that are used as examples in this chapter describe literacy events in which

---

they seemed to be coming to know it. The research strategy for this study, constructed and adapted during a four-month phase of exploration, combined audiorecordings of more than 100 story-reading events, informal and formal interviews with nursery school parents and teachers, and longitudinal participant observation of a broad range of nursery school activities. The study focused on group story-reading, which emerged as a key aspect of early socialization for literacy in the community, and, equally importantly, on the network of literacy events that surrounded and supported story-reading.

[2]Examples of adults mediating texts with older children are based on an informal exploration with two of my own children at home. Conversations about books were recorded as soon as possible after they occurred within the daily routines of home life. These conversations, therefore, are *not* verbatim but closely approximate conversations.

adults helped children use, understand, interpret, or apply written language.

A second concept that helps to frame this chapter is the distinction between contextualized print and decontextualized print. Contextualized print (e.g., street signs, grocery item labels, notes to the milkman, and so on) gets some of its meaning from the context where it occurs and from the way it is used. For example, with a stop sign, part of the meaning is the immediate print environment—that is, white letters on a red, metal, hexagonal sign on a pole in the ground. Part of the meaning is also the way print generally functions—to give directions to oncoming traffic; and part is derived from the situation—a sign on a corner facing the right lane of traffic where streets intersect. The actual definition of the word *stop* is only one cue to the meaning of this print. The situation, the function of the print, the environment where the print occurs, and the interrelations of all of these also signal meaning.

Decontextualized print, on the other hand, is written language whose meaning is relatively independent of the situational and environmental contexts in which the print occurs. For example, when we read a novel, its meaning does not depend on the chair or the room in which we read, or on the color of the paper or ink with which the book is printed. Rather, meaning comes from the definitions of words and groups of words, from syntax, and from the conventions of literature. To make sense of decontextualized print, we have to understand the demands and nature of the conventions of various literary genres. The physical environment of the print provides few cues to meaning. Decontextualized print must be interpreted quite differently from the ways contextualized print is interpreted. One important role of teachers is to mediate between children and both of these kinds of print; as they do so, they help children learn to use each.

In the pages that follow, we look carefully at the role of the teacher during mediation. The chapter begins with discussion of the process through which a teacher mediates between young children and environmental print. It continues with discussion of ways teachers can mediate between beginning readers or older readers and extended, narrative discourse.

Mediating Between Children and Environmental Print

The next several examples feature literacy events where a teacher mediated between children and contextualized, or environmental, print. The children in these examples were quite young. They were beginning to be able to recognize and, in some cases, write or copy their own names and recognize a few words in the environment. But it is important to note that none of these children could read and write in the conventional sense, and none could decode words decontextualized from the environment.

In these examples the teacher mediated by acting as an intermediary between children and written language in order to help the children get things done with print. The teacher carried out as much of the literacy event as she needed to do, depending on the skill and experience of the individual child. The two examples that follow make this point. Notice in these examples that the use of print as a name label to show ownership was identical, but the degree and kind of teacher participation in the literacy events varied, depending on the skills of the two children.

Example 1
   Alice is painting a picture at the easel in the workroom. The teacher walks by and says, "Here, Alice, let me put your name on that so that you'll know it's yours at going-home time." Alice looks up as the teacher prints her name in a corner of the picture. At noon when her mother arrives, Alice tells her she has painted a picture. Via the name label on the painting, Alice's mother verifies that the picture is Alice's and takes it home.

Example 2
   It is snack-time, and the children are finding places at the table. There is an argument between Linda and Jeffrey over a juice cup. Both children claim that the cup is theirs. Jeffrey will not give in until Linda demands that he look at the name printed on the cup. "Is this your name?" When Jeffrey admits that the writing does not seem to say "Jeffrey," Linda triumphantly announces that it says "Linda," which is her name and which means it's her cup.

In the first example, although the child, Alice, was directly involved, she really did little except to observe. The teacher dominated and controlled both the mechanical processes of encoding and decoding the name and the way print was used as a label. Both the teacher and, later, the parent, however, behaved *as if* Alice intended to use print as a way to show ownership and acted *as if* she herself had used the name label in this way. These adults assumed the child's intention "to mean" with print and hence, essentially allowed her to use print meaningfully. The child could not have used print in this way by herself, but adult mediation supported this for her. Linda, the child in the second example, on the other hand, independently understood the use of a name label to designate ownership and therefore demanded certain rights and obligations. She was able to initiate and control both this use of print and the decoding it required. Her literacy event was initiated, guided, and terminated by Linda herself: She called Jeffrey's attention to the name label on the cup, required that he attempt to read the label, verified the label herself, and announced the outcome of the situation.

There are two important features to notice in these mediated literacy events and in the many others that took place daily at the nursery school studied. First, the teacher allowed (and indeed encouraged) all of them to occur. Second, her role as teacher in these events was to move easily along a continuum of participation to provide just the amount of help needed in order for the individual child to get something done with print. Description of an additional literacy event makes clear the way adult mediators respond to the needs and abilities of individual children depending on the context of the particular literacy event.

Example 3
Susie and I (the researcher) have been trying to make a sailboat out of half a walnut shell. We get the sail on but can't get the boat to balance — it keeps tipping and then sinking into the water. We finally make a second boat that looks like the first, but will float. At about the time we finish, the children all go outdoors to play. Susie hurriedly brings me a scrap of paper and asks me to write her a little note to place between the boats. She directs me: "It will say, 'this one will go in the water and this one will not,' so that no one will put the wrong one in the water and it will sink."

In this example the child herself completely controlled the literacy event. She stipulated the exact message to be written down, the context in which the message was to be used, and the way that the message was to be interpreted by passers-by in relation to the nearby water table and the two little boats. Her actions indicate that she clearly understood that print could be used in place of an oral message. The role of the adult was to mediate by acting as intermediary in the event — but only when the child needed her as encoder, as instrument for the child's own use of print. The teacher's role as mediator between children and environmental print has three critical parts: (a) to create and encourage an atmosphere in which it is very apparent to children that using print is an effective way to get many kinds of things done; (b) to judge the amount of mediation a given child needs in order to participate effectively in a given literacy event; and then (c) to mediate — that is, to offer the child just the amount of help needed to fulfill the child's own intention.

At the nursery school from which the three above examples were taken, dozens of literacy events occurred every day. These literacy events were jointly accomplished through adult–child participation, with the teacher (or other adult) mediating by acting as intermediary between child and print. In these situations we see the teacher-mediator filling in the gaps between what the child was able to do with print independently and what he or she could do with help. We see the child in these events as active learner, working to sort out the rules for using print by using them for his or her own purposes.

Several additional nursery school examples provide elaboration on these roles. These examples feature the teacher mediating reading and writing events to help children use print to express their feelings and emotions by writing down the child's angry or distressed words, or encouraging the child to join in a cooperative writing session wherein the teacher transcribed as the child dictated. The teacher used print in this way to reflect the child's feelings, that is, to acknowledge and give credibility to the emotions. In the following example, it is worthy of note that it was not the child's intention to use print, but to express anger. It is equally important to emphasize, however, that it was also not the teacher's primary intention to use or demonstrate a use of print. Rather it was her intention to help the child deal with his emotions. Despite the fact that literacy instruction was neither the intent nor the context of this literacy event, literacy instruction did occur: As the teacher helped the child carry out his own intentions, she modeled a way of using print in the world and mediated the child's use of that print.

Example 4

Mark has many strong feelings. He often explodes and lashes out angrily at other children. For several days he has been particularly angry with Alice, who wants to do what he does. After an episode that ends with Mark hitting and Alice crying, the teacher talks to Mark quietly. She suggests that he seems very angry with Alice. He agrees and elaborates. As he does so, the teacher reaches for a pencil and paper and, without comment, begins to transcribe:

I want some kids to follow me around, all except Alice. I want to show these notes to her.

(Teacher: You want her to see these notes. You want her to be upset?)

I want to upset her. I'm not going to be her friend. Her sister can be my friend.

(Teacher: You feel very angry with her?)

I feel angry. I hate some kids. She always wants to be in the same room with me.

(Teacher: She follows you and you don't like that?)

And she follows me around. I feel like a two-headed monster.

I'd like to have a wrecking truck to wreck Alice's house and furniture.

There were frequent episodes like this one with the teacher helping children use reading and writing as ways of expressing strong emotions. In these literacy events, the teacher used print as a technique for effective listening; the primary underlying message was the acknowledgment of feelings: "I hear you, I accept your strong feelings. You are permitted to have strong feelings here." There is little doubt that nursery-school children understood this message and came to expect the adults around them to be sensitive and accepting of their feelings. It is also significant, however, that the teacher elected to use print to convey this message about the legitimacy of children's feeling. There are, of course, many nonverbal and verbal nonprint alternative ways for dealing with children's feelings. At this nursery school, however, print was consistently chosen as an effective way to deal with feelings, and children had frequent opportunities to participate in literacy events of this kind. General evidence over an 18-month period indicates that the children were indeed learning to be literate (that is, learning ways to effectively use and interpret print) as a result of their repeated mediated experiences with print.

The two examples that follow represent two literacy events that occurred about 2 weeks apart but were directly related to one another. The second example illustrates dramatically that a child himself was coming to understand both the affective messages underlying expressive writing and the power of the print medium in which that message was expressed. Taken together, these two examples make the point that children who witness and participate in many mediated literacy events begin to internalize a great deal of information about print and the ways it functions.

Example 5
The children are playing outside. Alice crashes her "Big Wheels" into the wall of the building and hurts her hand. She is crying, sobbing that she wants her mother. The teacher picks her up, hugs her: "Of course you do. Would you like to write her a note?" Alice is crying too hard to respond. The teacher carries her inside where they sit down at the worktable. As Alice continues to sob, the teacher transcribes:
A: I want my mommy. (crying)
(The teacher asks something about whether her own mother or a car-pool mother will pick her up today.)
A: Grandma and Grandad are moving their clock today. It's a big clock. (crying)

A: Mommy, come get me!
I want to go home. (crying)
The teacher makes an envelope for Alice and addresses it to "Mommy". By the time the writing and envelope-making are completed, Alice has stopped crying. Still sniffling, she goes back outdoors to play, clutching the letter in one hand and the envelope in the other. Later in the day, when all the children have gone home, the letter is still lying on the table.

Example 6
The small afternoon group of children are playing indoors on the big sliding board. Mark falls and hurts his head. He begins to cry and goes to the teacher for comfort. He climbs into her lap, but immediately jumps up and says, "Let's write a note to my mother." He brings paper and pencil from the workroom, hands them to the teacher, and dictates without elicitation or interruption:
Dear Mom and Dad:
I fell down on a very hard place.
It hurt a lot.
And I love you, Mom and Dad.
I bumped my head.
Marilyn would like to come over soon, and I'd like her to (referring to plans for researcher-parent interviews).
When the teacher is finished writing, she reads the letter to Mark. He points to the first few sentences of the letter with a circular gesture, "Now this is the part about the fall, right?" The teacher replies, "Yes, and this (pointing to the third sentence) says, 'I love you.' Then this (pointing to the fourth sentence) says you bumped your head, but it should be up here (drawing an arrow connecting the fourth sentence to the first two)." Satisfied, Mark nods and rolls the letter into a scroll, which he deposits in his lunch box to take home later. His hurt is apparently forgotten.

In the incident of Mark, the child in Example 6, the teacher mediated by acting as an instrument for the child: At his request, she encoded and commented on the organization of the child's letter. The child himself, however, controlled the literacy event and the expressive use of reading and writing. He himself initiated, directed, and concluded the entire event. His actions indicate that, to a certain extent, he had internalized the use of reading and writing as a way of expressing strong emotions: When he fell, he immediately sought comfort in writing a note to his mother. In many instances in which print was used for self-expression, the written message was never delivered. Rather, it was the act of writing, the literacy event itself, that was important.

These examples make it clear that the role of the child in mediated literacy events was not a passive one. Rather, the child was actively involved in employing print for his or her own social purposes and, in the process of doing so, sorting out the rules for using and interpreting print in various situations. But it was the teacher-mediator who allowed and encouraged all of this to happen. The teacher modeled ways that individuals could use print for various purposes. The teacher helped children complete the parts of literacy tasks that they could not do on their own. The teacher offered just enough help to allow the child to be effective. With children who seemed to have very little control over the uses of print, the teacher used print for the child by initiating literacy events, encoding or decoding the necessary printed words, and following through for or with the child with the appropriate response or interpretation of the print. Throughout all of these activities, the teacher behaved *as if* children themselves were using and wanting to use print effectively. By doing so, the teacher empowered the children with control of print. They became both consumers and producers of print, both readers and writers, who were not intimidated by print. They saw it as a tool that could serve them and their purposes. Little by little children took over the various roles in literacy events, with control of the uses of print *preceding* control of the mechanical skills of decoding and encoding.

A critical point to stress about the teacher's role in helping children use print is the nature of the contexts within which the literacy events in the above examples occurred. The context was never "instruction in the uses of reading and writing." Rather, it was a variety of everyday situations into which various uses of print were routinely interwoven. As we saw above, for example, the context of incidents in which reading and writing were used for children's self-expression was not instruction in this purpose so that children would learn that written words could be helpful in sorting out feelings. Rather, in each incident the context was a situation in which there was an angry or confused child, and the goal was to help the child deal with his or her emotions. Reading and writing were used in these situations because the teacher saw them as effective ways for people to deal with their feelings, not because she felt obligated constantly to instruct children in the development of literacy skills.

In this way the children were learning a kind of literacy that included using print for a wide range of purposes, but they were exposed to all of these purposes within the environment of everyday classroom life. The preschoolers who figure in the above examples were not so much "surrounded with print," as the expression suggests, but surrounded by teachers and other experienced language users who chose to help children use print because it was effective in many aspects of their everyday lives.

In the children's own lives too, literacy was meaningful and relevant—it could, for example, help them claim ownership, establish their pretend play settings, provide them with information about the world around them, and celebrate their important occasions. There were, therefore, many reasons for them to be interested in print: It functioned effectively in many ways in their lives and was not restricted to any single context. As Schieffelin and Cochran-Smith (1984) have pointed out, a prerequisite for literacy cross-culturally seems to be that literacy is functional, meaningful, and relevant both to individuals and to their larger social groups. The children of this nursery school had no difficulty meeting this prerequisite, and they were, indeed, beginning to acquire facility with literacy at a very early age.

The children's knowledge and experience with so many ways of using reading and writing provided them with a readiness for the technical skills of decoding and encoding that is outside of the meaning of the term as generally used in educational contexts. The preschoolers in the above examples were not "ready" merely by virtue of appropriate cognitive or emotional developmental levels; they were also ready with knowledge of various ways to use reading and writing to meet specific goals in their lives and ready with the desire to use print to meet those goals.

One way to think about the literacy events that occurred in this classroom is in relation to the notion of "whole" or "authentic" written language. Following the work of Goodman and Goodman (n.d.), Harste and Burke (1977), and Smith (1985), Edelsky and Draper (1983) suggest a distinction between real, authentic reading and writing events and inauthentic, artificial "reading" and "writing" exercises (which Edelsky and Draper denote by enclosing the terms in quotation marks). Authentic reading and writing occur when a reader or writer interprets or creates text with all four of the interdependent systems of language—graphophonic, synctactic, semantic, and pragmatic—intact. However, as Edelsky and Draper point out, classroom instruction in literacy is primarily inauthentic: It is almost always comprised of the "reading" of "textbooks" created specifically for "reading" instruction or the completion of exercises covering specific, isolated "reading" and "writing" skills. Edelsky and Draper assert that children do not become literate by "reading" and "writing." Rather, they become literate by using reading and writing for actual purposes.

The dozens of literacy events that occurred in the nursery school from which the above examples have been taken were, with almost no exceptions, authentic reading and writing events, even though the youngsters involved could not decode or encode. Because they could not yet read and write independently, the children often asked adults to write down messages for them or to read to them the print on particular signs, labels, or pages. For example, as we saw above in Mark's letter home to his mother, Mark asked the teacher to encode his message, "I fell down and hit a very hard place." In one sense, then, the event was not authentic: Mark himself was not dealing with graphophonic information, but rather he asked his teacher to supply it for him. The syntax and meaning of the message were his own, however, as was the organization. And the pragmatic function of the print—as a way to express to his mother his distress at falling down—was certainly his idea.

The way to understand the literacy events that occurred in this nursery school is to see them as events with all four language systems intact and undistorted, although not all dealt with by the same person. As we have seen, the teacher often mediated between children and print by handling the graphophonic information with which the children could not yet deal. But the teacher did not assign the children literacy tasks, create or use texts created only for instructional purposes, or distort the pragmatic functions of literacy events. In these ways the teacher created an environment where written language was an indivisible whole and where, as their literacy attempts show us, children were learning written language *for themselves* (that is, to return to Meek's phrase, they were "picking their own ways" to literacy).

What I am suggesting, then, is that, in order for children to become readers and writers, whether special learners or not, they need to have many opportunities to use print for real reasons. They need to have teachers who help them to use print for these reasons by modeling ways to use, interpret, and relate it to the contexts in which it occurs, and who mediate between the skills of the child and the kind of reading required by the print itself. These kinds of opportunities do not occur when children spend most of their time filling out workbook pages on specific skills or copying dummy sentences from the board. Rather, they occur in classrooms where being able to use print matters because it is effective for children themselves.

Mediating Between Children and Narrative Texts

I have been talking about the kinds of experiences that helped young learners gain some of the skills necessary to make sense of and use contextualized print. I want now to look at children's mediated experiences with the decontextualized print of narrative texts—print that does not rely for its meaning on the context in which it occurs. Rather, as I noted earlier, decontextualized print (the most common examples of which are books, magazines, newspapers and other connected, essayist-style pieces of literature) depends for its meaning on the lexical and syntactic features of printed texts themselves and on the conventions of literature. Making sense of decontextualized print requires a great deal more than the decoding of printed symbols; it also requires understanding the demands and nature of the conventions of literary genres and other texts.

There are two main points that I argue below: First, in teacher-mediated storyreading or discussion sessions, children are able to understand and respond to more sophisticated, complex written language than they are able to handle independently; and second, through mediated experiences with texts over time children are exposed to a model for making sense of decontextualized print that they begin to internalize and apply to other reading situations. The teacher plays the key role in this process.

Mediating Narrative Texts for Younger Children

The best way to explain what I mean by mediating a narrative text is to contrast a mediated storyreading with one that is not mediated. The two examples below feature children who are about the same age (between 3 and 4 years), looking at the same wordless picture book. The text, implied in the pictures, is about a bird and a fish who become friends after sharing a worm together. The first example is from a study by Whalen-Levitt (1977) of individual children who were instructed to look at the book and tell the story to the researcher; the child teller in Example 7 was 3 years, 9 months of age. The second example features a teacher sharing the same book with a small group of children, three years, three months to four years, nine months in age. The important thing to notice about these two tellings is their striking contrast.

Example 7
    A bird. A tree./1 A bird on a tree./2 A fish and a bird./3 A fish and a bird./4 A bird and a fish./5 A bird. A tree and a Christmas tree./6 A bird and a fish./7 A big fish and a big bird./8 A big fish and a big bird./9 A bird and a fish./10 A brown fish and a purple bird and a yellow sun./11

Notice that, in this telling of the *Good Bird* story, the child offered a catalog of the separate items pictures on individual pages; these items were not related or connected to one another in any way. The child did not infer that actions had taken place in between the pages or even that action was implied within the individual pictures themselves. The child did not structure the story around the framework of a problem that required a solution or a theme that was implied in the outcome of events. Rather, the child listed the objects shown in the pictures.

The child in this example was asked to present a demonstration of his ability to comprehend the story; implicit within this request is the assumption that literary understanding is a product. Clearly, there is much that this child could not do with stories and books. In a certain sense, it seems reasonable to wonder whether the child's lack of literary skill is simply a developmental issue — perhaps children of 3 or 4 years of age are not yet able to deal with plot, theme, and the interrelationships of story in any substantial way. But to those of us who have had a variety of practical experiences with young children in both home and school settings, and who have read accounts of others' experiences with children and books, lack of developmental readiness does not seem to be an adequate explanation. Indeed, the second *Good Bird* telling in Example 8 below makes the case to the contrary and suggests that, within a certain framework and with certain kinds of support, children of the age of 3 or 4 can deal very well with these aspects of literature. In the example below a teacher was reading to a small group of children. Notice the striking contrast between this teacher-guided storytelling and the preceding telling of a child independently handling the text implied in the pictures.[3]

This teacher-led storyreading is clearly very different from the one we looked at earlier, and is probably closer to the kind of story mature readers would interpret from the same series of pictures. Notice that this second story was embedded within the social interaction of an adult and several children. The adult read *with* the children (not just *to* them), and

---

[3]The transcription system used in examples is adapted from Ochs' (1979) "basic transcript." The behaviors of the storyreader appear on the left and behaviors of the storylisteners appear on the right side of the page. In each case, verbal behaviors are in the first column and nonverbal behaviors in the second column. Information about the situational and discourse contexts is enclosed in parentheses. Except for overlapping behaviors (indicated by horizontal placement), the transcript is temporally arranged and should be read in a continuous left-to-right, top-to-bottom manner. Utterances follow the usual conventions of capitalization and punctuation. Book information appears in the first column of the left side of the page. Description of illustrations (LP, RP, or PIC) appears in the transcript immediately after the storyreader has turned the page (TP). Picture information is enclosed in brackets. The words of picture book texts are enclosed in quotation marks; within quotation marks reader modifications are enclosed in parentheses. The storyreader's utterances that are *not* direct readings from the text are transcribed in capital letters.

Example 8.

Focal Points	Reader		Listeners	
	Verbal	**Nonverbal**	**Verbal**	**Nonverbal**
	Amy: ALL RIGHT . . .			
		holds up book	(many children talking)	
		opens to first page		
	[PIC: bird flying downward toward evergreen tree] ONCE UPON A TIME . . .		Mark: Once upon a time . . . (exact intonation as reader)	
	THERE WAS A . . .	pats picture of bird	Curt: Birdie! Mark: Birdie Susie: Birdie Curt: Flying! (excited)	points to picture
	THIS IS CALLED THE . . . good . . . /beh/ . .	turns back to cover, points to words of title		
		TP	Susie: I want a scary, scary story.	on knees
	[PIC: bird sitting on tree; house with fishbowl in window off to side of picture] AND HE FLEW . . .	makes downward motion with hands, tracing path of bird		
			Curt: To a tree! Andrew: De tree, and then he flew to a house!	

Focal Points	Reader		Listeners	
	Verbal	**Nonverbal**	**Verbal**	**Nonverbal**
			Mark: A house!	
	NEAR A HOUSE . . .			
			Susie: With a fish!	pointing to fishbowl
			Mark: With a fish	
			Andrew: With a fish . . .	
		TP	(louder)	
	[PIC: fish lands on windowsill of house, sees fish swimming in bowl]			
			Curt: And *then*, the bird flew in the, to from the window open, yeah!	
			Shshpish!	makes flying noise and motions flying with arms
		TP		
	[PIC: close-up, bird looks at fish through glass, fish is sad]			
			Andrew: The fi--, fib . . . I cannot tell a fib, I name in the contest . . .	
			Curt: Do you hafta figure out what . . .?	
			Mark: And water . . .	

Focal Points	Reader		Listeners	
	Verbal	**Nonverbal**	**Verbal**	**Nonverbal**
	AND WHAT DID HE DO?	points to fishbowl	Curt: Peck, peck. He pecked on the glass . . .	
	AND THE LITTLE FISH . . .	points to fish's frown	Curt: Was afraid. Mark: Scared.	
		* * *		
	[PIC; bird is right beside fishbowl with worm in mouth] AH, CUTE . . . RIGHT OVER TO THE . . .	points to fish	Mark: Fish Susie: Fish ?: Fish	
	his friend, the . . .	TP		
	[PIC: bird perches on edge of fish-bowl and gives fish worm]	* * *		
	AND WHAT DID HE DO WITH THAT WORM? MARK, WHAT DID THE BIRDIE DO WITH THAT WORM? HE GAVE . . . HALF OF IT TO HIS . . . THE FISH, AND HE KEPT HALF OF IT . . .		Susie: Half Susie: friend Curt: For hisself . . . Bobby: Half for hisself . . .	
		TP		
	[PIC: night comes, fish and bird asleep] AND THEN . . .			

	Reader		Listeners	
Focal Points	Verbal	Nonverbal	Verbal	Nonverbal
	WHAT IS IT?	points to picture	Mark: Them sick? Curt: Well... it was the *night* time!	
	THE MOON CAME OUT...		Mark: night time, and then, and then, and... (Andrew makloud noises)	
	AND IT WAS NIGHT... THEN THE...		Mark: And then the bird and the fish were all alone.	
	ALONE, ASLEEP QUIETLY, THE BIRD OUT IN THE AIR AND THE FISH IN HIS WATERY TANK.	TP		
	[PIC: bird on plain white background]			
		closes book	Curt: That's... Mark: And then... Curt: Good night, little birdie! Goodbye, little birdie! (singing)	
	DO YOU THINK HE WAS A GOOD BIRD, MELISSA?	turns back to front cover	Melissa: Yes. Curt: Goodbye, little birdie.	

the reading was neither an adult performance (often a more dramatic type of storyreading where quiet listening is the only audience participation called for) nor a demonstration by a child of the product of his or her independently achieved literary understanding, as was the telling by an individual child in Example 7. Rather, this teacher-led reading was a cooperative venture shaped by a conversational network of adult–child verbal give-and-take. The result of this give-and-take was the joint construction across utterances of a thematically and narratively connected story about a bird and a fish.

It is important to notice the active role taken by the teacher in this second reading. The title of the book, *The Good Bird*, was the only printed text that had to be decoded for the children. The teacher could have chosen simply to show the pictures to the children, turning the pages one by one as the children looked on and presumably silently created their own individual tellings of the story. Or, the teacher could have encouraged the children jointly to tell a story as she turned the pages. She also could simply have displayed the pictures to the children while she herself orally rendered the implied text. But she did none of these. Instead, she took an active but not solitary role and mediated or aided the reading so that it became a cooperative venture.

It is worthwhile to look more closely at the way in which the teacher mediated the story. She initially framed the telling as a narrative by using the words of the formulaic story opener, "Once upon a time . . .," in the traditional intonational pattern. The reading was further framed as a narrative about a bird by both the reader's continuation of the opening phrase, "There was a . . .," while patting the picture of the bird, and her emphasis on the book's cover picture and title. The teacher's focus at that point on the only words in the book reinforced the idea that a bird would be the main figure in the narrative and also instructed the children that they should evaluate this figure as a literary "good guy."

As the narrative progressed, the teacher provided connectives between characters and events, supplied temporal markers, and cued the children in how to evaluate particular outcomes. The teacher also kept them on the track of the plot of the story by asking questions such as "And then what did he do?" when the children began to stray from the point. Essentially, what the teacher was doing was helping the children to infer the events that happened in between and within the pages. When the bird was seen flying with a worm in its mouth, for example, the teacher helped the children infer that the bird must have found the worm in the apple pictured on the previous page. She also helped the children to connect thematically the events in the story by emphasizing that the bird was the fish's friend and was sharing with him what he had.

Unlike the little boy in the first example who was asked to tell a story unaided, the children in the second example were not limited to viewing the pictures in the book as a series of items unrelated to one another temporarily, spatially, or thematically. Through the teacher's active role as mediator, the participants together constructed a story that was much more narratively and linguistically sophisticated than the story created by the same age child working alone. In these contrasting versions of *The Good Bird*, we see the effect of the teacher's mediation between children and print: The children in the second mediated storyreading were able to do significantly more with the written language of narrative discourse than the same aged child was able to do without mediation in the first storyreading.

When teachers are working with emergent and beginning readers who are at, roughly, preschool through second grade reading levels, storyreading mediation often has the general shape of the *Good Bird* reading. That is, the teacher often dominates the storyreading event by mediating heavily between children and text. The teacher's mediation structures for the children what is important about each individual text by calling their attention to the central aspects of a story and then framing their responses to the text in relation to those aspects.

The framework constructed by the teacher is different for every storyreading. It is tailored to the specific subtleties of structure and style that characterize the individual piece of literature. In the picture storybook *Pinkerton Behave*, for example, a mother and child are unsuccessfully trying to train their dog who responds incorrectly but consistently to each command. This saves the day at the end of the story when a burglar appears on the scene and the mother calls out commands anticipating the "wrong," but needed, response. The key to understanding this story is recognizing the consistently turned-around relationship between what the dog is commanded to do and what he does. The brief excerpt below indicates that, as the teacher mediated this storybook text, she repeatedly emphasized this turned-around relationship to prepare the children to understand the resolution of the story (see Example 9).

In *The Snowman*, another storybook, the teacher emphasized the conflict that was brewing between two little boys as they built a snowman together. The teacher's emphasis framed the growing conflict as the centerpiece of the story. Later in the storyreading, when it became apparent that the story listeners had failed to make some of the inferences necessary for understanding the story, the teacher went back through the book, pointing to pictures and picking out bits of text that

Example 9.

	Reader		Listener	
Focal Points	Verbal	Nonverbal	Verbal	Nonverbal
	NOW BEHAVE PINKERTON, BE-HAVE! (in scolding voice)	holds up book		
	PINKERTON, YOU BEHAVE, IT SAYS.	points to words of title		
	IS HE BEHAVING?		Neal: No Several: No-oh	
	LET'S SEE WHAT HE DOES	turns to first page		
	[LP: above-mother and child with Pinkerton on leash; below-Pinkerton jumps out window] NOW "every puppy has to learn (how) to behave. First I'll teach Pinkerton to come when he's called." (explaining, conversational voice for mother)	points to mother		
	"Come" Pinkerton!		Lauren: That a lit-tle—	
	DID HE COME?	holds book out fur-ther	Several: No, no, oh . . . Lauren: He ran out the window! (excit-ed)	pointing to pic-ture
	[RP: Mother & child point out window to Pinkerton in ru-ined flowerbed; below-Pinkerton de-stroys newspaper] NOW HERE IT SAYS "He can learn to bring us the news-paper."	points to text above RP		

Focal Points	Reader		Listener	
	Verbal	**Nonverbal**	**Verbal**	**Nonverbal**
	"Fetch!" (very commanding voice)	points arm & index finger in command gesture		
	WHAT DOES HE DO?	points to bottom picture		
			Neal: Rip!	points to bottom picture
	OH NO! LOOK! HE RIPPED THAT PAPER TO SHREDS.	points to bottom picture		
			* * *	
	ALL RIGHT, "get that burglar Pinkerton!" (commanding voice)	points with forefinger & arm in command gesture TP	(several children talking quietly, most listening)	
	[LP: Pikerton licks dummy, Mother & Child look dismayed)			
	WHOOPS!	puts hand to mouth		
	WHAT IS HE DOING?			
			Lauren: Licking (very quietly)	
	THE DOG'S LICKING HIM.	points to picture		
			* * *	
	(READING CONTINUES: everytime the dog is given one command he does something else. For example, when he is told to come, he jumps out the window).			

	Reader		Listener	
Focal Points	**Verbal**	**Nonverbal**	**Verbal**	**Nonverbal**
	[LP: real burglar enters through window: Mother dreaming in bed of Pinkerton fetching obediently: Pinkerton dreaming of destroying the newspaper as before (no text other than 'fetch' in Pinkerton's dream)]	* * *		
	[LP: burglar aims gun at Mother and child, Pinkerton watching] "Pinkerton fetch! Pinkerton fetch! (in a very dramatic, commanding voice) [RP: above-Pinkerton grabs Burglar's coat; below-Pinkerton wrestles burglar to floor] AND LOOK, WHAT DID PINKERTON DO?	points to pictures	Annie: He's gonna, he's gonna get him! (excited)	
	SEE, WHAT DO YOU DO WHEN YOU SAY FETCH TO PINKERTON? WHAT DOES HE DO?	points to pictures	Xenia: He rips Sarah: He rips (laughs)	
	HE RIPS WHAT?		Sarah: Clothes off, he rips clothes off! (laughing)	points to Pinkerton grabbing burglar's jacket
	WHAT DOES HE USUALLY RIP? (laughs) NEWSPAPER . . .	TP		

explained the outcome in relation to the conflict that had been established early on.

The nature of storyreading mediation changes as children become more skilled language users and more independent readers and writers. Nonetheless, as we shall see below, text mediation continues to play a vital, but often underestimated, role in helping children grow and develop as readers.

Mediating Narrative Texts for Older Children

The literary experiences of older children can and should be extended through mediated, interactive read-aloud and/or text discussion sessions. When teachers or parents read to or discuss books with children who can read on intermediate to upper elementary grade levels, they can continue to mediate between children and print. With older children adults often mediate as they read or as they have ongoing discussions by explaining key vocabulary (e.g., "Do you know what a rickshaw is?"), extending or broadening important concepts (e.g., "A 'computer nut' is a person who is really interested in computers and wants to spend all her time working on them"), and emphasizing story events that are pivotal to what is still to come (e.g., "Oh boy, Paul still has the Little League permission form in his hand, but now he knows his father's not going to sign it in time for the big game. Hmmmm. . . . I wonder what's going to happen"). Although it is often less extensive, the function of mediation of texts with older children is not unlike the function of the mediation teachers do with beginning readers. It helps to structure texts for the children by filling in whatever gaps they themselves are not able to fill independently. Eventually, through this process of mediation children become able to read and interpret texts by themselves.

A great deal of recent reading research indicates that we do not teach comprehension very well in the schools. We test it, measure it, evaluate it, and often expect children to practice it on a variety of reading passages, but we do not show them how actually to "*do* comprehension" within real texts. Mediating texts as we read them aloud to and with children can be a powerful strategy for teaching comprehension skills. Mediation is an effective strategy precisely because it externally clarifies and demonstrates the internal process of reading. In other words, it makes explicit many of the mental moves that fluent, experienced, adult readers make implicitly as they read written texts.

Several years ago my 10-year-old son, Brad, became interested in the stories of Encyclopedia Brown, boy detective extraordinaire. Brad was intrigued by the mysterious cases. He especially liked the idea that

Encyclopedia, a boy who was close to him in age, could solve the mysteries faster and better than could the adults around him. But Brad could never figure out the cases for himself. We tried reading several of the stories aloud, discussing the events as we went. It was clear to me from our readings that Brad knew the vocabulary and the concepts necessary to understand the story. I realized, though, that what he did *not* know was how to read for clues—how to pick out those key details of each mysterious episode that would prove to be tip-offs for Encyclopedia Brown. As we began to read a new story aloud, I started commenting on these. "I think that's going to have something to do with solving the mystery," I remarked after we read that the knife was stuck three inches into the watermelon. Or, "I have a feeling that there's a clue somewhere right in this part," I suggested as Brad read aloud a paragraph detailing the grocer's testimony about the robbery that had allegedly taken place at his store. It was not long after I began mediating his reading of the cases in this way that Brad was able to solve most of the Encyclopedia Brown mysteries independently. And even when he could not solve a case completely, he had the correct sense of where in the text the missing clue was probably located. "I don't know quite how he did it, Mom, but I know it has something to do with the rainy weather," Brad would tell me.

I was surprised that Brad could solve the cases independently so soon after we began to read the stories aloud, and I was puzzled by what had happened. When I thought carefully about it, I realized that his newly developed competence had nothing to do with a sudden improvement in vocabulary skills or a marked increase in reading level. Rather, Brad had begun by solving the mysteries with help, and then solving them with less and less help, until eventually he was able to solve them independently. I realized that our discussions had mediated for Brad the way to read a very particular genre of mystery story by helping him recognize how these texts were structured and how clues were embedded within evidence, testimony, and action.

I certainly had not realized, however, how far-reaching and unexpected the effects of mediation could be. Two years after my Encyclopedia Brown discussions with Brad, I sat down with his 9-year-old younger brother, Michael, to watch on television Agatha Christie's "Murder on the Orient Express." The movie begins as many passengers hurriedly board the train, but cuts over several times to a murky scene where a young child is being kidnapped. "Why do they keep showing that?" Michael asked, annoyed on the one hand and puzzled on the other. "I think it's going to have something to do with the story later on—something to do with the murder on the train," I answered. "Oh," Michael replied. "You mean it's gonna be a key? I know what that is because I've read Encyclopedia Brown and stories like that. And when they tell you something like 'the knife was stuck three inches into the watermelon,' then it's usually a key to something that's happening in the mystery case, and you know it's gonna be an important clue later on." Amazed, I nodded in silent agreement.

Michael had been in the room during those conversations with Brad, I remembered, and he had indeed read Encyclopedia Brown stories for himself during the past year. It was hard to believe that he had remembered for two years my "lessons" in how to read those stories. That Michael mentioned as an example of the key to a mystery exactly the same clue that I had used in talking with Brad 2 years before certainly surprised me. But it was equally surprising to me that Michael, a beginning third grader, talked so assuredly and off-handedly about how, why, and when he used a particular comprehension strategy. Brad and I had not talked specifically about what to do with the clues we noticed, and I knew Michael had not been instructed in reading Encyclopedia Brown or other mysteries in his classes at school. But Michael's casual remark was actually quite a good statement of his metacognitive awareness, at least for that particular kind of story. Of course, I will never know for sure how to trace the route Michael took to becoming a reader of mysteries, but hand-me-down mediation coupled with his own continued reading experience seemed to play a role.

Earlier in this chapter, I discussed the importance for children's written language development of having experiences with authentic language, with Edelsky and Draper's (1983) reading and writing as opposed to "reading" and "writing." Close examination of teacher-mediated read-alouds and discuss-alouds sheds light on one of the reasons children learn to read and then learn to read better by having experiences with real texts that are not designed to teach specific, isolated comprehension skills. When teachers, parents, or other adults mediate extended, connected, narrative discourse for children, they are helping children learn the skills of comprehension in three critical ways: (a) *as they interrelate to and interact with other comprehension skills;* (b) *as they bear upon a specific text which is a member of a particular genre;* and (c) *as they relate to what the child readers themselves can and cannot already do with written texts.* Because there are an infinite number of ways in which the individual skills of comprehension can be combined and applied to make up something called "text understanding," it is ineffective to instruct children by pulling out separate, supposedly discrete comprehension skills. There is no way to teach and develop comprehension skills in these three ways *outside of* the reading and/or discussing of real texts.

Mediation is a useful instructional strategy because it provides for children a model for understanding texts *within the context of understanding texts*. This may sound like a circular argument, redundant at best, but when we look closely at individual mediated storyreadings, it becomes clear that children can be instructed in comprehension as they struggle to comprehend, and that is is impossible to give them the same kind of instruction outside of this context. Description of another book discussion with Michael, at 8 years old, illustrates this point.

Second-grader Michael, had just finished reading *J.T.*, a poignant novel about a boy who befriends a badly hurt alley cat whom he names Bones. When he finished the story, Michael told me that one of the reasons he liked it was that, at the end, J.T. got to keep the cat. Knowing that Bones was hit by a car and killed near the end of the story, I asked Michael whether he was sure that the book ended that way. He nodded and, when I still looked doubtful, he found the part near the end of the book where the kind storekeeper brought a cat to J.T.'s apartment. There was even a picture showing J.T. holding the kitten on his lap. I looked closely at the picture that Michael offered up as evidence of his interpretation. The two cats in the book's photographs had the same markings, and although I was sure the picture of the kitten at the end of the novel was supposed to look smaller and different from Bones, it really did not. It was very possible to mistake the kitten at the end of the story for Bones, the cat J.T. had cared for throughout the book.

Michael and I talked for a long time about the cat. I suggested that maybe the cat at the end of the book was not Bones but a new kitten that the storekeeper had brought to J.T. because he felt so bad about the loss of Bones. Gently I asked Michael about the scene in the book where Bones is killed by a car. Michael persisted. Yes, he knew Bones had been hit by a car, but he had good textual evidence to support his conclusion that the cat had reappeared. He found the part earlier in the text where J.T., fearing that Bones would die outdoors, had begged his mother to let him keep the cat. Michael pointed out this conversation and read aloud to me J.T.'s mother's answer: " 'Well,' his mother replied, 'a cat's got nine lives. Losin' one won't matter much.' " Then Michael turned to the end of the book and showed me again the section where the grocer had brought J.T. a cat. We studied the text carefully, I trying to read it as Michael must have read. " 'I found him in the street,' Mr. Rosen explained. 'I thought maybe the boy would take care of him.' " The kitten in this passage was simply referred to as "a cat," "the cat," or "him"; there was nothing that said explicitly that this cat was new and different, a cat which had just entered into the story. Michael had correctly understood that Mr. Rosen, the shopkeeper, had found a cat in the street several days after the accident; based on the "fact" that cats have nine lives and not picking up on the implicit clues that Mr. Rosen had brought a new, tiny kitten, Michael had incorrectly concluded that "the cat" was Bones.

I tried to untangle my own understanding of the story. I took it for granted that Bones had died and Mr. Rosen had brought J.T. a different cat, a new kitten, to try to cheer him up after the accident. How had I known that? I looked back over the text and reread with Michael a passage describing the accident: "J.T. picked up the cat's broken body and carried him over to the little house. He could feel that life was gone as he put him inside." As we talked, it became clear that Michael was not quite sure about those phrases: "broken body" seemed to suggest to him something that was in need of repair but could be fixed, and "life was gone" fit well with Michael's idea that the loss of one life would simply leave the cat eight lives to spare. Nowhere in the text did it state explicitly that Bones had died. We talked about the meaning of the "nine lives" expression, and I explained to Michael what I thought had happened in the story. Eventually, after we had re-examined each of the key passages, Michael agreed that Bones must have been killed. This realization did not change his general opinion of the story. He still liked the book, deciding that it ended "sort of happy and sort of sad" since J.T. began to perk up and take an interest in the new kitten and also returned a stolen radio, an act which Michael correctly realized signified J.T.'s changed outlook on the world.

From the above book discussion we could conclude that there were several skills with which Michael needed help—interpreting idiomatic or common expressions, understanding pronoun referents, making inferences, and so on. These are skills that are commonly listed on the scope and sequence charts of basal reading materials and then systematically drilled with various exercises. But the book discussion described above raises questions about the efficacy of this approach. The book discussion emphasizes both the interconnectedness of comprehension "skills" and the unique ways in which these skills are applied by individual readers to individual texts. It casts considerable doubt on the wisdom of having Michael (or any reader) do comprehension exercises like matching up lists of idioms with their common usages. And it makes the alternative critical point that I *was* helping Michael with these comprehension skills as we discussed the book, reviewed bits of text and pictures, and negotiated jointly how these fit together. Careful consideration of mediated storyreadings and story discussions emphasizes that the various skills we use in order to make sense of texts are isolable neither from one another nor from the larger context of understanding individual texts.

Conclusion

Classroom teachers can provide many opportunities for mediated text experiences for children. As this chapter has argued repeatedly, one of the best and easiest is for the teacher to read extended texts aloud. But the teacher is not the only possible mediator in the classroom. Children can be very effective at mediating stories for and with each other. Small group discussions where children are encouraged to talk about stories and relate their interpretations to textual and pictorial passages can be effective in helping children come to fuller understandings of texts than they can come to independently and individually.

The writing and storyreading examples used throughout this chapter demonstrate an important characteristic of mediation as an instructional strategy. Mediation is most effective as a teaching strategy when it occurs within what Vygotsky (1978) has called the child's *zone of proximal development*. Vygotsky's notion of the zone of proximal development stems from his theory concerning the relationship of learning and development in school-age children. Vygotsky's work is based on the premise that learning should be matched in some way with the child's developmental level. This is not a claim with which educators would take issue. However, Vygotsky asserts that we need to know at least two developmental levels. He calls the first the child's *actual developmental level* or already-completed developmental cycle. This level is indicative of what the child can do alone; standardized tests aim to measure this level of development. But Vygotsky raises an important question about using only this kind of information. He argues convincingly that "what children can do with the assistance of others might be in some sense even more indicative of their mental development than what they can do alone" (p. 85).

Vygotsky suggests that the child's actual developmental level characterizes mental development only retrospectively by identifying functions that have already matured. The zone of proximal development, on the other hand, characterizes development prospectively by identifying those functions that are *in the process of maturing*. Vygotsky urges that it is the zone of proximal development that is most important to educators, because what is the zone of proximal development today will be the actual developmental level tomorrow.

The zone of proximal development helps to explain the difference between *The Good Bird* story of the 3-year-old who was asked to create the text on his own (a bird/a tree/a bird and a tree) and *The Good Bird* story of the 3- and 4-year-old children with whom an adult mediated the text ("And then what did he do with that worm? He gave half of it to his friend, the fish, and he kept half of it for himself"). My son's ability to solve the Encyclopedia Brown mysteries with help and then eventually solve them on his own is also a case in point.

Mediation is an instructional strategy that can be used by teachers of reading and writing whether they work with special learners or not. But mediation can also function as a useful assessment strategy. The book discussion about *J.T.*, described above, is an especially good case in point. The discussion demonstrates that, as I mediated Michael's understanding of the novel's resolution, I also gained a great deal of critical information about the comprehension strategies Michael was able to apply to the text. This information prompted important insights and gave me important information to go on as I talked with Michael about other novels. In the classroom, this kind of information can help the teacher plan discussion questions, response projects, and book selections. It can help the teacher arrange for book discussion groups or book discussion pairs.

I would like to close by returning to the quote from Margaret Meek's *Learning to Read* with which I began this chapter: "we are certain only that good readers pick their own way to literacy in the company of friends who encourage and sustain them and that . . . the enthusiasm of a trusted adult can make the difference" (p. 13). One important way we, as teachers, can sustain and encourage our young friends in their attempts to use and effectively understand written language is through the process of mediation.

Children's Books Cited in Examples

Erskine, Jim. (1978). *The snowman.* New York: Crown Publishers.

Kellogg, Steven. (1979). *Pinkerton behave!* New York: Dial Press.

Sobol, Donald. (1978). *Encyclopedia Brown, boy detective.* New York: Bantam Books.

Wagner, Jane. (1969). *J.T.* New York: Dell Publishing Company.

Wezel, Peter. (1969). *The good bird.* New York: Harper & Row Publishing.

References

Anderson, A., Teale, W. H., & Estrada, E. (1980). Low-income children's preschool literacy experiences: Some naturalistic observations. *The Quarterly Newsletter of the Laboratory of Comparative Human Cognition, 2*(3), 59–65.

Bruner, J. S. (1978). The role of dialogue in language acquisition. In A. Sinclair, R. J. Jarvelle, and W. J. M. Levelt. (Eds.). The Child's Conception of Language. NY: Springer-Verlag.

Cazden, C. (1980). Peekaboo as an instructional model: Discourse development at home and at school. *Papers and Reports in Child Language Development, 17.*

Cochran-Smith, M. (1984). *The making of a reader.* Norwood, NJ: Ablex Publishing Corp.

Edelsky, C., & Draper, K. (1983). *Reading/'reading'; writing/'writing'; text/'text.'* *Unpublished manuscript.*

Goodman, K., & Goodman, Y. (n.d.). *A whole-language comprehension-centered view of reading development.* Unpublished manuscript, University of Arizona.

Harste, J., & Burke, C. (1977). A new hypothesis for reading teacher research: Both teaching and learning of reading are theoretically based. In P. D. Pearson (Ed.), *Reading: Theory, research, and practice* (26th Yearbook of the National Reading Conference). St. Paul, MN: Mason Publishing Company.

Heath, S. B. (1978). *Outline guide for the ethnographic study of literacy and oral language from schools to communities.* Unpublished manuscript, University of Pennsylvania.

Heath, S. B. (1982). Protean stages in literacy events: Ever-shifting oral and literate traditions. In D. Tannen (Ed.), *Spoken and written language.* Norwood, NJ: Ablex Publishing Corp.

Meek, M. (1986). *Learning to read.* Portsmouth, NH: Heinemann Educational Books.

Ochs, E., & Schieffelin, B. B. (Eds.). (1979). *Developmental pragmatics.* NY: Academic Press.

Ochs, E. Transcription as theory. In Ochs, E., & Schieffelin, B. B. (Eds.). *Developmental pragmatics.* NY: Academic Press.

Schieffelin, B., & Cochran-Smith, M. (1984). Learning to read culturally. In H. Goelman, A. Oberg, & F. Smith (1984). *Awakening to literacy.* Exeter, NH: Heinemann Educational Books.

Smith, F. (1985). Reading without nonsense. New York: Teachers College Press.

Vygotsky, L. S. (1978). *Mind in society.* Cambridge, MA: Harvard University Press.

Whalen-Levitt, P. (1977, June). *A study of children's strategies for making meaning of visual narrative in Peter Wezel's The Good Bird.* Paper presented at ALA, Research Forum on Children's Books.

Chapter 7

Spontaneous and Natural Reading for Daily Living: Implications for the Special Learner

Carolyn N. Hedley

Fordham University

Shirley Brice Heath (1983), in her study of the literate traditions of two communities of the Piedmont Carolinas, Roadville and Trackton, has defined a new kind of reading task: reading for daily living. Reading for daily living is described by Heath as reading to learn before children go to school to learn to read; reading set in a context of immediate action; print surrounded by oral communication; reading that fosters activity; reading as a way to do and reading as a way to be. These descriptions of reading imply that, like the people of Trackton, learners, whether special or normative, use this kind of reading spontaneously, naturally, and successfully.

Heath described how members of the Trackton community across age levels used newspapers, car brochures, advertisements, church materials, homework, and official information that came to Trackton every day. "In addition, there are other rather more permanent reading materials in the community: boxes and cans of food products, house numbers, car names and license numbers, calendars and telephone dials, written messages on television, and name brands which are part of refrigerators, stoves, bicycles, and tools" (p. 190). Some writers (Cochran-Smith, in a previous chapter in this book) may describe these kinds of activity as contextualized reading tasks or literary events, but they are more than that.

In communities more middle class and urban than the Trackton and Roadville communities, reading is an activity engaged in to help us progress in such projects as preparing food, building a house, or getting along with peers. This kind of referential communication or reading activity that helps us with tasks of daily living and problem solving may be much more critical in a modern, middle class, metropolitan community than in a rural mill town. Like the people of Trackton, we are engaged in reading tasks that are surrounded by oral language and social activity; we read to be and to do, but at a different level of need.

Before the discussion of referential and contextualized reading continues, especially with regard to the special learner, the reader should be aware of two factors underlying the discussion. First, since reading for daily living occurs as much in the home and community as in the school, and such reading involves sharing with members of the family and community, we are not talking about age-related reading development. Rather, the discussion deals with across-age reading ability, in the preferred social milieu for such reading tasks. Second, we are discussing reading for daily living in terms of the special learner, particularly the learning-disabled person, who seems to pick up reading for daily living or survival reading skills reasonably well. However, reading tasks for daily living are a form of reading that all of us engage in. Thus, we will discuss how the normative learner manages these daily living reading tasks and then suggest how these ideas can be adapted to the special learner.

Levels of Referential Communication and Social Need

In a high-tech, mobile society, where persons will necessarily have to learn a great deal just to keep up with the demands of modern living, we need to analyze this fragmented, situation-related communication involving reading. We must become adequate learners and teachers of referential, context-dependent, functional, and informational reading tasks associated with the spontaneous, contingency-based communication. These functional reading tasks are as much a part of the highly educated, technologically advanced environment as they are part of life for the unskilled rural or the educationally less advanced. Indeed, we do so much of this spontaneous and unnoticed kind of reading that we have not really analyzed the various *levels of referential communication* and what is happening when we engage in such tasks.

At levels of *personal need*, learning the new dial system, or putting a tape on your telephone, reading to run the microwave, reading to work the new VCR, reading medicine bottles or prescriptions, using directories, or television guides, or doing banking, we read manuals and directives. In the realm of *career development*, we fill in forms and read manuals, read want-ads, take care of personnel actions, log our activity, learn how to use sales slips, and follow directions. In the area of *transportation and travel*, we learn to read maps, street signs road advertisements, and menus, look for services, read schedules, sign into motels, read directives on hotel doors, and learn by literature in hotels how to orient ourselves to a new community. Other reading activities help develop ideas for functioning in the world of *leisure, recreation, and sports.* In this category, we have directives for learning games, programs for music and art; programs for watching television, for attending plays, concerts, and brochures and flyers for taking tours, riding buses or boats for sightseeing purposes, as well as directives for conducting one's self in such settings.

Clearly, many of us, whether handicapped or not, have mastered many of the functional reading tasks of daily living. Indeed, in the area of special education, these reading skills have been called literacy for basic living or survival reading abilities. For the more normative learner, we think of such reading as referential communication or contextually based reading activity. Because we have to read the newspaper, the television guide, the junk mail, and other materials which are part of the literate society, we have become casual in our analysis of what is going on in terms of reading. However, the examination of reading in daily activities may have some implications for reaching the special learner.

Categories of Reading Tasks for Daily Living

Wells (1987a) describes the kind of literacy that we are talking of here as *functional literacy*, dealing with the concerns of being able to cope with the literate demands of everyday life. He writes: "In practice, teachers who emphasize the functional level of literacy tend to assume that the processes of coding and decoding have been learned; however, because they recognize that the form of written language varies according to the purpose that the writing serves, they devote much of their attention to getting students to practice on those types of texts that they judge to be functionally most important for them in life outside the school" (p. 43).

In his discussion, Wells categorizes levels of reading tasks into (a) performative (tasks that emphasize the graphic substance and the mechanics of reading and writing) (b) functional (literate demands of everyday life) (c) instrumental (reading and writing for information) and (d) epistemic (reading and writing which encourages the personal construction, evaluation, and reconstruction of knowledge or a way of transforming knowledge and experiences that are, in general, unavailable to those who have never learned to read and write). Wells writes: "there is a relationship of inclusiveness between the four proposed levels." However, he rejects the notion that these four levels conform to some kind of developmental progression. Wells points out that all four levels of literacy described in the model benefit children involved in literacy events. That is, all four levels of literate behavior are included when one is engaged in any one of them, at any age. Thus, children are able to engage in all levels of literacy in the model. However, students come to school with rather different conceptions of the purposes that written language can serve; thus, all four levels of the reading task may not be brought into play.

Given the success that all learners experience at this level, functional literacy for daily living may be a good level to emphasize when teaching the special learner. From this emphasis, the teacher can move to emphases on other levels, such as the mechanics of reading, reading for information or reading to construct, test, and reconstruct experience. Wells summarizes his presentation with the following points:

- The extent of a child's command of written language is the single most important predictor of his or her educational achievement at the end of the elementary years. Teachers are right, therefore, to give high priority to the acquisition of literacy in setting their goals for this stage of education.
- The development of literacy begins in the preschool years and, in a literate society, all children have already developed some understanding of written language and the purposes that it serves before they come to school.
- As with the development of spoken language, the early development of understanding of the form of written language takes place spontaneously and follows a common sequence, which is not dependent on deliberate or systematic instruction.
- With respect to understanding of the functions that written language seves, however, there is much greater variation among children; this is dependent on the sorts of literacy events that they have observed and participated in their local communities.
- Literacy events that emphasize all four levels in the proposed model of literacy provide the most adequate opportunities for children to become fully literate; shared story reading appears to be particularly beneficial from this point. (pp. 45–46)

Following these astute observations formed from Heath's work and his own studies done in Bristol, England, Wells (1987a) develops lessons for the teacher on how to instruct and create the literacy events that use the four levels of his reading model. We will not deal with instruction and construction of literacy events in this disussion but, rather, analyze the nature of referential communication and its implications for reaching the special learner.

The Uses of Reading and Writing: Language Integration

Heath, in describing the literacy events in both Roadville and Trackton, finds that the following categories of events emerge, though in different forms, in both communities:

Uses of Reading in Trackton and Roadville

Instrumental: reading to accomplish practical goals of daily life, such as dealing with checks, bills, clocks, and street signs.

Social interactional: reading to maintain social relationships, make plans, and introduce topics.

Recreation: reading for temporary entertaining, funny papers, brochures for camp grounds, and story telling.

News-related: reading to learn about third parties or distant events, local news items, and community center circulars.

Confirmational: reading to gain support for attitudes or beliefs already held: Bible, brochures on cars, loan notes, and bills.

Uses of Writing in Trackton and Roadville

Memory aids: writing to serve as a reminder for the writer and occasionally others—calendar and telephone numbers.

Substitutes for oral messages: writing used when direct oral communication was not possible or was embarrassing—notes to teachers, greeting cards, and letters.

Financial: writing to record numerals, and amounts, accompanying notes—checks and income tax preparation.

Public records: writing to announce the order of the church services and forthcoming events, and to record financial and policy decisions.

Social interactional: writing to give information and extend courtesies, and greetings for maintaining social linkages.

What is clear from Heath's analysis of reading and writing in these two communities is that oral communication, reading, and writing are language activities that are integrated into social events as well as into literacy events, simultaneously. The differences in learning to function in these two oral-literate communities, Trackton and Roadville (and in the modernized, urban community) is in degree and in kind; the activities are related to daily livings tasks of a similar nature. Finally, we do not find an oral tradition versus a written tradition; rather, there are integrative communicative activities centered around a task or an event. As Heath writes: The modes of expression serve to supplement and reinforce one another (1983, p. 230).

In both communities, children learn to accommodate reading for daily living. "Talk is the thing," and reading is social, for the most part. In Trackton, particularly, reading follows the flow of daily social transactions, with the community building bridges from print to practice. There are very few books in Trackton which children can use to relate to reading practice. Using Wells's analysis, the first emphasis in reading is functional, with performative, informational, and epistemic forms of reading flowing from functional reading. In analyzing the way in which children and adults learn to read in these communities, functional literacy is a primary and learned form of reading, though learned in the family and community. Formal instruction and the literacy of schooling follow, but literacy events are created by the community, in the community. Wells describes how the reading instruction of the school should be managed in order to continue the fluency of functional literacy into other forms of literacy. However, the cognitive processes, strategies, and skills inherent in functional literacy activity have not been analyzed by either Heath or Wells.

Cognitive Bases of Contextualized Reading

What knowledges and strategies are assumed and used to read and write in these communities? First, a primary knowledge of social structures, procedures, and traditions is requisite. That is, *cultural literacy* is basic to actual literacy. Literacy tasks are meaningless without an understanding of how they relate to the community and to particular events in the community. A knowledge of social structures and procedures is basic to literacy events and an understanding of social roles and needs is requisite to participating. Heath describes persons who read in isolation in the community as being somewhat apart from the community—they are regarded as being the "difficult people" in a community which expects and thrives on participation.

Second, a kind of *psychological decentering* is necessary in order to follow through on the reading-as-transaction task. Egocentrism has been contrasted with decentering or role-taking. Referential communication, by definition, requires the reader/actor to put himself or herself in another's place, to see the world through another's eyes in order to imagine doing the task. Thus, the participant in social literacy events of daily living takes roles in order to imagine how he or she can perform reading tasks related to social need. Such role-taking involves judgments about complex situations; it involves self-control and an understanding of individual versus situational viewpoints. A good referential reader must be quite sophisticated in his or her social development.

Third, these literate reactions are related to social and personal need. Therefore, *intentionality* or purpose for reading is basic to literacy task for daily living and coping—reading menus, reading literature from church, paying bills by check or cash, and the like. In fact, intentionality is pervasive when one reads to be and to do. Since we understand that language is a social and cultural phenomenon, we know that signs and symbols are created to communicate something to someone; and that they are purposeful and meaningful. Hence, intentionality is inherent in languaging, and it is pervasive in languaging at many levels. If one uses directions to explain how to make cookies from the box, the first reading of the package is to get an overview of the process. The next reading might be to find what utensils would be needed to carry out the task. Thus, the intention for reading varies within the accomplishment of the task, but the general intention is to make cookies. Intentions set into motion cognitive search strategies which propel the literacy event and literacy learning—it is not useful to ignore the meaning and intent contained in signs and symbols (Harste, Woodward, & Burke, 1984).

Notions of intentionality are probed and conveyed by the "why" questions. Why are you reading this? Why are we discussing this? Why are we arguing? How important is this notion? The "why" question gets at intentionality. "What motivates them individually and collectively?" is an underlying theme in probing the intentionality of social and literary events.

Intentions are inferences made on the basis of already inferred meanings. Thus, we do not have easy access to intentionality in reading and social behavior. Motivations are complex. In many cases, intentionality can be arrived at only through speculation, personal empathy, and other heuristic means, especially when one is looking for intentionality in the referential reading act, and speculation goes beyond a straightforward instrumental interpretation of language.

Within the notion of intentionality as part of communicated meaning are several social and cognitive structures that are part of the pervasiveness of intentionality in social reading transactions. One of the dimensions of intentionality in social and functional reading is *motivation*. "Why are we doing this?" "What's the point?" "Is there a point?" During reading that is surrounded by oral communication and social activity, the initial layer of intentionality should be fairly obvious, but there are other layers of intentionality that are more elusive.

Engagement in the literacy event suggest that feelings, and attitudes or *affect* (a dimension of motivation, within the context of intentionality) enter into why one participates and suggests what feelings one has about the outcomes of social participation and read-along strategies. "Do you enjoy getting bulletins and Sunday School papers from church?" "How do you feel when you don't get there?" "How do you feel if you don't understand some of the notes from the nursery school?" Depending on the nature of contextualized reading tasks, feelings about reading and its functions come into play with regard to the efficacy with which participation and reading occur. The affective dimension in the referential reading act is, in part, a function of motivation; but concerns about affect can be made by queries to determine affect quite apart from motivation. One can feel motivated to accomplish a task without feeling good about doing it. It is obvious that affect is both personal and social, that attitudinal concerns about oral language, reading, and writing are casual, when compared to the feelings that one might have about the personal and social relationships where reading occurs.

The notion of intentionality and its pervasiveness in the social literacy event or the referential reading act encompasses a number of other cognitive events. *Belief systems about the importance of language and reading,* about how language is used, and about life in communities is inherent in the referential reading act. *Expectancy as to what will be accomplished* by participating in socially and contextually relevant reading and writing acts is another dimension of intentionality that reflects these belief systems. Queries to the reader can get at these dimensions of intentionality. "Do you think that you are reading when you are looking at the manual as you set up the VCR?" "How helpful is the manual when you are putting together the bookcase?" "Do you think that reading the directions on the food package helps you get a better dinner?"

To say that contextualized reading and writing acts reflect complex cognitive behaviors is to generalize about the social judgments that occur in the process to the point of making such judgments trivial. Contained within the notion of intentionality about performing functional kinds of reading are not only motivational factors and belief systems, but *cognitive acts that direct behavior.* One cannot look at ends (intentions) without looking at means (the processes involved for the achieving the ends). Once engaged in a functional literacy event, one must make judgments about how to accomplish the task, how to organize activity, and how to make decisions regarding the various means to achieve one's ends, in a context. Queries of the learner with regard as to how he or she intends to achieve his or her purpose may be ascertained by means–ends analysis. Thus, we must try to understand not just the motivation (why?) behind a literacy event, but the means (how?) of accomplishment as well. "How will you accomplish this?" "What things will you do to make this happen?" "How can you do that?"

Strategies for Reading for Daily Living

The analysis of the social-functional literacy event takes us beyond the social and psychological processes and perspectives of the learner. Using a top-down approach, that is, going from the psychological and sociological factors underlying the referential reading task, a next step is to explore reading strategies used in reading for daily living. What does the reader *do* when one is participating, motivated, and talking, listening, reading, and, perhaps, writing—when one gets thr junk mail and looks through it, when one looks at the telephone directory or the *TV Guide*, when one consults maps and motor guides, when one is making muffins from the package?

The answers and discussion which follow, pointing out cognitive and metacognitive behaviors, contain a caveat. Too much analysis of strategies to be used in formal instruction may vitiate the contextually based, spontaneous, and natural reading act. Thus, this discussion is not intended as a guideline for instruction. Rather, such discussion helps us rationalize reading and social behaviors that are close to living, so that we may understand communicated meanings better. To attempt to *teach* these cognitive and metacognitive strategies as part of the functional reading task is to be premature in our action and probably wrong-headed in our method. The rationalization of the social reading experience has to be a satisfactory goal for our purposes. Simply understanding the nature of reading in the contextualized reading act may lead us to opportunistic means for enriching the literary-social event.

What happens while reading for daily living? What strategies are used by the reader/actor? Let's do a walk-through. First, the reader is usually involved in social transaction; he or she opens or finds a message in print that augments his or her discussion or causes it to take a different direction. "What do the minutes say?" "What's the special on today's menu?" From these initial acts, skimming, scanning, and advance organizers aid the reader-participant to use print material. He or she looks for specific information: headings, lists, numeration, and sequencing. Often the reader does previewing, and looks for organizational patterns. Whatever he or she is reading calls for activity, or for social participation, or in some ways regulates his or her behavior (the STOP sign). Remember, however, that this reading activity is sporadic— he or she looks, talks, and checks with others in the group. He or she may discuss, gain new insights from others, and gain new knowledges from the message that he or she is reading. The reader is engaged in higher level thought processes which involve his or her judgment, not only about the nature, purpose, and appropriateness of the material, but about its usefulness in the reference to his or her actions and/or discussions.

Reading itself involves using graphic visual material and integrating this material with print: using pictures, graphs, models, flow-charts, and sequence pictures. Reading of main words, headings, captions, salutations, dates, or survival words, such as *caution, poison, peas, help wanted, ladies, hamburger heaven, restaurant, food-gas,* and the like are just the sort of short messages that the special learner can accommodate. If the reader is not experienced enough to tackle sentences and paragraphs, at least these short eliptical messages can be useful and manageable.

The value of these social-literacy events is that they provide the frames of experience to which to relate print. Another positive outcome of these social encounters with print is that patterns of literate behavior are provided the learner; we know that modelling for the special learner is a powerful mode for learning. In these reading transactions, where oral language and social activity surround print, the learner can see how reading occurs, get help when difficulty occurs, and use the model of others to direct his or her reading and social behaviors.

So far, in our walk-through, the reader has participated in the literal comprehension in reading, combined with do-able tasks. But reading set in a context of immediate action involves higher level thought processes often not found in the academic task, much of which involves only translation of information. (Most school textbook learning involves comprehension tasks related to finding the main idea, reading for details, testing vocabulary, and, rarely, inferencing from text). In functional literacy tasks, inferences and activities derive from literal comprehension. Reading for daily living fosters activities that involve high level and high impact thought.

But while contextualized reading occurs, recall of past experience, problem-solving, reflection, decision-making, questioning, evaluation, discussion of relevant ideas, contrasts, and comparisons are made. Critical analysis, persuasion, and evaluation also occur. Goals are set, community life occurs, personal and group behaviors are organized. From this activity, knowledge and experiences are being internalized through the cognitive processes of assimilation and accommodation.

While these social and psychological processes are addressed, the learner is reading sporadicaly, often eliptically, gathering information from many sources. Reading is integrated into many other social and communicative acts. Reading rates are flexible and responsive to need; the social context while reading provides for vocabulary development; the written word gathers meaning from the social context. Messages often occur in short bursts which are manageable for the learner who is having difficulty with print.

The Special Learner and the Referential Reading Task

As Bereiter writes in a previous chapter, we should teach and work with the special learner opportunistically, as well as through direct instruction. Our actions with regard to referential reading, and the creation of literacy events should be couched in social activity. There is every reason to feel that survival reading is an effective way to reach the special learner. What is learned can be useful to his or her gaining control over himself or herself and the society in which he or she must live. As he or she is learning to master print in casual and natural ways, the learner is also involved in higher order social thought, the sort of thing that many special learners handle quite easily and well.

What are some caveats for the person helping the special learner with the referential reading task? When print is surrounded by oral communication and social activity, and the learner is special, then take time and be relaxed and positive during such activities; be sure that the learner is involved and attending; keep directions simple and concise; stress the sequences in language-integrated activity; point out materials for learners to read to help them in discussion and action; put ideas in both oral and written form; demonstrate and model ideas; complete a project together; display and praise the completed action or project; monitor the social-literary event after the learners have begun working on their event; ask for periodic status reports on long-term, sequenced, literary events. It is during the functional literacy task that other aspects of learning from print can occur opportunistically. The other levels of reading occur simultaneously—performative reading, emphasizing the mechanics of reading and writing; instrumental reading, reading and writing for information; and epistemic reading, the personal construction, evaluation, and reconstruction of experience—can be emphasized.

For too long, we have dealt with the special learner as an individual who is psychologically different and socially apart from the more normative learner. If there is one area where the similarities of psychological and social development can be seen, it is during the functional, referential reading act; we need more analysis of what is going on during this interplay between reading and living—there may be much that we can learn from survival reading tasks of special learners and the functional reading tasks of normative persons. Referential reading in social contexts may be the point of collaboration where the special learner and the regular learner can work together.

References

Anderson, R. C., Hiebert, E. H., Scott, J. A., & Wilkinson, I. A. G. (1985). *Becoming a nation of readers.* Washington, DC: National Institute of Education.

Cochran-Smith, M. (1983). *The making of a reader.* Norwood, NJ: Ablex Publishing Corp.

Cook-Gumperz, J. (1986). *The social construction of literacy.* Cambridge, England: Cambridge University Press.

Fillion, B., Hedley, C. N., & DiMartino, E. (1987). *Home and school: Early language and reading.* Norwood, NJ: Ablex Publishing Corp.

Flavell, J. H., & Ross, L. (1981). *Social cognitive development.* Cambridge, England: Cambridge University Press.

Goelman, H., Oberg, A., & Smith, F. (1984). *Awakening to literacy.* Portsmouth, NH: Heinemann Educational.

Gorlitz, D., & Wohlwill, J. F. (1987). *Curiosity, imagination, and play.* Hillsdale, NJ: Erlbaum.

Harste, J. C., Woodward, V. A., & Burke, C. I. (1984). *Language Stories and Literacy Lessons.* Portsmouth, NH: Heinemann Educational Books.

Hayes, J. R. (1981). *The complete problem solver.* Philadelphia, PA: The Franklin Press.

Heath, S. B. (1983). *Ways with words.* Cambridge, England: Cambridge University Press.

Hedley, C. N., & Baratta, A. N. (1985). *Contexts of reading.* Norwood, NJ: Ablex Publishing Corp.

Kovac, C., & Cahir, S. R. (1981). *When is reading?* Washington, DC: Center for Applied Linguistics.

Levin, B. J. (1981). *Real life reading skills.* New York: Scholastic Book Services.

McNeil, J. D. (1987). *Reading comprehension* (2nd ed.). Glenview, IL: Scott Foresman.

Meek, M. (1983). *Achieving literacy.* London: Routledge & Kegan Paul.

Nickerson, R.S. (1986). *Reflections on reasoning.* Hillsdale, NJ: Erlbaum.

Odell, L., & Goswami, D. (1985). *Writing in nonacademic settings.* New York: Guilford Press.

Overton, W. F. (1983). *The relationship between social and cognitive development.*

Hillsdale, NJ: Erlbaum.

Romaine, S. (1984). *The language of children and adolescents.* London: Basil Blackwell.

Rush, R. T., Moe, A. J., & Storlie, R. L. (1986). *Occupational literacy education.* Newark, DE: International Reading Association.

Santeusanio, R. P. (1983). *A practical approach to content area reading.* Reading, MA: Addison Wesley.

Stein, N. L. (1986). *Literacy in American schools.* Chicago, IL: University of Chicago Press.

Stubbs, M. (1986). *Educational linguistics.* London: Basil Blackwell.

Taylor, D. (1983). *Family literacy.* Portsmouth, NH: Heinemann.

Wells, G. (1981). *Learning through interaction.* Cambridge, England: Cambridge University Press.

Wells, G. (1987a). The learning of literacy. In B. Fillion, C. N. Hedley, & E. DiMartino (Eds.), *Home and school: Early language and reading.* Norwood, NJ: Ablex Publishing Corp.

Wells, G. (1987b). *The meaning makers.* Portsmouth, NH: Heinemann.

Werner, O., & Schoepfle, G. M. (1987). *Systematic fieldwork* (Vols 1 and 2). Beverly Hills, CA: Sage Publications.

Chapter 8

Comprehension Strategies for Special Learners

Patricia A. Antonacci

Fordham University

There are many children in our schools who are not learning to read. Reasons for their failures are numerous; classifications of their reading disabilities are also mounting. Whatever the factors related to students' failures, it is certain that the design of effective strategies to teach learners with special needs must consider the nature of the reading process as well as the reader.

Text Comprehension and the Reader

The reader plays the central role in the comprehension process. Ten years of the application of schema theory to reading is rather convincing of the reader's importance: the printed page is in itself devoid of meaning. Comprehending text is an act of creation which commences when the reader begins to infuse meaning into the written message as he interfaces with the author (Anderson, Reynolds, Schallert, & Goetz, 1977).

According to the schema-theoretic view of reading, it is the readers' utilization of their prior knowledge that allows them to construct meaning from the text (Anderson, 1986). The word concepts within the text provide a set of directions to its readers suggesting a blueprint for meaning construction based upon their previously acquired knowledge. Adams and Collins (1985) offer an explanation for this occurrence: The words of the text evoke in the reader associated concepts, their past interrelationships, and their potential interrelationships, while "the organization of the text helps him to select among these conceptual complexes" (p. 406). That the role of the reader's prior knowledge in shaping meaning from print is clear, for without its interaction with text, it is unlikely that the reader will build bridges between the "old" and the "new" information (Pearson & Johnson, 1978).

Use of Prior Knowledge by Poor Readers

Research demonstrates that there are critical differences between good and poor readers in their abilities to activate prior knowlege to use as a facilitator in text comprehension. While fluent readers are able to use their experiences to evaluate text, poor readers are incapable of this task (Bransford, 1979). At the high school level, disabled readers could not relate past experiences to what they have read (Sullivan, 1978). However, Bransford (1979) demonstrated that nonfluent readers could be instructed to utilize their prior knowledge to comprehend text.

Selection of efficient strategies for the special learner must be guided by the following findings:

1. Comprehension is an active process which occurs as the readers create meaning through relating their own conceptual knowledge to those concepts suggested by the text.

2. When students do not have the prerequisite prior knowledge to comprehend text, background knowledge should be supplied.

3. Poor readers lack competency in relating their own experiences and knowledge to the text.

4. Comprehension of text can be facilitated through direct and meaningful instruction with special learners on how to relate personal experience and prior knowledge to the text.

The purpose of this chapter is to suggest effective instructional strategies for readers who are special learners. The strategies suggested here emphasize activating the readers' prior knowledge to comprehend text, building conceptual knowledge through vocabulary development, and developing concepts for structures in narrative and expository text.

Interactive Vocabulary Instruction

Earlier in this chapter it was suggested that comprehension can occur only when readers are active processors of text, that is, when they deliberately choose to create meaning from the printed page. What happens to commence this act of creation? As a reader interacts with the text, his conceptual networks or schemata are activated. The reader's schemata are directed to come into play by the word concepts or the conceptual networks within the text; the activating command signal can be carried out only when there is a match between the reader's and the text's conceptual networks. This instantiation of prior knowledge is a prerequisite for the reader's construction of meaning (Dreher, 1986). When students do not have the necessary knowledge to deal with the text, comprehension is restricted. In other cases, students may possess the necessary knowledge but lack the linguistic referents or the labels for their knowledge structures (Beck, 1984; Pearson, 1984). This second case also restricts comprehension. Without the vocabulary labels for the concepts, the instantiation of the appropriate schemata utilized in comprehending text is impossible (Thelen, 1986).

There is no dispute over the central role that vocabulary knowledge plays in reading comprehension: It has been established that word meaning is strongly related to fluent reading (Barrett & Graves, 1981; Davis, 1972; Hunt, 1957). Poor readers have been earmarked as those who are deficient in word knowledge (Anderson & Freebody, 1981); further they are limited in their comprehension to certain word concepts within text (Antonacci, 1982).

The directive for enhancing word knowledge is quite clear: Comprehension strategies for special learnes should incorporate interactive vocabulary instruction that aims at building knowledge networks along with the appropriate linguistic referents derived from and related to those conceptual networks within the text. Fulfilling the criteria listed above for strategies for vocabulary development are semantic mapping and semantic feature analysis.

Semantic Mapping

As an instructional strategy for vocabulary development, semantic mapping is a powerful tool that puts demands on the students to become actively involved in their own learning. This procedure leads to the development of a visual schematic of categorically structured information (Johnson, Pittelman, & Heimlich, 1986). Throughout the process students are required to relate their own knowledge and personal experiences to pre-selected word concepts from the text. Learners are further asked to organize the information into rational categories (Johnson & Pearson, 1984). Rather than presenting word meanings as isolated, unrelated lists of words (Heimlich & Pittelman,

1986), semantic mapping provides the reader with an opportunity for viewing word meaning as a network of knowledge derived from personal experiences and self-knowledge but related to concepts within the text.

Procedure for Using Semantic Mapping as an Instructional Strategy for Vocabulary Development

The following procedure has been adapted from a strategy for semantic mapping suggested by Johnson and Pearson (1984, pp. 12–13).

1. Select the critical word concepts. After careful reading of the students' text, select the word concepts that are important to comprehending the passage.
2. Write the word concept. Working with one concept at a time, write the target word on the chalkboard.
3. Brainstorm related words. Encourage the students to brainstorm as many words or groups of words that are related to the target word. Write the students' responses on the chalkboard.
4. Categorize groups of related words. With the students, analyze the words for the purpose of placing them in an appropriate category.
5. Name each category. After discussing the nature of the relationship among the words within a given category, have the students select a title for that category.
6. Complete this procedure (Steps 2–5) with each target word selected from the text.
7. Discuss word relationships. The categorical arrangement of words is a visual representation of the knowledge network that relates the "old" information (students' prior knowledge) to the "new" information (text information). The focus of this discussion is on this relationship which provides the students with the preparation of the text reading that is to follow.

Discussion makes this strategy effective (Stahl & Vancil, 1986). There is a greater depth in processing of word meaning by active discussants, because they are called upon the generate lists of related words, to categorize words correctly, to draw relationships between new words and knowledge they already have.

Semantic Mapping as a Prereading Activity

As a prereading activity, semantic mapping serves many functions. Primarily it is used as an alternative to the traditional techniques to develop vocabulary. When semantic mapping is used before reading the text, the teacher taps the readers' prior knowledge, organizes it with them, and helps them to connect their old ideas with the new information. Additionally, students see new linguistic labels, previously unknown to them, assigned to their preexisting knowledge structures. Finally, the use of semantic mapping as a prereading strategy allows the teacher to sufficiently evaluate the students' related knowledge. If a paucity of prerequisite knowledge is found, the teacher must make a decision: Attempt to build the students' knowledge base needed to comprehend the text or choose a different text to read.

Semantic Mapping as a Postreading Activity

The postreading semantic map, as an instructional strategy, can be an equally effective activity (Johnson et al., 1986). In building a semantic map of the text after its reading, students are provided the opportunity of recalling, organizing, and graphically representing textual information they have just read. The students may design this knowledge map during or after reading the text; they may construct a second postreading-semantic map or expand the prereading map. In any case, the postreading schematic should be quite expansive, because it represents a fusion of the "old" with the "new" information from the text. Figure 1 illustrates the differences between the pre- and the postreading semantic maps, showing the second map as an elaborate version of the first.

Semantic Feature Analysis as a Strategy in Vocabulary Development

Semantic feature analysis is another very powerful strategy, because it is derived from the theoretical construct of ways that humans process and organize information. Further, as a strategy to develop vocabulary, it is highly effective, because it builds on the students' personal knowledge as they are actively involved in their own learning.

Categorization is one way that human organisms deal with the vast stimuli in the environment. This process enables us to learn and to retrieve large quantities of information while conserving our finite resources; we are, so to speak, cognitively economic (Rosch, 1978). For example, for each encounter we have with a tree, we do not need to learn about the features of each individual tree, because we already possess a concept for "tree," that is, a knowledge structure of features

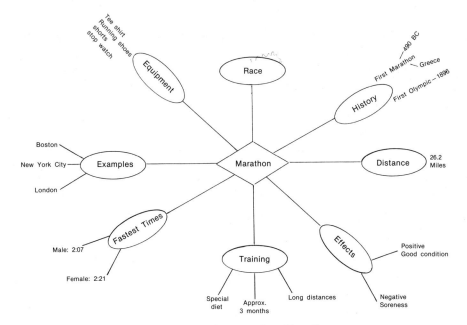

Figure 1a. Prereading semantic map for Marathon

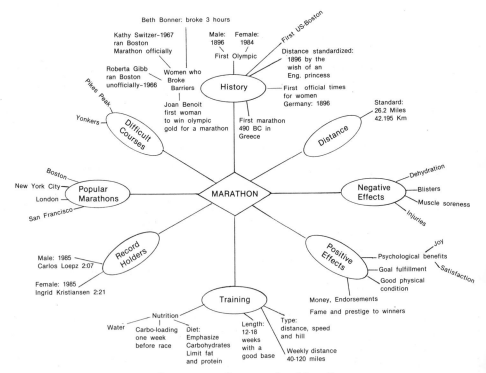

Figure 1b. Postreading semantic map for Marathon

common to all trees. Therefore, we assign the tree to its correct category, making it possible to process the tree and then go on to the next object. However, as we learn more about different trees, the category becomes too large; not all trees share the same features. These distinct features among objects represent elaborate concepts that need an equally elaborate language to make this knowledge useful.

Semantic feature analysis is an effective instructional strategy to achieve this end: It is a singular procedure proposed to expand conceptual knowledge and language. While its design is a corollary to the architecture of the structure of information and the category system of the human organism, it works to explore the nature of knowledge and to reinforce vocabulary concepts through categorization.

Procedures for Using Semantic Feature Analysis as a Strategy for Vocabulary Development

1. Select a single category. Since the purpose of this strategy is to develop vocabulary related to the text, the category selected should represent the topic of the text.

2. List in a column at the left of the paper or the chalkboard concepts within the category. Once again, these should be related to the text that is to be read.

3. List in a row, at the top of the page or on the chalkboard, features, properties, or descriptors shared by some words.

4. Place a plus beside each word, beneath the feature, if it shares that property.

5. Place a minus beside each word, beneath the feature, if it does not share that property.

6. Students may brainstorm to add additional words and features.

7. If the text to be read by students is long and includes several topics, it may be necessary to repeat this process with other categories so that the students have sufficient background knowledge before reading the text.

Figure 2 depicts a semantic feature chart for the category, *kitchen tools*, which serves as an example.

Additional Activities Involving Semantic Feature Analysis

After the students have gained experience with semantic feature analysis, there are other extended activities that use the same general

Figure 2. Semantic Feature Analysis

Kitchen Tools	Features					
Terms	Sharp	Electric	Measure	Stir	Cut	Scrape
Bread knife	+	±	−	−	+	−
Peeler	+	±	−	−	−	+
Scissors	+	∓	−	−	+	−
Beater	−	−	−	+	−	−
Spatula	−	−	∓	+	−	+
Strainer	−	−	−	−	−	−
Measuring cup	−	−	+	−	−	−

N. B. A plus (+) and a minus (−) together indicates that the object could possess either feature.

procedure and will enable children to take closer look at their language for even finer differences among related word meanings (Johnson & Pearson, 1984). Utilizing these strategies should continue to foster word awareness in readers as they internalize the concept of precise word meaning.

1. *Listing words that share a feature.* Write a feature on the chalkboard. Have children list words that share the feature.

2. *Ranking words on a single shared feature.* All word concepts do not share the same feature equally; this difference may be on the basis of intensity, strength, seriousness, or any other quality. On the chalkboard, write words in a list that share a feature. Let the students determine the rank order of words on the basis of the single shared feature. A rationale for ranking the words in a particular order should be provided by the students.

3. *Determining the shared feature from a list of words.* Provide a list of words with at least one shared feature. Do not tell the children the feature; they must determine the shared feature. A systematic procedure for doing this is the following: Have the students generate all possible features for each word. Then direct them to search for the feature common to all words within the given list.

Comprehension Strategies for Two Types of Text

The task of progressing through the stages of reading development for young children is not quite simple. Beginning reading instruction commences with very simple stories, as the young readers quickly advance to longer stories that are more complex in nature. By the time children reach grade 4, they must make the very difficult transition from understanding stories (narrative text) to reading and learning from their subject matter textbooks (expository texts). Additional demands are placed on maturing readers as they are challenged with increasingly complicated literature.

Reading programs that rely heavily on the basal readers and the teachers' guides to supply necessary instruction in comprehension to adequately prepare children for comprehending different forms of text have been questioned by authorities (Durkin, 1978–1979). One of the major criticisms of the basal-reader programs is their heavy reliance on questioning as a means to teach comprehension. If special learners are to develop strategic processing skills needed to comprehend text, they need direct instruction.

Two comprehension strategies which suggest direct instruction and student involvement are presented here. The first strategy includes a procedure for assessing students' understanding of stories along with a method for developing their story schemata. The second strategy is instruction in comprehending expository text. Through a writing approach students are taught to recognize the main idea.

Using Story Grammar Strategies to Improve Comprehension for Stories

How is a person able to recall all of the important parts of a story? What does it mean to have a schema for a story? When do people acquire a story schema; does it ever change? For 10 years researchers have been involved in studying these and other questions related to story comprehension. Much of their research has focused on procedures to analyze the structure of stories, the developmental aspects of story schema in children, the knowledge of story structure and its effects upon comprehension as well as the use of instructional strategies for improving story comprehension.

Story grammar research.   Initial research in story grammar began with the construction of a number of different procedures for analyzing stories. Varying sets of rules for studying stories and classifying their elements or parts were developed by Kintsch (1977), Mandler and Johnson (1977), Rumelhart (1975), Stein and Glenn (1979), and Thorndyke (1977). That schema is used by a reader or a listener as a set of expectations for story structure, to aid in story comprehension, and to improve memory for the story (Mandler & Johnson, 1977; Stein, 1979) was an important finding. Applebee (1981) noted developmental differences between younger and older children's story schemas. As children are exposed to more stories, they gain greater competence over story elements: They progress from telling stories comprised of a few unrelated elements to retellings which are highly structured stories, containing all the story elements, many details, inferences, all related to common themes (McConaughy, 1980).

Finally, research has continued to focus in on the effects of instruction about story elements upon comprehension. Effective instructional practices include the development of a story map and story grammar frameworks for use in preparing questions in guiding the reader through the story (Beck & McKeown, 1981; Cunningham & Foster, 1978). For readers who lack comprehension for stories, these strategies may be especially useful (Fitzgerald & Spiegel, 1983). To help young children develop a sense of story, Galda (1982) suggested creative drama which demands active student involvement in all of the story's elements. A retelling strategy was designed to utilize children's story schema to make predictions about the story and to confirm and compare their predictions with those of their classmates (Cambourne, 1984).

In the next part of this section, a brief overview of story grammar is presented; its understanding is necessary for the implementation of any related instructional strategy. Following this brief overview are two detailed descriptions of story grammar strategies that may be used with special learners. Finally, specific suggestions to develop an awareness of story structure are made.

What is story grammar?   Story grammar may be described as an "idealized internal representation of the parts of a typical story and the relationship among those parts" (Mandler & Johnson, 1977, p. 111). It is a procedure which consists of a set of rules that defines a text's structure into its elements and their relationships. People possess a knowledge about the structure of a prototypical story which changes or develops as they read, hear, and see more and more stories. According to Stein and Glenn (1979), a story consists of two major parts, the *setting* and the *episode*. The *setting* introduces the main character, describes the time, place, and context in which the event occurred. The *episode* is the second major part which includes the five following categories: The *initiating event* sets the story in motion causing the main character to respond in some manner. The *internal response* is the main character's reaction to the initiating event which results in the establishment of the story's goal that motivates subsequent behavior. The *attempt* consists of one action or a series of actions to achieve the goal. The *consequence* is the element which notes goal attainment or the failure to achieve the goal. Finally, the *reaction* tells how the main character responded to the consequence.

While simple stories contain one or two episodes with few characters, more complex stories contain numerous interrelated episodes. Figure 3 shows how the *Mrs. Cow* story has been analyzed into its parts (Spiegel & Fitzgerald, 1986). This example of story analysis clarifies its process. Note that this simple story has one setting and a single episode.

A Strategy for Assessing Students' Story Schema

Teachers may wish to determine how well children remember a story they have read or heard. Instead of traditional questions used to check comprehension, student retellings may be evaluated. What is being measured is the completeness of the students' retellings of the story, determined by the inclusion of the story elements in their retellings. The student must organize and retrieve the important information related to the story. If a student has a well-developed concept for stories, his retelling should be complete; a student who has a paucity of knowledge for story structure should produce incomplete retellings.

Figure 3.   The Parts of *The Mrs. Cow Story**

Setting	One day Mrs. Cow was walking around the barnyard on Mr. Brown's farm.
Initiating Event	All of a sudden she spied Mr. Brown's garden, just outside the barnyard fence.The garden was full of ripe cabbages, tender green beans, juicy melons, and delicious squash.
Internal Response	Mrs. Cow said to herself, "My, those vegetables and fruits are very tempting. And I am sooooo hungry."
Goal	Mrs. Cow decided to get into the garden somehow.
Attempt	So she trotted all the way back across the barnyard, until she was as far away from the garden fence as she could get. Then she lowered her head and ran as fast as she could right at the fence. Wham! She hit the fence hard.
Consequence	The fence was old and it broke into 100 pieces. Mrs. Cow smiled in satisfaction and stepped daintily over the shattered fence, into the garden.
Reaction	Mr. Brown, of course, was not very pleased, and tied Mrs. Cow up in the barn for 3 days as a punishment. But Mrs. Cow was sure that it had been worth it!

**The Mrs. Cow Story* was analyzed by Spiegel and Fitzgerald (1986, p. 679). The same labels for the story elements were not used.

The following procedure for evaluating student retellings has been suggested by Marshall (1983).

1. Select an appropriate story for the individual student. While kindergarteners can retell very short stories that they listen to, children who are in the fourth grade may be able to retell longer, more complex stories.

2. Use regular reading instructional time. After children have read or heard the story, have one student retell the story while you record his responses on a checklist developed by Marshall (1983) for this purpose. To do this, write the story elements across the top of the page next to each other, creating a column for each element. At the side of the page, list the students' names so that each student has a set of boxes to represent the story elements.

3. If the student mentions the story element, record a plus (+) in the appropriate box; if he fails to mention the story element a prompt question should be asked by the teacher. (The prompt response is given in the form of a question designed for the specific story element the student fails to mention. Use the genetic questions in Figure 4 as a guide to develop prompt questions for specific story elements.) If the student responds correctly to the prompt question, record a check (ν) in the appropriate box; if he fails in his second attempt, record a minus ($-$).

4. Students are evaluated individually; however, each retelling may be conducted as part of the reading group activity. If this is done, the same story should not be used to evaluate another student's story recall, since he would have two exposures to that story. During the course of

Figure 4.   Generic Questions Used to Develop Prompt Questions

---

Setting

Character: Who is the main character? What is he like?
Time: When does the story take place?
Place: Where does the story take place?

Episode

Initiating event: What happens at the beginning of the story to set it in motion?
Internal response: How does _____ realize he had a problem?
Goal: What is _____'s problem?
Attempt: What does _____ do to solve the problem?
Consequence: Does it work?
Reaction: What happens to _____?
How does _____ feel at the end of the story?

---

the school year, each student should get an opportunity to retell four different stories.

5. Some stories contain story parts that are implicitly stated, creating greater demands on the comprehension processes of the students. To recall implicitly stated text, readers must make inferences. Therefore, this should be noted by recording inferred story elements with an additional symbol; underscore the plus (+), the check (✓), or the minus (–) for the recall of implicit story parts.

Story grammar as an assessment technique can provide greater insights into students' reading achievement. In many of the traditional teacher-made tests that are used to evaluate reading performance, test items measure isolated skills in reading, many of which are not fairly represented on a test. However, this is not the case in the story grammar assessment strategy where the integrated processes of comprehension are emphasized as students retell the entire story and the teacher observes how well the important information from the story is recalled (Marshall, 1983). Moreover, the teacher who wishes to make effective decisions regarding the selection of appropriate instructional strategies needs to be guided by valid assessment techniques.

An instructional strategy to develop story schema.   Poor readers who have a limited knowledge of story structure may be given a framework to help them recall the important elements of the story (Fitzgerald & Spiegel, 1983; Spiegel & Fitzgerald, 1986). Generally, the framework consists of a set of generic questions that follow the structure of a prototypical story. Students and teachers may use the questions in a number of ways, but the purpose is the same: To provide a systematic cueing system that serves the reader in retrieving the important information from the story, since questions follow "the progression of ideas and events in the story" (Beck & McKeown, 1981, p. 915).

The following strategy is one that has been adapted from several researchers (Fitzgerald & Spiegel, 1983; Sadow, 1982). It uses the generic questions along with a graphic aid—a visual map of the story. The procedure consists of the following steps:

1. The teacher prepares the materials in advance. They are as follows: (a) an appropriate story for the students for listening or for reading; (b) a set of prompt or cue questions designed from the generic questions in Figure 4; (c) an "empty" story map with the appropriate number of boxes to match the elements of the story.

2. The teacher prepares the class for the reading of the story. Since it is important that students become actively involved in the story, establishing a purpose for reading is a critical phase of instruction. One way to prepare students to read the story is to discuss the setting and

the problem that confronts the main character. Then ask students to make predictions about possible solutions or attempts at the goal.

3. List the students' predictions.

4. Display the story map with empty frames. Ask students the parts of the story that you have already told them. As they respond, fill in the frames, telling them that each box represents an important part of the story.

5. Next, ask the students to read the rest of the story independently or read it to them.

6. The completion of the story is followed by the discussion which focuses on which of the listed predictions were confirmed within the story.

7. Ask students to recall the story by using the prompt questions that were designed from the generic questions. As students respond with story information, fill in the appropriate frames on the story map. Show students how each question is designed to cue the recall of a specific story element. Figure 5 shows a completed story map and prompt questions for *The Mrs. Cow Story.*

8. The discussion should stress the relationship of the story parts. For example, if Mrs. Cow were not hungry, would she have broken through the fence to get into the garden to eat the delicious fruits and vegetables?

9. Throughout the discussion, refer to the visual display of the story elements on the story map, making deliberate attempts to explain the relationships among the parts of the story.

For poor readers, the combination of the prompt questions and the visual display of the story parts promotes a greater depth of processing of the text, facilitates memory for story, and heightens the students' awareness of story structure. As the line of questions progresses through the story, the readers begin to retrieve story information systematically. Frequent use of this strategy will provide special learners with a basic framework to develop their own strategies for recalling important story information.

Additional suggestions to develop story schemata.   1. *Read every day.* Children love to be read to, regardless of age or ability. They enjoy hearing enthusiastic teachers reading interesting literature. An increased exposure to good stories, possessing a well-developed structure, ensures the listeners a heightened awareness of story structure.

2. *Promote silent reading.* Because reading achievement is significantly related to the amount of independent silent reading that children do in school (Allington, 1984), it is important that the time children engage in silent reading in school be increased. It is equally important that during

Figure 5.   A Story Map for *The Mrs. Cow Story*

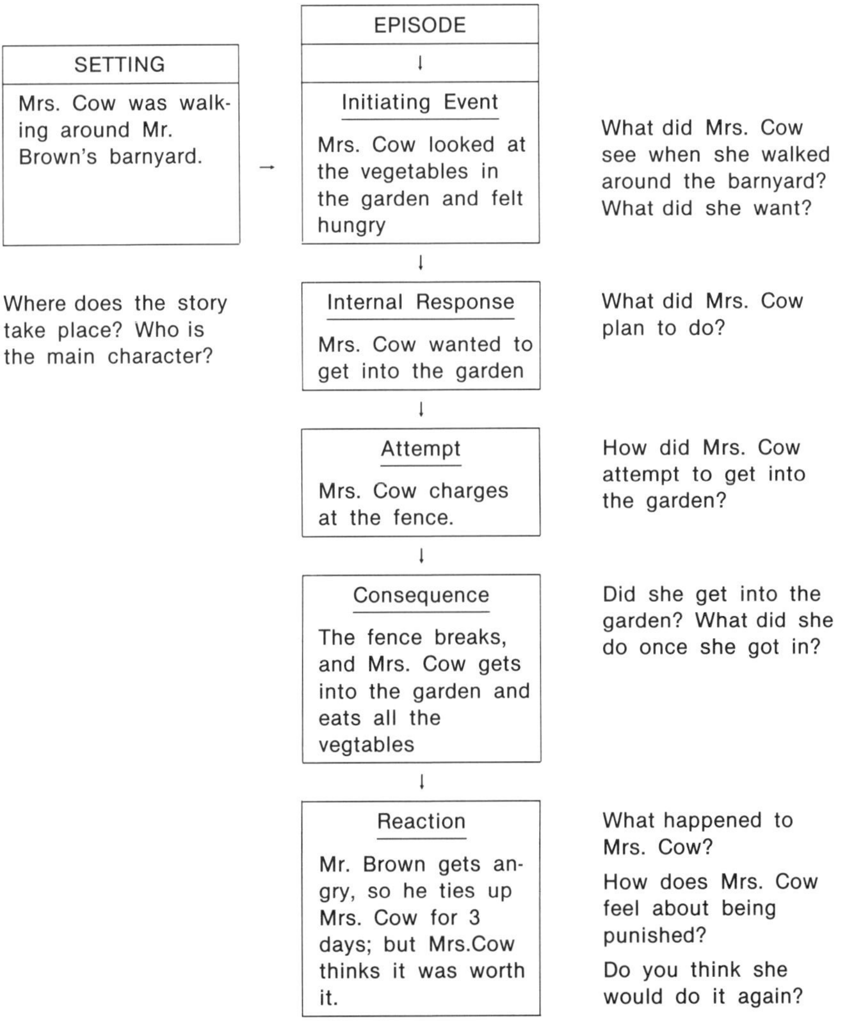

SETTING	EPISODE	
Mrs. Cow was walking around Mr. Brown's barnyard.	↓ Initiating Event Mrs. Cow looked at the vegetables in the garden and felt hungry	What did Mrs. Cow see when she walked around the barnyard? What did she want?
Where does the story take place? Who is the main character?	↓ Internal Response Mrs. Cow wanted to get into the garden	What did Mrs. Cow plan to do?
	↓ Attempt Mrs. Cow charges at the fence.	How did Mrs. Cow attempt to get into the garden?
	↓ Consequence The fence breaks, and Mrs. Cow gets into the garden and eats all the vegtables	Did she get into the garden? What did she do once she got in?
	↓ Reaction Mr. Brown gets angry, so he ties up Mrs. Cow for 3 days; but Mrs.Cow thinks it was worth it.	What happened to Mrs. Cow? How does Mrs. Cow feel about being punished? Do you think she would do it again?

this silent reading period the teacher fosters quality literature that is both comprehensible and interesting to the readers.

3. *Guide students in predicting deleted parts of incomplete stories.* Waley (1981) suggests the use of a macro-cloze task designed after the

traditional cloze activity where words in a text are deleted. In the macro-cloze task, a story part is omitted which may be represented by one or more sentences. In place of the deleted story part, lines are drawn to indicate where the missing story element appears in the text. After students read the story, they are asked to write the missing story part. Acceptable responses need not match the content of the story, but they should fit the condition of the deleted story element. A discussion, guided by the teacher, should bring children to understand what story part is deleted, the type of information that would be appropriate, and why inappropriate responses do not fit into the structure of the story.

Story grammar strategies are beginning to find their way into the classrooms. As with any other strategy, its success depends upon how well it is implemented. One word of caution in its application—Story grammar is a means to an end. That is, the technical terminology should be avoided wherever possible. Teaching readers to dissect a story will not make them fluent readers. The purpose of story grammar strategies is to provide a prop or a framework for those students who have difficulty in locating the important information in a sotry and organizing its parts into a whole. The framework is merely an organizer allowing the reader to match and to assemble the ideas from the story in a systematic progression fitting the blueprint of a story.

Comprehension Strategies for Expository Text

In the primary grades, children's first experiences in learning to read are with stories, narrative text. There is good reason for this: By the time children enter school most have already acquired a sense of story structure (Applebee, 1978) from hearing stories at bedtime, being read to in nursery and kindergarten, and viewing stories on television. Further, stories are a natural form of entertainment, providing the motivation that a child may need to learn to read. So stories are a good starting point in beginning reading instruction. However, when students reach fourth grade, greater demands with respect to the text are placed on their learning (Flood & Lapp, 1986).

Transition from Narrative to Expository Text

Intermediate grade students must now read to gain information from content textbooks. Their exposure to a new type of discourse, expository text, with a different text structure, presents increased text processing demands: In addition to learning a new technical vocabulary, children must acquire an inner sense for expository writing (Meyer, 1975). This period represents a difficult transition when children come from reading familiar narrative text to the unfamiliar expository (Flood, Lapp, & Farnan, 1986). Comprehending content textbooks does not come automatically to children; for some it is a slow process; but for poor readers it appears to be an almost impossible daily task. However, with direct instruction and practice, poor readers can be sensitized to the structural factors in expository writing needed for comprehension.

Finding the Main Idea from Expository Text

Throughout their school lives, children are asked to read content text and remember the important information. Teachers agree with researchers that this assignment is the source of much difficulty for their students (Winograd & Bridge, 1986). Instruction of main idea as a skill (or set of skills) in reading across the wide range of grade levels only emphasizes its importance as well as its difficulty. Ability to synthesize information in the text, to find or to generate the main idea, is critical to successful learning (Brown, Campione, & Day, 1981). While fluent readers are more sensitive than poor readers to important information in the text (Winograd, 1984), most readers find difficulty in locating the main idea even in simple texts (Baumann, 1983). Therefore, a strategy designed for effective instruction of main idea would not only promote fluency in reading for the students but would equip them with a useful tool for efficient learning.

A Writing Strategy for Learning to Read Main Idea

Researchers have come quite a distance in studying the reading/writing connection. Not only are these two processes complementary and reciprocal (Squire, 1983), but there is a strong influence of writing on developing effective reading strategies (Stotsky, 1983). Calkins (1986) explains the effects of authorship on this relationship:

> I have found authorship is also a process. . . . (I have) new insights into what I read, finding new layers of meaning in the work of other authors. I have become an insider in reading . . . being an author changes how I read. The amazing thing is that even five-year-olds can make these connections. (pp. 220–221)

If there are difficulties in teaching children to locate the main idea, make them authors! Let them as "insiders" discover how to write the main idea in order to find it in the works of other authors. Calkins' point of view of turning students into writers to make them better readers, critics of the printed page, is a strong argument for teaching the main idea through a writing strategy to all students.

The following instructional strategy has been adapted from one suggested by Flood and Lapp (1986). Changes of the original procedure include modelling the process by the teacher and elaborations with regard to the directions.

Procedure

Step 1: Modelling the writing process. Objective: The purpose of this step is to demonstrate to the writers the behaviors of the composing process in which they will be engaged. The teacher thinks aloud the students' thought processes of the writing procedure in Steps 2 to 5.

1. To prepare for this step, the teacher should have the title of each step, its objective and set of directions printed on large chart paper. The language should be appropriate to the students' age and ability. Additional chart paper and a felt pen should be on hand for the composing process.

2. The teacher explains the purpose of the strategy and provides a general overview of the procedure, along with a discussion of how she will model the process.

3. For each step, the teacher explains its purpose and the set of directions, referring to the chart. After describing the directions for a step, the teacher will "do" the step. It is critical that the students see and hear the teacher in the actual composing process, thinking aloud as she engages in writing. The teacher writes on the chart paper as the students look on. After this step is completed the students are encouraged to begin the process at Step 2.

Step 2: Prewriting. Objective: The purpose of the prewriting step is to generate a topic of interest, to determine facts and ideas the writer already knows, related to the topic, and to gather information from various sources about the topic.

1. The teacher and the student have a conference which is similar to an interview. Through questioning by the teacher and the writer, brainstorming, and reflection, the topic is generated.

2. Now the teacher probes to determine how much information the writer already knows. This fact-finding session is conducted with open-ended questions. As the writer responds with the information he already knows, he lists the facts.

3. The conclusion of this step is gathering information from the experts. The written sources include encyclopedias, reference books, books related to the topic, pamphlets, newspapers, magazines; other sources include teachers, adults familiar with the topic, and librarians. Each piece of information and its source are recorded.

Step 3: Theme composing.   Objective: The purpose of this step is to analyze the information, to decide the information to be included in the paragraph, and to generate, in sentence format, a main idea for the information.

1. Study each fact and begin to select only those pieces of information that will be used in the paragraph.

2. Cross out any repetitious information.

3. Begin to narrow: This demands a classification of information. Group two related facts. Decide the basis of their relatedness. Determine which facts belong to the group. When you have one complete group of related facts, begin the process over again until you have exhausted the list of facts. After the categorization of information, the student decides on the group he will write about.

4. This group of facts is studied by the writer who asks, "How are the facts related?"

5. Based upon the answer to the question above and the body of facts, the writer constructs a main idea sentence which he records on a separate paper.

Step 4: Elaboration on the theme.   Objective: The purpose of this step is to use the main idea sentence and the selected category of facts to write a paragraph.

1. Students are asked to write a paragraph to expand the main idea.

2. The writer studies the main idea and the information. He uses the information to expand and explain the main idea in a paragraph format. The sentences are written under the main idea in paragraph form.

Step 5: Feedback, rewriting, editing.   Objective: The purpose of this step is to construct a good text, one that is comprehensible by the writer's peers. The writers are helped by their peers and teacher who are the listeners and editors.

1. Feedback: Writers may pair with a partner or be part of a small group. Each member reads his paragraph for the purpose of receiving reactions from the group on clarity of ideas. A copy can be given to each group members so that revisions may be made.

2. Revision: The writer and the teacher confer, studying the sug-

gested changes. The writer will then incorporate these into a rewritten paragraph of the original text.

3. Editing: The focus of this stage is the form of the paragraph. The mechanics of language, such as spelling and punctuation, are corrected. The final copy is recorded on a separate paper.

Presented in this chapter are suggestions for helping the special learner reach the stage of fluent reading. Active student involvement in comprehension and drawing upon his knowledge resources in learning to comprehend text are emphasized in the suggested strategies. Whatever instructional procedure is selected to teach understanding, its focus should work to recruit the reader as the primary figure in meaning construction.

References

Adams, M. J., & Collins, A. (1985). A schema-theoretic view of reading. In H. Singer & R. B. Ruddell (Eds.), *Theoretical models and processes of reading* (3rd ed.). Newark, DE: International Reading Association.

Allington, R. L. (1984). Oral reading. In P. D. Pearson (Ed.), *Handbook of reading research*. New York: Longman.

Anderson, R. C. (1986). Role of the reader's schema in comprehension, learning, and memory. In H. Singer & R. B. Ruddell (Eds.), *Theoretical models and processes of reading* (3rd ed.). Newark, DE: International Reading Association.

Anderson, R. C., & Freebody, P. (1981). Vocabulary knowledge. In J. T. Guthrie, (Ed.), *Comprehension and teaching: Research reviews*. Newark, DE: International Reading Association.

Anderson, R. C., Reynolds, R. E., Schallert, D. L., & Goetz, E. G. (1977). Frameworks for comprehending discourse. *American Educational Research Journal, 14,* 367–382.

Antonacci, P. A. (1982). *Effects of varying protypicality and argument-repetition on sentence comprehension by high- and low-ability readers.* Unpublished doctoral dissertation, Fordham University

Applebee, A. (1978). *The child's concept of story.* Chicago: The University of Chicago Press.

Baker, L., & Brown, A. L. (1984). Cognitive monitoring in reading. In J. Flood (Ed.), *Understanding reading comprehension*. Newark, DE: International Reading Association.

Barrett, M. T., & Graves, M. F. (1981). A vocabulary program for junior high school remedial readers. *Journal of Reading, 25,* 146–150.

Baumann, J. F. (1983). Children's ability to comprehend main idea in content textbooks. *Reading World, 22,* 322–331.

Beck, I. (1984). Developing comprehension: The impact of the directed reading lesson. In R. C. Anderson, J. Osborn, & R. J. Tierney (Eds.), *Learning to read in American schools: Basal readers and content texts.* Hillsdale, NJ: Lawrence Erlbaum Associates.

Beck, I., & McKeown, M. G. (1981). Developing questions that promote comprehension: The story map. *Language Arts, 58,* 913–918.

Bransford, J. D. (1979). *Human cognition: Learning, understanding and remembering.* Belmont, CA: Wadsworth.

Brown, A. L., Campione, J. C., & Day, J. J. (1981). Learning to learn: On training students to learn from texts. *Educational Researcher, 10,* 14–21.

Calkins, L. M. (1986). *The art of teaching writing.* Portsmouth, NH: Heinemann.

Cambourne, B. (1984). *Retelling as a pedagogical strategy: Summary thoughts.* Presentation at Miscue Update Conference, Detroit.

Cunningham, J., & Foster, E. O. (1978). The ivory tower connection: A case study. *The Reading Teacher, 31,* 365–369.

Davis, F. B. (1972). Psychometric research on comprehension in reading. *Reading Research Quarterly, 7,* 628–678.

Dreher, M. J. (1986). Spontaneous instantiation of general terms. In H. Singer & R. B. Ruddell (Eds.), *Theoretical models and processes of reading* (3rd ed.). Newark, DE: International Reading Association.

Durkin, D. (1978–1979). What classroom observations reveal about reading comprehension instruction. *Reading Research Quarterly, 14,* 481–553.

Fitzgerald, I., & Spiegel, D. L. (1983). Enhancing children's reading comprehension through instruction in narrative structure. *Journal of Reading Behavior, 15,* 1–17.

Flood, J., & Lapp, D. (1986). Getting the main idea of the main idea: A writing reading process. In J. F. Baumann (Ed.), *Teaching main idea comprehension.* Newark, DE: International Reading Association.

Flood, J., Lapp, D., & Farnan, N. (1986). A reading-writing procedure that teaches expository paragraph structure. *The Reading Teacher, 39,* 556–562.

Galda, L. (1982). Playing about a story: Its impact on comprehension. *The Reading Teacher, 36,* 52–55.

Heimlich, J. E., & Pittelman, S. D. (1986). *Semantic mapping: Classroom applications.* Newark, DE: International Reading Association.

Hunt, C. L. (1957). Can we measure specific factors associated with reading comprehension? *Journal of Educational Research, 51,* 161–171.

Johnson, D. D., & Pearson, P. D. (1984). *Teaching reading vocabulary* (2nd ed.). New York: Holt, Rinehart, & Winston.

Johnson, D. D., Pittelman, S. D., & Heimlich, J. E. (1986). Semantic mapping. *The Reading Teacher, 39,* 778–783.

Kintsch, W. (1977). On comprehending stories. In J. Just & P. Carpenter (Eds.), *Cognitive processes in comprehension.* Hillsdale, NJ: Lawrence Erlbaum Associates.

Mandler, J. M., & Johnson, N. S. (1977). Remembrance of things parsed: Story structure and recall. *Cognitive Psychology, 9,* 111–151.

Marshall, N. (1983). Using story grammar to assess reading comprehension. *The Reaching Teacher, 36,* 616–620.

McConaughy, S. H. (1980). Using story structure in the classroom. *Language Arts, 57,* 157–165.

Meyer, B. (1975). *The Organization of prose and its effects upon memory.* Amsterdam, The Netherlands: North Holland.

Pearson, P. D. (1984). Guided reading: A response to Isabel Beck. In R. C. Anderson, J. Osborn, & R. J. Tierney (Ed.), *Learning to read in American schools: Basal readers and content texts.* Hillsdale, NJ: Lawrence Erlbaum Associates.

Pearson, P. D., & Johnson, D. D. (1978). *Teaching reading comprehension.* New York: Holt, Rinehart, & Winston.

Pichert, J. W. (1979). *Sensitivity to what is important in prose* (Tech. Rep. No. 49). Urbana, IL: University of Illinois, Center for the Study of Reading.

Rosch, E. (1978). Cognition and categorization. In E. Rosch & B. B. Lloyd (Eds.), *Principles of categorization.* Hillsdale, NJ: Lawrence Erlbaum Associates.

Rumelhart, D. E. (1975). Notes on a schema for stories. In D. G. Bobrow & A. M. Collins (Eds.), *Representation and understanding: Studies in cognitive science.* New York: Academic Press.

Sadow, M. (1982). The use of story grammar in the design of questions. *The Reading Teacher, 38,* 518–522.

Spiegel, D. L., & Fitzgerald, J. (1986). Improving reading comprehension through instruction about story parts. *The Reading Teacher, 39,* 676–682.

Squire, J. (1983). Composing and comprehending: Two sides of the basic process. *Language Arts, 60,* 581–589.

Stahl, S. A., & Vancil, S. I. (1986). Discussion is what makes semantic maps work in vocabulary instruction. *The Reading Teacher, 40,* 62–67.

Stein, N. (1979). How children understand stories: A developmental analysis. In L. G. Katz (Ed.), *Current topics in early childhood education.* Norwood, NJ; Ablex.

Stein, N., & Glenn, C. (1979). An analysis of story comprehension in elementary children. In R.O. Freedle (Ed.), *Discourse processing: Multidisciplinary perspectives in discourse comprehension.* Hillsdale, NJ: Ablex.

Stotsky, S. (1983). Research on reading/writing relationships: A synthesis and suggested directions. *Language Arts, 60,* 627–642.

Sullivan, D. E. (1978). Comparing strategies of good and poor comprehenders. *Journal of Reading, 21,* 710–715.

Thelen, J. N. (1986). Vocabulary instruction and meaningful learning. *Journal of Reading, 29,* 603–609.

Thorndyke, P. (1977). Cognitive structures in comprehension and memory of narrative discourse. *Cognitive Psychology, 9,* 77–110.

Waley, J. F. (1981). Story grammar and reading instruction. *The Reading Teacher, 34,* 762–771.

Winograd, P. (1984). Strategic difficulties in summarizing texts. *Reading Research Quarterly, 19,* 404–425.

Winograd, P. N., & Bridge, C. A. (1986). The comprehension of important information in written prose. In J. F. Baumann (Ed.), *Teaching main idea comprehension.* Newark, DE: International Reading Association.

PART III

SPECIFIC PROGRAMS FOR
THE SPECIAL LEARNER

Chapter 9

A Specific Reading Program for the Nonreader in the Special Education Classroom

Betty Van Witsen

Fordham University

Most children learn to read in first grade, when they are between 6 and 7 years old. If a youngster reaches second grade, between the ages of 7 and 8, and is still not successful in learning to read, he usually becomes discouraged and resistant to repeating the same unsuccessful activities. Even when he appears to be cooperative, his previous experience makes it unlikely that he will be able to focus on tasks that do not produce instant success, since they have not been effective in the past.

In some cases children do mature enough when they are between 7 and 8 for reading to be learned easily. Many other children continue to find the task insurmountable. These children confuse *b* and *d*, and sometimes *m* and *w*, forget the sounds of letters, and forget previously learned words from one day to the next. They seem to be unaware of visual similarities and patterns in words, even when pointed out, and, despite the fact that they appear to have language adequate for grasping the content of instruction, they cannot remember or apply material taught in class. They do not translate their awareness of time sequence (for example, eating breakfast *before* going to school, watching a particular TV show *after* dinner) to spatial left-to-right sequence, as most other children do, but will attempt to read a word (when they are willing to do so) from either end, randomly. They frequently do not recognize their own names in a group of similar ones, and when they do learn to do this, they do not perceive the similarity between their own names and words that have the same phonic elements. For example, Mark, who has learned to recognize his name, sees no similarity between the printed word *Mark* and the printed word *bark*, even though he can rhyme orally. He will agree when the *ark* element is pointed out to him, but later, when he encounters the word *park*, the same phenomenon will occur. If presented in a list, however, the words *Mark, bark, lark,* and *hark* can be decoded, once he is started off in the right direction, and if he remembers the sounds of the initial consonants.

This difficulty seems to occur only in reading. The child often can match geometric patterns, sequence pictures, find a design that's different from the others, and do many similar visual perception "readiness" activities, or if he can't do these, he learns them fairly quickly. It is only in reading that he hits a blank wall.

This kind of child is not uncommon in our schools. Sometimes he is called immature, which, in reading, he is. Sometimes he is called a remedial reading case, which he is. Sometimes he is called learning disabled, which he is. But only in reading. His math is usually OK, and he is, as a rule, at least adequate on the ball field and socially.

This child can be taught to read through direct instruction.

Teaching reading to a nonreading second or third grader involves the following assumptions:

1. He has at least average intelligence.

2. He has been exposed to reading instruction, including letter names and sounds, books, and other written and printed material.

3. He has language adequate to express his ideas and to grasp the meaning of simple narratives involving everyday situations.

Two additional elements that must be present are:

4. Focus—The child must pay close attention to the tasks presented, even if for only 5 minutes at a time, at first.

5. Unfamiliar format

In beginning instruction with a child who has not succeeded in a task that he has seen others of his age accomplish, it is advisable to use a format that is different from any he has previously experienced. Therefore, since he has probably used books, workbooks, and word cards before, begin with a blank notebook.

One-to-one instruction is essential for short periods, followed by small group activities involving three to five children, to provide practice in the use of language elements, in word recognition and in word analysis.

Individual activities should be alternated with small group or two-child activities, as a device for varying the style of instruction. Most youngsters who feel inadequate to the task of reading are resistant to long periods of work, even on a one-to-one basis. Another important reason for small group instruction is to prevent children from becoming overdependent on the attention and social reinforcement that accompany individual tutoring.

Independent activity sheets can be devised that are consonant with the child's cognitive level that is more advanced than his decoding level. The reasons for this is that, while his reading skills are immature, his mind is not necessarily so, and such activities as word search and crossword puzzles, while too difficult for beginning readers of 6 or 7, are more interesting to 7½- to 9-year-olds than simple coloring, matching, and circling activities.

The activities that follow are in the order in which they should be taught. Children will soon develop favorites among these activities, particularly if they are successful at them and win games. Teachers should be careful to alternate among the games, varying the individual activities (words, or phonic elements, or phrases and sentences) according to the child's changing needs. If Mark, for example, is having trouble remembering *ight* words (this is not uncommon—a pupil who knows *right* as a sight word may still have a hard time decoding *fright, slight,* and *lightning*)—Mark's Game can be made, using phrases and sentences, in either a Go Fish format (see Activity 10 and Activity 15) or a Bingo format (see Activity 12). The other children enjoy playing the game of one child, who takes it home, if he wants to, only after all the words are mastered.

When the child has learned to use individually designed worksheets, he can be introduced to commercial workbook pages and worksheets that accompany basal readers. Hooking children into the more normalizing regular materials is important to their self-concepts, and they will, as a rule, be motivated to succeed with "regular" materials if they have the requisite skills, and can recognize the requirements of the task.

There are many paradoxes that confront the teacher in helping nonreading children develop the skills necessary to perform this important task. In the first place, while children love to feel special, they want to feel special because they're pleasantly unique, not because they're remiss. Special materials can be ego-damaging to the very children they are designed to help. Moreover, special materials sometimes make children more dependent on adult help than they need be at first, and they should be weaned away from that. One solution may be to use the same materials that other children use, but in an individualized way, in small doses with less on a page, with rebus clues, and with extra activities to remediate faulty sight-sound memory.

A problem with basal readers is that, when they are most interesting, there is not enough repetition of words at the beginning reading levels for the youngster who needs extra practice. Books that provide ample repetition are sometimes less interesting, and turn off the very children who need to be motivated to read.

Comprehension, aside from picture clues, depends on decoding skill. Children who are having difficulty learning to read frequently get most of their grasp of what is going on from the pictures and from listening to class discussion. They learn more and more to ignore the text, which gives them few clues to meaning.

Another seeming paradox is that many intelligent children can read and remember words in the context of a story, not by guessing, but because the context plus knowledge of initial consonants often acts as a trigger to their faulty memories. These children cannot recognize the same words on a list—they are lost without the semantic clues of the story. On the other hand, these same children can often sound out words in phonic drill activities and in games, but draw a blank when confronted with the word in the context of a passage.

Teachers need to build bridges between what a child can do and what is demanded of him. For example, the child who excels in phonic drill might be led by putting material from the drills into sentences on a worksheet, then into paragraphs, then into stories, mixed with other, nonphonic words, in a skilltext sort of format, which presents a story on one side of the page and follow-up activities on the other side.

An additional problem that arises in dealing with children who need much one-to-one instruction is that they sometimes become passive learners, waiting for the teacher to explain, to hint, to prompt, to encourage long past the time that they ought to be able to tackle tasks independently. In fact, such children frequently feel cheated and resentful when the teacher's attention is directed elsewhere. I do not think that these are "spoiled" children or children lacking in attention and affection at home. They have developed faulty habits, probably because the reinforcement that comes with doing independent work successfully has not been readily available to them. When they do want to show their skills, these children often race through pages of math or reading workbooks, substituting quantity for quality, hoping their diligence will win them the rewards that other children seem to earn, and that their errors will be excused. This must not be allowed to continue. The teacher must give the child work in which he can succeed, in small doses, and require independent effort from the beginning.

Evaluation or follow-up should probably be done at least annually, but no oftener than every 4 months, using standardized material so that the teacher stays on the track. Keeping records of children's performances helps keep perspective on progress that often seems incredibly slow. Frequent review of material covered, and gradual increase in task demands in terms of length and complexity, are necessary.

The more reading a child does, the better reader he will become. If you can help him enjoy reading by feeling successful, he will want to read by himself. When he does that, the very act of reading and grasping the meaning of what he reads will take over your job, to a great extent. Then he will know what he really needs help with, and will tell you how to provide it.

A blank notebook.

A preprimer and primer in a basal series or a skilltext, which is a soft-covered book with a story on one side of a page and follow-up activities on the other side.

A structured phonics program, such as Hegge, Kirk, and Kirk's *Remedial Reading Drills* (published by George Wahr Publishing Company, 304½ State Street, Ann Arbor, Michigan 41808).

File folders.

Small envelopes (pay envelopes are a good size).

Colored felt markers.

Oaktag.

Colored index cards: pink, yellow, blue, green, salmon, and white.

Alphabet tabs.

Envelopes of standard size.

A box to keep the envelopes in.

Colored construction paper.

Buttons and foreign coins of various kinds to use as game pieces.

Activity 1 — The Alphabet Dictionary

Purpose:　The Alphabet Dictionary is a visual-auditory device that teaches sound symbol correspondence, provides paired association techniques to aid faulty memory for sight words, and is a self-reference for the student.

Materials:　Blank notebook.
　　　　　Alphabetical index tabs.
　　　　　Colored felt-tip markers.
　　　　　Pencils.

Directions:　*The Alphabet Dictionary.* Alphabet tabs are placed, index fashion, along the edge of the pages of a blank notebook.

Page 1 is A. The child is told that "A" says 'a' (the short sound of a). The sentence "Allen asks an alligator for an apple" is written at the top of the page, every initial "A" in red marker, the rest of the letters in black marker. The child is then asked to draw a picture of Allen asking the alligator for an apple. If he is reluctant to draw, the teacher does it, fairly crudely, but making sure that Allen has an "A" on this T-shirt, that the alligator has an open mouth, as if he is saying "a," and that the apple is clearly there. Talk balloons may be added to pictures if they help. In this instance, Allen's talk balloon might say, "May I have that apple?"

The child repeats the sentence "Allen asks an alligator for an apple" a few times as the teacher points to the words. The following pages are done similarly. The child is asked for suggestions for the names of the protagonists of each one-sentence story.

The sentences in a book recently completed by Mark are:

Billy buys a blue balloon.

Carol catches a cow.

David delivers a dirty dog.

Edna educates every elevator (Mark's mother's name is Edna), etc.

By the time the book is completed, which takes about 6 six weeks, the child has probably memorized it. Each story is read every day during the creation of the book, and discussion of antecedent and consequent events relating to the stories occurs, to fix the ideas firmly. If the youngster hesitates in the reading of the stories, the words are told to him.

Activity 2—The Rhyme Game

Purpose: The Rhyme Game teaches and provides practice in matching words with the same vowel and final consonant sounds, and in varying the initial sounds to create rhymes.

Materials: None.

Directions: *The Rhyme Game:* The teacher says, "I'm thinking of a word that rhymes with blue." The children take turns guessing: "Is it shoe?" ("No, it is not shoe.") "Is it new?" ("No, it is not new.") "Is it flew?" ("Yes, it is flew.") The child who guesses the word thinks of a new word for the others, including the teacher, if possible, to guess.

It is difficult for some children to think up rhyming words. The teacher can take this kind of child aside, ask for two rhyming words, and then suggest which one to use.

Some good rhyming words to begin with are:

take	*hat*	*win*	*top*	*get*	*mug*	*seed*
coat	*time*	*spoon*	*men*	*feel*	*tire*	*went*

These words give practice in hearing the long and short vowel sounds and in discriminating final consonant sounds. Some children will think that *line* rhymes with *time*. The teacher must exaggerate the final sound in *time* to dramatize the difference. An incorrect rhyme must never be allowed to go uncorrected. The child should be asked for another word that rhymes with *time* if he has made this kind of error, and one may be suggested to him if he cannot think of one. If children spontaneously offer other kinds of words for rhyming when it's their turn, for example two syllable words like *party* or words that contain dipthongs like *flower* or *boil*, these should be accepted.

Activity 3—The Sentence Game

Purpose: The Sentence Game enhances the child's skill in syntax and auditory memory and provides models of correct usage and complete sentences.

Materials: None.

Directions: *The Sentence Game*: This game requires children to form sentences by adding successive words without repeating the previous ones, but remembering them so that the sentence makes sense. The teacher begins the game by saying any word that can begin a sentence. The children take turns saying single words that add to the sentence. The words must be syntactically correct. For example, *he* cannot be followed by *are* or *in*. If there is any question about the syntax, the child saying the word must tell the teacher the sentence he had in mind. Young children will not, as a rule, insert dependent clauses into sentences, but a gifted child or an older child might think up a sentence like "He, in taking the candy, disobeyed his mother" where the word *in* does indeed follow the word *he*. This kind of unusual use of words should not be discouraged, but it will not occur too frequently.

Sentences may be of any length, but after three or four words, the teacher may have to recap what has been said. As the children become more proficient at this game and make longer and longer sentences, a part of the game may consist of the teacher's pointing to a child at random and asking for a recap before going on. This practice insures attention. The teacher should participate in the game and try to insert less common words into sentences, such as *whether, wonder, ever, if, any, but,* and the like to keep the sentences from being the monotonous "I like to play baseball" or "My friend is coming to my house" variety, although, of course, some sentences will inevitably be of that kind.

When the game is first played, the sentence is stopped as soon as it is a sentence (except for two-word sentences like "I went" or "She plays") and the next player begins another sentence. When the children can do this with no trouble, the teacher can suggest continuing the sentence to make it longer.

Children who have a hard time thinking up appropriate words for sentences may be helped by having the sentence length limited to three or four words at first, and then by adding suggested modifiers. For example: "I went home," "How did you go?" "By bus." "Put that into the sentence." "I went home by bus." "When did you go?" "After school." "Put that into the sentence." "I went home by bus after school."

Activity 4 — My Grandmother's Trunk

Purpose: Alphabetical sequence, application of initial sounds in words, short-term memory.

Materials: None.

Directions: *My Grandmother's Trunk:* This game is familiar to most children. It provides practice in the sequence of alphabet letters, in using initial sounds, and in remembering a sequence of unrelated objects through association with letters and individuals. One child starts the game by saying, "I packed my grandmother's trunk with . . ." and then says the name of a group of objects that begins with the letter A for example "apples." The next player says, "I packed my grandmother's trunk with . . ." whatever the first player said and the name of a group of objects that begins with the letter B for example "I packed my grandmother's trunk with apples and books." Each player repeats all of the previous statements before adding his own. The teacher should give plenty of help to young children playing this game for the first time, and the alphabet should be prominently displayed somewhere in the room so that the children can see which letter comes next.

Activity 5 — Scrambled Sentences

Purpose: This activity provides practice in decoding sight words, in using correct syntax, and in copying and writing.

Materials: Oaktag, cut into strips ½ inch wide by 8 inches long.
Small envelopes.
Felt-tip pen.

Directions: *Scrambled Sentences*: The Alphabet-Dictionary sentences are written on oaktag strips ½ inch wide by 8 inches long. The child is shown the strips as they are written, when he is reading that page in his Alphabet-Dictionary. He is given three or four, randomly each day, to read independently. After he has read the sentence strips successfully (referring to the appropriate page in the Alphabet-Dictionary if necessary) the sentences are cut up into words. The words are placed into envelopes, one sentence per envelope. The child selects three envelopes each day, lays the words out on the table, and unscrambles the sentences by moving the words around. The first word of the sentence begins with a capital letter, and the last word has a period after it. These two clues enable him to find the first and last words of the sentence, and serve to reduce the size of the task. When the sentence is unscrambled, the child copies it onto paper, and reads the sentences he has written to the teacher.

Activity 6 — Phonic Drills

Purpose: To provide automatic response to phonograms in the English language.

Materials: Any structured phonics program. The one I have found most successful is the *Hegge-Kirk-Kirk Remedial Reading Drills*. Other valuable systems you can use for the same purpose are Glass Analysis (available from Easier to Learn, Inc., Box 329, Garden City, New York 11530) and the Phono-Visual System (12216 Parklawn Drive, Rockville, Maryland 20852). The *Hegge-Kirk-Kirk Remedial Reading Drills* are available from George Wahr Publishing Company, Inc., 304½ State Street, Ann Arbor, Michigan 48102.

Directions: *Hegge-Kirk-Kirk Remedial Reading Drills*: This activity teaches the child to blend individual sounds (and later common phonic elements) into words. Most children will need extensive prompting for the first few lessons of this drill. The drills consist of consonant–vowel–consonant patterns, pronounced separately, then blended into words. In the first lines of the drill the initial consonant changes, while the last two letters remain the same (following the style of Activity 2—The Rhyme Game). The child says, for *cat*, "cuh, a, tuh—cat." The teacher points to each sound, then moves a finger across the word as a cue to the child to say the whole word.

c a t	*m a t*	*f a t*	*s a t*	*r a t*
h a t	*b a t*	*p a t*	*t h a t*	*t a t*

In the next group of words, the final letter is varied:

s a c k	*s a t*	*s a g*	*S a m*	*s a p*
c a t	*c a n*	*c a p*	*c a d*	*c a b*
r a n	*r a m*	*r a t*	*r a g*	*r a c k*

The next section varies both the first and last letters:

s a c k	*m a t*	*f a n*	*r a g*	*c a b*
d a b	*s a p*	*b a d*	*f a t*	*r a c k*
r a t	*b a n*	*t a m*	*s a d*	*l a p*

The final section varies the first and last letters, and gives the word with its letters printed more closely together. In this section, the child is to read the words without breaking them up. If he has trouble with a word, the teacher helps break it up into its component sounds by pointing to each letter, going back to the earlier techniques.

man	*hat*	*rag*	*fad*	*back*	*cap*	*dab*	*Sam*
gag	*Jack*	*rat*	*sap*	*lad*	*fag*	*lack*	*bad*
cat	*fan*	*sad*	*tack*	*gap*	*Pam*	*cad*	*dam*

All of the words are real words. The child is told any sound he is not familiar with (*ck* and *x*, for example). The Drill begins with a short *a*, then teaches short *o*, short *i*, short *u*. It then introduces *ee* and other digraphs before gong on to short *e*, because of the difficulty most children have with that sound.

Activity 7 — Basal Reading

Purpose: The purpose of introducing the Basal Reader fairly early is to hook the child into whatever reading series is being used in the school, to provide a more normalizing experience. Children want to use the same materials their peers use. If the preprimers seem too babyish, a Skilltext kind of material can be used until the child is at a Primer level. Skilltexts published by Merrill and Addison Wesley, among other publishers, present a story on one side of the page and follow-up activities on the other side.

Materials: Preprimers or Skilltexts at the preprimer level.

Directions: A basal preprimer is begun. the child reads the story aloud. Any word he does not know is told to him, and if he does not recognize it the next day, it is told to him again, and entered into his Alphabet-Dictionary on the appropriate page, with a rebus picture. Many rebus pictures must be symbols rather than illustrations, since they must be small and simple to be accommodated by the lines of the note-book, and since only nouns and verbs, as a rule, lend themselves to literal pictures. Some rebus symbols I have used with children have been taken from *Rebus Reading*, by Woodcock et al. (SRA), while others have been devised by the children or by me. The use of talk balloons helps children remember more difficult words.

Some examples of useful rebuses:

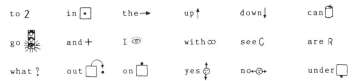

Since the child is doing the Hegge-Kirk-Kirk Drills at the same time as those words are being introduced, after a couple of weeks he should be able to sound out words like *can, an, on, with, that,* and other phonetically spelled short vowel words. Most children who have difficulty in learning to read will not do this spontaneously. They freeze when they encounter a word they do not remember. They must be encouraged to sound out these words in the context of reading a passage, even when it slows down the reading to a virtual standstill. Comprehension must be sacrificed at this point to decoding skill. For the first few weeks this procedure is very slow. The child is learning to rely on his own skill and on the use of reference material. When he encounters a word in a story that he does not remember, if the phonetic elements are familiar, he is asked to sound it out. If the elements are not familiar, he is told to look it up in his Alphabet-Dictionary. If the word is not there, it is promptly added.

At this point the child's daily lesson consists of unscrambling three sentences, reading a page or two in a preprimer, doing half a page of the Hegge-Kirk-Kirk Remedial Reading Drill and playing The Rhyme Game, The Sentence Game or My Grandmother's Trunk with the group.

Activity 8 — The Concentration Game

Purpose: The Concentration Game gives children practice in recognizing sight words and in using the skill of positional memory as an aid to word memory.

Materials: Oaktag of two different colors, cut into one-inch by two-inch cards.

A felt-tipped marker.

Directions: *The Concentration Game:* Eight words from the Alphabet-Dictionary (including some family names) and from the preprimer (but not necessarily words that the child has trouble remembering: he needs success, too) are written on one- by two-inch cards of two different colors. The words are placed face down on the table and mixed up. the child turns up a card of one color, reads it, and then turns up a card of the other color and reads that. If the words match, he keeps the pair and takes another turn. If they do not match, he turns them face down again, and the next player takes his turn. The unmatched cards should be put back in the same place as they originally were, since some children remember the words by the position they occupy, and the game becomes more than pure chance, since positional memory can be involved in finding matching words. If the child cannot read the turned-up word, he may look in the Alphabet-Dictionary, may sound it out, or the teacher may tell it to him. In this game it is not so important that the child look up the word, since he will have many opportunities to review it during the course of the game.

Activity 9 — Six-Bingo

Purpose: This activity introduces common letter clusters, or word "families," and changes the task of blending individual sounds to blending consonant sounds with word family clusters.

Materials: File folders.
         Felt-tipped markers.
         Half-inch by one-inch oaktag cards.
         Small envelopes.

Directions: *Six-Bingo:* file folders are ruled into columns and rows of spaces ½-inch by one-inch. Half-inch by one-inch cards are cut from oaktag, words from short vowel "word families" are written on the cards, and the cards placed into small envelopes with the "word family" name on the outside. for example, the *an* envelope could contain the words *man, can, tan, pan, ban, Dan, fan, Jun, Nan, ran, than, Stan, plan,* and *bran.* It will be noted that consonant blends are introduced in this game but they should not be too difficult for a child who has learned to put sounds together in the Hegge-Kirk-Kirk Drills.

         The first word elements, or "families" to be introduced should be *an, on, in, at, ot, it, ap, op,* and *ip.* Two groups are used the first two times the game is played, then three, and finally four. All of the cards are placed face down in the center of the table. The children and the teacher take turns selecting a card and reading it. The cards are placed in the spaces on the file folder of each player as he picks and reads a word. The first player to get six of the same "family" in a row (vertical, horizontal or diagonal) calls "Bingo" and wins the game.

can										
ran						lap	nap			
fan										
hit										
				top						
					hop					
						mop				
							flop			

This game gives practice in discrimination between similar elements in words. When a word is misread, the teacher should point to the envelope with the "family" name on it and repeat the sound. If the consonant blend or digraph is causing the problem (for example in words like *shop, chop, flop*), the teacher should say "*ch* says . . ." and make the *ch* sound. If the child still has trouble, the teacher says "*ch* says" and makes the *ch* sound, "*op* says" and makes the *op* sound, pointing to the letters as he says them, "so the word is . . ." and he moves his finger across the word slowly as the child pronounces it.

At this point the daily lesson consists of reading in the basal reader, unscrambling scrambled sentences and writing them, Hegge-Kirk-Kirk Drill, and a follow-up game, selected from The Rhyme Game, The Sentence Game, My Grandmother's Trunk, Concentration, or Six-Bingo.

Activity 10 — Go Fish

Purpose   This is a word recognition game that uses words in thecontext of sentences and phrases that requires the children to match phrases.

Materials: Oaktag cards, 2½ by 3½ inches.

Felt-tipped markers.

Directions: *Go Fish:* Phrases from the preprimers are typed onto 2½ by 3½ inch oaktag cards. Each phrase appears on two cards. Twenty-six phrases are used in making a deck of 52 cards. Five cards are dealt to each player, and the rest of the deck is placed face down in the center of the table. The first player calls another player by name and asks for a phrase that he has in his own hand. If the player has it, he gives it to the first player, who then puts the pair down in front of him and takes another turn. If the other player does not have it, he says "Go Fish," and the first player takes the top card from the center pile. If it is the card he requested, he gets another turn. The game proceeds around the table clockwise until all of the cards have been paired. The player with the most pairs wins the game. Examples of preprimer phrases:

Daddy will show you.	*Get your milk.*	*Go to bed.*
Give her a call.	*up the hill.*	*Mother will help him.*
Play with me.	*to ride in the car*	*in the house*

Activity 11 — The Basal Workbook

Purpose: Acclimating the child to classroom-like tasks in a format that is used by other children.

Materials: Pre-primer workbooks from a basal reader series.

Directions: *The Basal Workbook*: By now the child should be ready to begin to use the preprimer or primer workbook that accompanies the basal reader. He should be ready to begin the primer now. If not, the preprimer workbook pages are assigned *as independent work*, after the vocabulary is reviewed and the page explained.

Most primer workbook pages consist of matching sentences or words either to each other or to pictures, of filling in words to complete sentences, or substituting initial or final consonants in phonetically regular words, of selecting appropriate alternatives in answering questions, of coloring or marking the correct response to a question or of following a simple sequence and then numbering sentences in the correct order. After going over this kind of activity once or twice, the child should be strongly reinforced with praise, stars, and other forms of recognition for doing the work by himself, which entails silently reading the material and responding appropriately.

Words such as *underline, circle, draw, sentence, word, choose, find* and the like can be put into the Alphabet-Dictionary and into Concentration and Go Fish games, if necessary.

Activity 12—Vocabulary Bingo

Purpose: Sight-word recognition, out of context, using words in sentences.

Materials: 8½ by 11 inch oaktag cards
Felt-tipped markers
Envelopes—large manila, to accommodate the game cards, and small ones for the words and markers
Colored construction paper

Directions: *Vocabulary Bingo*: Forty-eight words from the primer vocabulary are put on six 8½ by 11 inch oaktag cards, ruled with a one inch border at the top and bottom, and a ¼-inch border on each side, into four columns of boxes two inches wide by three quarters of an inch long. The words are typed on four cards in random positions, and onto one other card, which is then cut up, and the word cards placed into an envelope with the name of the child or of the book he is reading on it. Another envelope, labelled "Markers," is filled with colored oaktag or construction paper rectangles of the same size. About 150 markers are needed. The spaces on the Bingo Cards are divided by a heavy line at the bottom of the first 16 words and the second 16 words, making a card that looks like this:

When the game is played, the cards are placed face down on the table and the markers are distributed around the table. The players take turns picking up the top word card, reading it, using it in a sentence and placing it back into its envelope. The sentences must use the exact word, not another form of it.

come	did	he	you
dog	I	and	do
tell	this	go	she
show	one	on	are
can	milk	good	dish
with	ate	will	see
mother	four	got	is
car	be	little	here
the	at	five	him
went	give	a	father
play	for	is	has
look	had	under	kitten

Activity 13 — Bingo Solitaire

Purpose: To review sight vocabulary on an individual basis in a familiar format.

Materials: The same as Activity 12.

Directions: *Bingo Solitaire*: A solitaire version of Bingo, played with the same cards as Vocabulary Bingo.

The child takes one Bingo card and a blank card that has been ruled like a Bingo card, but has no words on it. He shuffles the Bingo word cards thoroughly, then places them face down in three piles of 16 cards each. Selecting from each pile in turn, left to right, he reads the word, finds it on the Bingo card, and places it in the corresponding space on the blank card. When he gets four cards in a row, vertically, horizontally, or diagonally, he scores a point on a score sheet. Three Bingos wins the game. He leaves the filled card for the teacher to check, and reads the words to her when she checks. The player may use his Alphabet-Dictionary if he needs it.

This game may be played by two children as a form of double solitaire. In playing, the children take turns selecting from the packs of word cards, which might be divided into four rather than three piles. Each child has his own Bingo card and blank Bingo card to match, and the words are read aloud, then shown to the other player. This version might help a child who is unsure of words, but it also has the danger of permitting children to confirm each other's errors, so it should be used with caution.

Activity 14—Circle Spelling

Purpose: To teach the spelling and to facilitate the recognition of consonant–short vowel–consonant pattern words. This activity provides practice in auditory discrimination of initial and final consonants and short vowels, gives practice in auditory sequencing, and requires a written response, adding a kinesthetic element as an aid to memory.

Activity Pattern

Materials: Rexograph of activity pattern
Pencils

Directions: *Circle Spelling*: This activity gives practice in discriminating the sounds of short vowels, and beginning and final consonant. The teacher names the pictures and emphasizes the vowel sound.

Then he dictates consonant–vowel–consonant pattern words to the children, who write them on the lines of the circle, rotating the page so that when they have written the eighth word, they are back at the starting position. The children are told that one sound changes in each new word, and only one sound, or one letter. In beginning this game, the following practice run can be given:

The teacher says "Write 'cat' on the first line: *cuh - a - tuh*, *cat*. On the next line write 'can,' *cun - a - nnnuh*. Only one letter changed. Which letter was it? Right, the last letter. The 'T' changed to an 'N'. Now, on the next line, write 'man', *muh - a - n-n-nuh*. Which letter changed this time?

Yes, the first one. The 'C' changed to an 'M'. In the next space write 'map', *muh - a - puh, map*. Now write 'mop', *muh - o - puh, mop*. Which letter says *o*? If you're not sure, look at the pictures at the top of your page. Each one begins with a vowel letter. Which picture begins with the sound (making the short o sound) *o*? If no one says *ostrich*, the teacher then names the pictures again.

The above role-playing example probably will not benecessary for most children by this time, but in dictating the following lists, the teacher should stand or sit near the weakest spellers, and give similar prompting if it is needed, *after* the other children have written the word.

Some lists for Circle Spelling:

1	2	3	4	5	6	7	8	9	10
fit	*cup*	*pin*	*pet*	*dim*	*red*	*but*	*tap*	*lab*	*get*
fat	*cop*	*tin*	*peg*	*rim*	*rid*	*bet*	*tag*	*lag*	*got*
hat	*cob*	*tan*	*leg*	*him*	*rod*	*set*	*tug*	*rag*	*hot*
hag	*job*	*man*	*log*	*hem*	*hod*	*wet*	*hug*	*rig*	*hop*
wag	*rob*	*mat*	*lot*	*ham*	*had*	*wit*	*hum*	*dig*	*hip*
wig	*rub*	*sat*	*hot*	*tam*	*lad*	*bit*	*ham*	*dim*	*nip*
win	*rut*	*sit*	*not*	*Tom*	*lid*	*big*	*ram*	*dam*	*nit*
fin	*cut*	*sin*	*net*	*Tim*	*led*	*bug*	*rap*	*dab*	*net*

The pictures of the apple, elephant, Indian, ostrich and umbrella should be enlarged and displayed in a prominent place in the room to be used as a reference by groups in playing phonics games like Six Bingo or at any other time.

More activities:

At this point, several activities for sight word recognition should be integrated into reading activity:

1. Advanced Go Fish (in which 2 different phrases using the same word, underlined, are matched, and the player asks for the word.)
2. Bookmarks with Sight Words
3. Words of the Month Bingo (using holiday, seasonal and special event words.)
4. Six Bingo
5. Seven Bingo (similar to Six Bingo, except that the words do not rhyme but contain the same phonic element such as *cars, parking, carpet, yard, charming, sharper* and *barn*.)

Activity 15 — The Silent E Game

Purpose: To teach discrimination between short vowel words and those with silent E.

Materials: A file folder
Felt-tipped markers, red and black
A long sandwich-toothpick
One die
Playing pieces, such as buttons, foreign coins, or similar tokens

Directions: *The Silent E Game*: By now the child has learned the silent E rule in the Hegge-Kirk-Kirk Drill, but many youngsters have trouble discriminating words with and without the E. They tend to use the long vowel sound in all unfamiliar words, even after carefully structured teaching of short vowel sounds. The silent E Game gives practice in visual discrimination between short vowel words and silent E words.

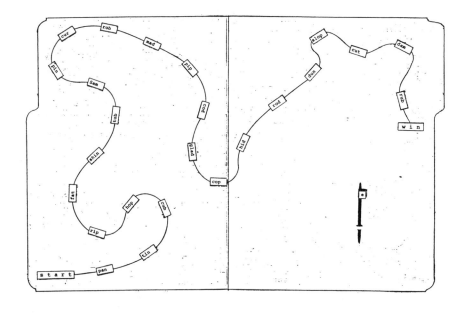

On an open file folder, 24 boxes of one inch by ½ inch are drawn in a path winding around the playing board, leading from START to WIN, connected by a red line. The following words are written in the boxes: *pan, tin, cub, hop, rip, fat, shin, tub, Sam, pin, cur, rob, mad, pip, cod, glad, cop, hid, rod, dun, slop, cut, dam, rub.* The letter *e* is written the same size as the letters in the boxes on a small square of oaktag, and glued to a sandwich toothpick or to a strip of oaktag. A slit is cut in the lower right hand corner of the playing board to hold the silent E. The first player takes the silent E. He then tosses a die (from a pair of dice or one made from a cube with numbers from 1 to 6 written on the faces), and moves that number of spaces, following the path and reading each word, first without the silent E and then with it, placing the E at the end of the word as he reads it, so that the word's appearance changes. He places a playing piece (a button or a coin) next to the word he landed on, and hands the E to the next player. At the end of the game, the players must toss the exact number to get out, reading *win-wine* as the final play.

Activity 16 — Blendograms

Purpose: This activity gives practice in combining consonant blends with common letter clusters, and requires the players to distinguish between real words and nonsense words. It requires auditory sequence and sound blending.

Materials: 1½ by 3 inch pink cards (80)
1½ by 3 inch blue cards (80)
1½ by 3 inch yellow cards (84)
1½ by 3 inch orange cards (80)
1⅔ by 3 inch green cards (80)
Felt-tipped markers

Directions;   *Blendograms*: This game, based on one that is commercially available, gives practice inputting consonant blends with letter clusters to make words. The game consists of 80 1½ by 3 inch pink cards, 80 blue cards, and 84 yellow cards. There are two of each of these letter clusters in pink and two in blue:

ack	ang	ay	ick	og
ag	ank	can	ight	ook
ail	ant	ear	ill	op
ake	ape	ell	ing	out
all	ar	ent	ink	ow

ame	*at*	*et*	*ip*	*own*
an	*ate*	*ew*	*ock*	*ump*

There are three each of the following blends on the yellow cards:

bl	*cl*	*fl*	*gr*	*sc*	*shr*	*sm*	*spr*	*sw*
br	*cr*	*fr*	*pl*	*scr*	*sk*	*sn*	*st*	*tr*
ch	*dr*	*gl*	*pr*	*sh*	*sl*	*sp*	*str*	*tw*

And three blank yellow cards.

The yellow cards are divided into two packs, one placed face down in the center of the table, and the other placed face up. The pink and blue cards are placed separately, face down next to the yellow cards. Each player takes four "cherry" and "blueberry" cards, or any combination of cherry and blueberry to make four, and places them face up in front of him. The first player takes the top card from the face up, or open yellow pile, and places it in front of his cherry and blueberry cards, in turn, pronouncing each resulting word. He must pronounce it even it it is not a real word. If it is a real word, the player puts the two cards to one side, and takes the next face up, or open, yellow card, and places it in front of his remaining cherry and blueberry cards. He proceeds in this fashion until he can no longer make a real word. He then places the yellow card back on the open pile and takes a card from the closed yellow pile, and tries to make a word with that one. If he can make a word, he continues to take cards from the closed yellow pile until all of his cherry and blueberry cards are used, or until he can no longer make a word. He then passes the yellow card in his hand to the next player, and fills out his hand with cherry and/or blueberry cards, and the next player takes his turn. The blank yellow cards are used with letter clusters that make real words, such as *ape* and *in*.

Much prompting is usually necessary when children begin this game, but the constant repetition of the word elements helps most youngsters retain the sounds after a time.

The letter clusters selected for this game are the commonest ones found in early reading materials. They can be varied by the teacher, and a second set of more advanced letter clusters on green and orange cards can be made for more advanced youngsters. The hardest clusters can be taken from Glass Analysis materials or the following ones, which have been helpful with older children who still have decoding difficulties, may be used:

aid	*ain*	*ange*	*eet*	*oat*	*oint*	*oon*	*ought*
ail	*air*	*are*	*ew*	*oid*	*oist*	*oop*	*ound*
aim	*ait*	*aw*	*ied*	*oil*	*ool*	*oud*	*uit*

At this point, the child's daily lesson consists of reading two to three pages orally in a primer or 1^2 basal reader, orally answering questions based on the reading, doing a workbook page independently, 5 to 7 minutes of Hegge-Kirk-Kirk Drill, and a selection of any of the above auditory language or phonics game. Varying the follow-up games from day to day serves to keep interest high.

Used by permission of American Learning Aids, P.O. Box 16552, Covina, CA 91722.

Chapter 10

The Making of a Writer As a Maker of Worlds

Janet Emig

Rutgers University

The primary, fundamental, and continual activity of the brain is nothing less than the creation of the worlds. *Thought* in its broadest sense is the construction of the worlds, both "real" and imaginary, *learning* is their elaboration and modification, and *language*—especially written language— is a particulary efficacious . . . medium by which these worlds can be manifested, manipulated, and sometimes shared. (Smith, 1983, pp. 118–119)

Writing is the symbolic process of creating worlds through texts; and then, if those text-worlds prove unsatisfactory, of re-creating them through revision. These text-worlds can easily and readily be shared with others. They can be abandoned after they have been partially or wholly created. New text-worlds can take their place. To write, then, is to become empowered in profoundly, uniquely human ways. These stunning attributes of writing hold especial value and hope for those who experience powerlessness in the literal world, as do many exceptional children and adults. Among the modes of symbolic action— dancing, sculpting, painting, playing musical instruments, singing, even talking—writing represents for many the most available, the most accessible source of expression and power.

To claim that writing is a process of creating worlds is to commit this essay to a certain intellectual tradition. That tradition is constructivism.

Among those who have helped construct constructivism is the philosopher Nelson Goodman (1984), who characterizes it as "a philosophy of understanding." Here is Bruner's (1986) explication of Goodman's philosophy.

> Its central thesis, "constructivism," is that contrary to common sense there is no unique "real world" that preexists and is independent of human mental activity and human symbolic procedures construct the world. . . .

> The activity of world making is, for Goodman, a diverse and complex set of activities, and however else it may express itself it involves "making not with hands but with minds, or rather with languages or other symbol systems." (pp. 95–96)

Constructivism emanates from a very different set of assumptions from those that govern behaviorism, the paradigm informing almost all prior research studies and curriculum designs and programs involving exceptional children and writing (indeed, exceptional children and all learning). Reid (1978) describes the features and assumptions of such "empiricist" curriculum designs:

> The areas of methods of diagnosis are both standardized and preestablished. . . . Specific behavioral objectives are delineated either early in or even prior to the beginning of the teacher–learning sequence. These practices assume a passive learner, a fixed body of knowledge and skills to be diagnosed and remediated, and fixed approaches to learning problems. (p. 227)

In contrast, constructivism espouses these assumptions:

> an active learner who constructs her own symbolic world of knowledge, skills, and beliefs;
> a fluid view of what knowledge and skills, consequently, will be required for such constructs;

and

> fluid, individualized approaches to aid the individual learner as a builder of symbolic worlds.

A wide literature states or suggests that the following resources and modalities are essential for our becoming writers as creators of symbolic worlds:

moving and gesturing
seeing
hearing
remembering and forgetting
languaging: possessing phonological, syntactic, semantic, and
    pragmatic verbal competences
conceptualizing: conceiving, imagining, rehearsing and planning,
    sequencing and organizing

and orchestrating all of these,

an intact brain, and a certain level of intellectual functioning.

But are all of these competences and entities equally crucial if writing is regarded centrally as the symbolic creation of text-worlds? Or are some competences more crucial, more bedrock, than others? Which are which? And how do we know? And what, as educators of exceptional children, can we do, or not do, about the matter?

In this essay I will suggest that some competences and processes previously characterized as requisite are not, and that certain liabilities and disabilities can be offset by the substitution of alternate modalities, by technologies, and by various forms of human assistance, both from teachers and from peers. I will also note which competences are not amenable to any of these interventions or enhancements. I will discuss these in reverse order from the catalogue above.

An Intact Brain with Appropriate Wiring

Appropriate wiring refers to the actual circuitry of the brain and the organization of synapses therein. In June 1986, in the Science section of *The New York Times*, Blakeslee (1986) reported on some recent findings and hypotheses concerning synaptic density and organization. The researchers posit a highly dynamic brain, with the brains of children, according to Dr. Peter Huttenlocher of the University of Chicago, having far greater synaptic density than those of adults. There seem to be twice as many synaptic connections in certain regions of children's brains as in adults.

Children learn well and easily other languages and playing musical instruments. "Children as a group are poor, even once they may have a brilliant idea, in sustaining it, elaborating it, developing it fully and logically in all of its manifestations and implications" (p. 12). The value of density seems to be in initiation and invention.

The number of synapses seems to fall in half by early adolescence. A vast pruning occurs. How does the brain decide which synaptic connections to eliminate? And what if the brain makes the wrong decision? Is a learning disability, for example, a case of bad wiring? Is schizophrenia? Once again, what psychologists have called developmental stages may literally be neurological changes occurring at fairly regular chronological ages within the cortex.

After adolescence, even a slight aphasia, as Gardner (1975, p. 89) notes, can prove sufficient to destroy an individual's literary talent. At the same time, what he calls the "highly situate" nature of lesions can make for anomalies in the processes of writing and reading, whereby if one system for written scripts has been destroyed, another can be functioning. Gardner (1975, p. 88) suggests that children can master an alternate route for written scripts, substituting, for example, ideographically based systems for those phonologically based. Here is an instance of the substitutions possible for the development of literacy in certain exceptional children.

Conceptualizing: Conceiving, Imagining; Rehearsing, Planning; Sequencing, Organizing

To treat these processes separately from a consideration of the brain and its functioning is, of course, an inaccuracy. Many would regard them all as programs of the brain that become activated and interactivated through the learner's experience.

To treat them separately has, however, a rhetorical usefulness: It makes possible noting how imagining, planning, and rehearsing represent as well significant features of the processs of writing. Much has been written, some of it by me, about the process approach to writing. From a constructivist perspective, these processes represent crucial actions and portions in the creation of text-worlds. We are not yet at all clear which we as educators can influence: perhaps planning, sequencing, and organizing, although a wide band of texts and curricular materials provide units, activities, and assignments that purport to enhance them all.

Language

In *Frames of Mind: The Theory of Multiple Intelligences,* Gardner (1983) develops the thesis that humans have multiple intelligences, each with an essential core of traits and operations. In that text he analyzes six:

linguistic, musical, logical-mathematical, spatial, bodily-kinesthetic, and personal (since its publication, he and his colleagues have identified an additional 14).

For each intelligence, he describes one or more possessors of those abilities in heightened and highly sophisticated forms. In his discussion of linguistic intelligence, for example, Gardner describes T. S. Eliot. He also gives his catalogue of traits and attributes for the making of a poet like Eliot: (a) sensitivity to the interaction among linguistic connotations; (b) an exceptional sensitivity as well to phonology, "their musical interactions upon one another"; (c) a mastery of syntax; and (d) an appreciation of the "pragmatic functions, the uses to which language can be put: the different speech acts, ranging from the lyric of live to the epic of description, from the directness of an order to the subtleties of a plea" (p. 75).

In "The Natural History of Language," the psycholinguist Eric Lenneberg (1967) set forth the hypothesis that, if children do not develop the rudiments of these core operations of a first language before adolescence, they do not develop them at all. (Adolescence, he, too, defines neurologically as the time when the brain—notably, its cortex—becomes physiologically mature.) Lenneberg claimed, however, that the onset of language is almost irrepressible, blocked only by a markedly low level of intellectual functioning (an IQ of 40), by appalling abuse, or by no interaction with humans at all, as with the very occasional child raised by wolves or other animals. The development of language, then, observes critical periods, albeit somewhat generous ones. (Linguistic competence here must be differentiated from linguistic performance. Children can demonstrate that they possess language without the ability to produce it, through their response to talk and signing and reading.)

Remembering and Forgetting

Must we be able to remember in order to write? With memory have we come to an essential feature of mind for which we can substitute no other process? No offsetting technologies? Or, to use Bruner's overclinical metaphor—no prosthetic devices?

If writing, by definition, is constructing text-worlds, endowing experiences with meaning, then it is obvious that a writer must have access to the memory of those experiences. Our memories provide the materials, the stuff of which many of our text-worlds are constructed, as they represent the source of schemas that govern the classification and organization of those worlds.

Case studies of persons with amnesia describe persons who find writing an agonizing chore, or even a total impossibility. The most famous instance is Z. Zaaretsky of Luria's (1972) study *The Man with a Shattered World*.

Without memory we may stay sentient and even moral beings; but without memory we cannot become, or stay, literate beings, able to write, able to read.

Hearing

From the studies of Lenneberg forward, the evidence is compelling that deaf children acquire natural language—for example, babbling—on roughly the same developmental timetable as hearing children. More recently, it has been observed that very young deaf children devise their own gestural and signing systems, either on their own or in tandem, that bear marked analogies to natural language "for example, in the manner of construction of two-word utterances" (Gardner, 1975, p. 52).

Some studies involving the deaf support the hypothesis held by Vygotsky and Luria, among others, that speaking and writing emanate from quite distinct zones of the brain. When Suzuki and Notoza (1984) compared the development of oral and written language in six deaf infants from the time they were 1 and 2 until they were 5 and 6, they found that written language acquisition was not dependent upon oral language; that written language could be initiated when children were 1 year of age; and that extremely young children found written language easy to learn. These findings correlate with those regarding hearing children as observed by Harste and Burke, Goodman, and others.

The use of the microcomputer seems to aid the acquisition of writing and reading skills among deaf children, if the program is based upon a theory of learning that emulates the way children acquire a first language—that is, as a responsive, interactive, and exploratory process (Prinz & Nelson, 1985).

Seeing

By seeing, I mean the active and selective transformative process perceiving. After reviewing a considerable body of literature, I claimed in my 1978 essay "Hand, Eye, Brain: Some Basics in the Writing Process" that seeing as perceiving was a requisite to the symbolic transformation of experience and that I could find no instances of highly skilled writers or other artists who were congenitally blind. I singled out sculptors perhaps because, as with writers, I found research studies concerning them.

Only this year did I read *The Man Who Mistook His Wife for a Hat*, an anthology of case studies by the gifted and eloquent neurologist Oliver Sacks (1985), studies the belie many of our conventional views not only regarding congenital blindness and world-making but also of many other forms of exceptionality.

The case of Madeleine J, which Sacks reports, contradicts my generalization and reveals a stunning surrogate for sight—literacy itself. Madeleine J was a congenitally blind 60-year-old woman with cerebral palsy who had never used her hands, which she described as "just lumps of putty." By putting her food, initially a bagel, just beyond reach, Sacks led Madeleine to reach and take it to her mouth.

As Sacks describes this action:

> it marked her birth as a "motor individual" (Sherrington's term for the person who emerges through acts). It also marked her first manual perception, and thus her birth as a complete "perceptual individual." (p. 59).

Soon thereafter, she began to explore with her hands, first objects, then person; and within a year she began to model heads and figures, "half or three-quarters life size, with simple but recognizable features, and with a remarkably expressive energy" (p. 60).

Why was Madeleine J able to overcome the double liability of congenital blindness and cerebral palsy? Sacks attributes her triumph to high inherent intelligence and imagination and to literacy, to the fact she had, through experiences with talking books and others reading to her, cultivated "an imagination filled and sustained, so to speak, by the images of others, images conveyed by language, by the *word*" (p. 59). As with moving and gesturing, language and literacy can themselves serve as surrogates that offset the terrible losses represented by blindness.

The print-handicapped can also be aided by other technologies: In the Exceptional Children Project in El Cerrito, California, talking computers are proving of great assistance to children as they compose, as they write.

Moving and Gesturing

Many theorists claim that the ability to move and to gesture is an absolute requisite to the development of written language. Piaget posits a sensorimotor period as an essential stage in cognitive/symbolic development. The Russian psychologist Lev Vygotsky (19778) claims that the gesture is "the initial visual sign that contains the child's future writing as an acorn contains a future oak"; and he calls gestures "writing in air."

But both psychologists note that gesture is but one mode of early symbolic practice and activity. Both cite, as others do, play and dreaming. Once language is acquired, a powerful form of play is pretending and creating oral stories; and engaging in word games, such as punning, joking, making riddles, and creating metaphors. Since as we know, many children with cerebral palsy and degenerative muscular diseases such as muscular dystrophy become highly skilled writers, the linguistic/symbolic do come perhaps to substitute for the motoric/symbolic activities. The motoric competence then seems not to be a bedrock requisite for the development of the writer as a creator of worlds.

In this brief, almost telegraphic review, we see that, by defining writing as a symbolic, transformative activity of creating text-worlds, we can far more discerningly determine which contributory processes we can influence and which we cannot. For seeing, hearing, gesturing (including handwriting), we can tap within the learner alternate modalities; borrow technologies; provide peers who can act as surrogate eyes, ears, hands, mouths, sensibilities; and we ourselves can serve in a range of contributory roles. In the cases, however, of a missing memory, a natural language not acquired by adolescence, a traumatized or synaptically disorganized brain, we can do very little, or nothing.

Recommendations

What then can educators do? Here is a set of recommendations from a constructivist perspective.

1. Work from a constructivist view of literacy, learning, and teaching.

2. Sponsor literacy events, which Heath (1985) defines as "any occasion in which a piece of writing is internal to the nature of participants' interaction and their interpretive processes."

3. Build on presences; offset absences. Tap all available modalities and processes.

4. Focus on the learner's abilities to construct worlds of meaning. Regard the presentation of such skills as punctuation and usage as subsidiary and contributing, but not as the focus of composition teaching.

5. As teachers, assume a wide and versatile range of roles:

Model

- one who writes and reads in the learner's presence
- one who writes and reads to the learner

Scaffolder

- one who constructs the blueprints and frames to make the construction of text-worlds possible

Co-Participant

- one who records, via script, typing, or word processor, the writer's evolving or completed text
- one who reads aloud the writer's evolving or completed text

Provider

- one who provides an enabling environment
- one who provides a wide range of writing invitations
- one who provides peer groups for solace, advice, response
- one who provides appropriate technologies to support the construction of texts

Evaluator

- one who evaluate the commitment, authenticity, and success of the writing ventures.
- one who knows that the value of writing a good story, a powerful narrative, is as symbolically valid as constructing an explanation or an argument.

Animal symbolicum: that is how the philosopher Ernst Cassirer describes us all. To be human *means* to be able to transform experience symbolically. Some even claim that to be human means to be able to comprehend and to create text-worlds. Holding constructivist views, educators of exceptional learners can proceed imaginatively, nonstereotypically, to find ways, perhaps not yet known to any of us, to sponsor their unique humanness and to give them the power and control writing well represents.

References

Blakeslee, S. (1986, June 24). Rapid changes seen in young brain. *New York Times*, sec. C1, p.10.

Bruner, J. (1986). Language, mind and reading. In *Actual minds, possible worlds.* Cambridge, MA: Harvard University Press.

Donaldson, M. (1978). *Children's minds.* New York: W. W. Norton & Company.

Emig, J. (1983). "Non-magical thinking" and "Hand, eye, brain: Some basics in the writing process." In *The Web of meaning: Essays on writing, teaching, learning, and thinking.* Montclair, NJ: Boynton/Cook.

Gardner, H. (1975). *The shattered mind: The person after brain damage.* New York: Alfred A. Knopf.

Gardner, H. (1983). *Frames of mind: The theory of multiple intelligences.* New York: Basic Books, Inc.

Giordano, G. (1983). The pivotal role of grammar in correcting writing disabilities. *Journal of Special Education, 17,* 473–481.

Goodman, N. (1984). *Of mind and other matters* Cambridge, MA: Harvard University Press.

Graham, S. (1982). Composition research and practice: A unified approach. *Focus on Exceptional Children, 14,* 1–16.

Graham, S. (1987). Writing assessment. In C. R. Reynolds & L. Mann (Eds.), *Encyclopedia of special education* (Vol. 3). New York: Wiley-Interscience

Graham, S., & Harris, K. R. (1987). Writing remediation. In C. R. Reynolds & L. Mann (Eds.), *Encyclopedia of special education* (Vol. 3). New York: Wiley-Interscience.

Heath, S. B. (1985). Being literate in America: A sociohistorical perspective. In J. A. Niles & R. V. Lalik (Eds.), *Issues in literacy: A research perspective* (34th Yearbook of the National Reading conference). Rochester, NY: NRC, Inc.

John-Steiner, V. (1985). *Notebooks of the mind: Explorations of thinking.* Albuquerque, NM: University of New Mexico Press.

Lenneberg, E. (1967). *Biological foundations of language.* New York: John Wiley & Sons.

Luria, A. R. (1972). *The man with a shattered world.* New York: Basic Books.

Luria, A. R. (1973). *The working brain: An introduction to neuropsychology.* New York: Basic Books.

Moulton, J., & Bader, M. S. (1985). The writing process: A powerful approach for the language disabled student. *Annals of Dyslexia, 35,* 161–173.

Popper, K., & Eccles, Sir J. (1977). *The self and its brain.* New York: Spring International.

Prinz, P., & Nelson, K. (1985). Alligator eats cookie: Acquisition of writing and reading skills by deaf children using the microcomputer. *Applied Psychology, 6,* 283–306.

Reid, D. K. (1978). Genevan theory and the education of exceptional children. In J. McCarthy Gallagher & J. A. Easley, Jr. (Eds.), *Knowledge and development: Vol. 2. Piaget and education* (pp. 199–241). New York: Plenum Press.

Sacks, O. (1985). *The man who mistook his wife for a hat and other clinical tales.* New York: Summit Books.

Selfe, L. (1977). *Nadia: The case of extraordinary drawing ability in an autistic child.* London: Academic Press.

Smith, F. (1983). A metaphor for literacy—Creating worlds or shunting information. In *Essays into literacy.* Exeter, NH: Heinemann Educational Books.

Suzuki, Shigetada, and Notoza, Masako. (1984). Teaching written language to deaf infants and preschoolers. *Topics in Early Childhood Special Education, 3,* 4, 10–16.

Teale, W. H. (1984). Reading to young children: Its significance for literacy development. In H. Goelman, A. Oberg, & F. Smith (Eds.), *Awakening to literacy.* Exeter, NH: Heinemann Educational Books.

Vygotsky, L. (1978). The prehistory of written language. In M. Cole, V. John-Steiner, S. Scribner, & Ellen Souberman (Eds.), *Mind in society: The development of higher psychological processes.* Cambridge, MA: HUP.

Welty, E. (1983). *One writer's beginnings.* Cambridge, MA: Harvard University Press.

Chapter 11

Using Microcomputers to Teach Reading, Writing, and Spelling to the Special Child

John S. Hicks

Fordham University

When reviewing material for this chapter, it became evident that, during the past 30 years, almost every conceivable reading program had been applied to nearly every conceivable type of self-contained special education classroom. It was difficult to make sense out of the seemingly endless array of "special" reading approaches and programs which have been presented, adapted, researched, and/or discounted through the years. One is tempted to believe that the ever-consuming American society has not spared our field. Approaches are introduced, met with hope and enthusiasm, applied everywhere, found to be valuable in some limited situations, and too often abandoned when next year's model comes along. The claims of companies which survive by selling their products to schools must be approached with caution, since recent research suggests only limited application for most of the reading programs which are available for the special student. What appears to be a permanent change in the ways in which special children are taught reading is the utilization of microcomputers to facilitate the process.

Self-contained classes vary dramatically from school district to school district. Historically, children have been placed in self-contained classes because there was a strong enough need to remove the child from the mainstream. Too often this "strong enough need" could best be understood in terms of behavior, not learning style or learning skills. Children were placed in self-contained classes simply because they could not behave, or compete in the regular classroom. Often, children were and are placed in self-contained classrooms because that was what was available if the student was going to receive remedial services. Yet the history of the mainstreaming movement indicated that, once the child was put in a special class, the learning slowed down even further. The classical small group or individual remediation did not produce significant academic gains, although, many times, the small group did improve the behavior of the child. The microcomputer is seen as one key to reversing those academic losses while at the same time being interesting enough to the child to allow impact on his or her behavior.

One has only to review books such as that of Salvia and Ysseldyke (1985) to understand how imprecise are our diagnostic and classification systems. Often, self-contained classrooms which are thought to contain groups of children with similar educational problems are in reality a group of children all having the same label, but many different reading problems. At the same time our faith in the diagnostic model remains intact. We believe and hope that the diagnostic systems will appear which will allow us to make decisions which will clearly link diagnostic labels to specific remedial strategies in the classroom. Perhaps one lesson from the medical diagnostic model has been learned at this point. For example, of all patients with high blood pressure, many will have commonalities and yet the treatment is patient-specific—tailored to the individual.

The situation we are faced with in learning disabilities is that there are some commonalities, but an overriding demand is that the program be individualized just the way a medical doctor takes a variety of living habits into consideration before deciding on an individual's prescribed medication. One has the feeling that there is a tremendous disparity between the degree of knowledge in our field of special education, which is a relatively new venture, compared with the degree of information available in the field of medicine. As frustrating as it may be to realize that educators may never reach the goals set forth by the medical field, we must move ahead, sorting out the reading programs and methods which have worked with students in self-contained special education classrooms. My assertion is that microcomputers will help us approach the level of skill which the medical profession has practiced for years.

Utilizing the Microcomputer in Reading Readiness and Preschool Programs

Many special children in the preschool and primary grade self-contained classrooms would be considered to be developmentally delayed. The task of the preschool teacher is to make certain the handicapped child accomplishes the typical readiness tasks of a preschool child. It may take a class of moderately to severely retarded children several more years to master these skills, simply because their rate of learning is slower. The skills they must develop fall into the categories of prereading skills relating to semantics, verbal language, and social use of language with other children and adults. The microcomputer can be an invaluable tool in developing these language skills.

Prereading skills related to semantics in early childhood suggests that the young child should acquire basic concepts and ideas about the physical world—objects, people, feelings, and activities that occupy his or her space. These are the basic building blocks of conceptualization, which most children master during the preschool period, not only in school, but at home. The young learner explores the physical world of space, shape, size, motion, texture, and other aspects of his or her world. Children learn that a rubber ball is round and soft, and very different from a tree or house. Much of this is done with the help of children's television. If one looks closely at children's programs such as *Sesame Street* or the *Electric Company*, one sees very close approximation of software packages—short, sequential packets of activity, highly structured and sequential. These brief spots follow the formats which one builds into simple software.

The basic concepts are then incorporated into classification systems, which lead to deeper and deeper layers of semantic meanings. Initially, those experiences are associated with verbal language, not usually written language. What is important is that concepts are incorporated— built into the student's cognitive structures. The process of semantic mapping has begun in its initial forms—a process begun long before words are written down and reading takes place.

The field of special education has developed extensive programs which have attempted to provide this semantic map for children before the reading process is formalized as instruction. Often, these programs have been established and researched, with the expectation that a direct causal link could be established between these prereading conceptual and perceptual structures and the facility of the child to use the written word. In many of the research findings (such as the Frostig program) a direct link between these conceptual and perceptual skills and reading progress has not been established. But these preschool programs have proven to have a positive effect for the skills they were stressing, which were valuable in themselves.

There are many examples of these programs: the Frostig-Horne program (Frostig & Horne, 1964) was designed to develop visual perception skills of young children. The Kephart program was developed to strengthen coordination and body awareness. The Barsch (1965) program was developed to strengthen visual skills. Perhaps one of the most well known was the Doman-Delacato program, at the Institute for Human Potential (IHP). In the IHP program children were laboriously taken through progressive muscular development systems (patterning) in an attempt to regenerate the neural pathways between the brain and the larger motor muscles. In all of those systems, the primary intention was to help the retarded, the brain-injured, or the learning-disabled student to better understand the concepts of three dimensional space we live in and their body's position in this universe. The programs were often classified as perceptual-motor training systems and were used extensively when a child's "real" developmental maturation was judged to be at a preschool level. It mattered not whether the child was retarded, brain injured, cerebral palsied, or whatever label was attached. The point of the programs was to develop a conceptual system of "meanings" which was strongly embedded in three-dimensional space in which we live. While many of these programs are widely used today, their value has not been proved, in terms of developing better reading abilities.

Many software programs are available for preschool children which focus on just those skills—size and shape recognition, discrimination of colors, discrimination of direction, and recognition of letters and simple words. The programs help the young child develop the basic perceptual discriminations which lead to word recognition. The microcomputer software has the added advantage of acting like a child's own TV set, one which he or she controls by pushing certain keys which can be color coded. At this point in time, almost every school district has software libraries, technical staff who can advise the teacher on the quality of software, and, usually, lend-lease programs where software can be "borrowed" as easily as an interlibrary loan of a book.

Learning to Use Language

Developing verbal language skills and learning to use language in a social way is critical in the preschool program. The simple production of language is critical in those preschool years when the child is developing understanding of concepts, syntactic order, and phonic regularities of our language. For some children these abilities are more critical than for others. Deaf or hard of hearing children have many problems which call for the maximum production of sounds early in childhood. Autistic children have long been recognized as being reticent or unable to produce adequate verbal language. The early work of the "talking" typewriter, and the work of Lovaas (1977) in helping autistic children to produce speech which then leads to reading, can be considered an example of the importance of the development of verbal production.

For the student to develop adequate auditory discrimination of sound, in some cases it may be necessary to teach the differences in sounds when discriminating them in words. The difference in the *i* sound in *bit* and *bite* needs to be heard if the student is to develop adequate language to accomplish reading tasks. Many of the standard verbal games, rhymes and songs, etc., which are part of the typical preschool program, are essential to the handicapped child who must learn the basic language of learning and living to succeed in reading.

Early in life, even in infancy, children learn that words have magic; that is, words cause people to do things. The child cries and the mother picks up the child and comforts him or her. When he or she is older and beginning to issue one-word commands, the caregiver will respond to even the rudiments of a statement. The egocentric use of language is usually followed by learning to communicate with other children and the understanding that there is a natural sharing or social interaction among people. Children at play learn to share, compete, take turns, and in short become social.

These lessons lead the child to understand that language, spoken, written, or read, is a basic tool for communicating with other people in the world. Reading and writing then become the basics of a child's ability to share ideas, feelings, events, etc., with others and the basis through which others share their own experiences. Usually, the use of verbal language is achieved well before a child starts school. For many retarded and behaviorally disordered children these basic language abilities are learned slowly. Thus, the written word is not understood as a means for communicating with others.

There has been considerable criticism of computers in the classroom to the effect that sitting at a computer tends to produce an "isolate" or antisocial child who tends to want to work alone. This, obviously, is being understood as an exaggeration. All children need to learn to work independently on many tasks. The use of microcomputers in the classroom can facilitate that learning. Also, some software asks for cooperative play or competition between two "users" and teaches social skills such as taking turns and cooperation. Simple networking allows children to send messages back and forth, facilitating social understanding of other children.

When these skills are successfully learned the child develops into a reader who understands that the written word conjures up a whole world of other people. The child understands that the newspaper and magazines tell of other interesting and "important" people. The child learns that books can take you to distant lands, or help one explore inner feelings. The child learns to express ideas and feelings to others as part of the social use of language. This reinforces the child's motivation to learn to read, because children understand that those "make believe" experiences of books or computers can be theirs when they learn to read.

Teaching the Special Child to Read:
The Beginning Reader and the Microcomputer

For the most part, exceptional children are still in the regular classroom when initial reading instruction takes place. That is to say, when the child is first shown the printed word by a teacher and it is explained that the oral language that the child has used can also be written down on paper by using the symbols that adults call letters or words. Recognizing, of course, that much of children's television on a preschool level begins this process very effectively, it must be realized that at some point in time a teacher begins what we call "formal" instruction of reading. The experience of the past decades in special education tells us that, unless the child is severely handicapped, that moment in time will happen in the regular classoom. Most of the children who end up in self-contained, special education classrooms have been identified only after initial reading instruction has failed. Beginning reading instruction for most special children follows the pattern which exists in the school district where they reside. One of the most successful uses of microcomputers is in the "Learning to Read by Writing" series in which the child begins his or her own written vocabulary through assitance from the computer. Instead of a child compiling his or her own notebook, or word file full of "words" that he or she has learned to write, the file becomes a "floppy disk." The rest of the approach is very similar—the child's life experiences are the basis for the beginning reading stories in the classroom. This program simply adds in one other element, the child's fascination with a machine that responds to him or her. Beginning reading instruction has entered the high-tech age.

Millions of words have been written about the necessary skills a child must have to begin to read, and I hesitate to try to add to that. However, for the purposes of review, the special child must learn some of the following principles to become a successful reader, all of which are possible through existing software for microcomputers.

1. The child learns that sounds can be written down using symbols we call letters (b, d, a, z, etc.).

2. The child learns that these written symbols can be put into

sequences called words, which have meanings attached to them (*cat*, *dog*).

3. The child learns that the sounds of the symbols sometimes change or vary (*cat*, *city*), or are silent (*kiss*, *knee*).

4. The child learns that certain left to right sequences are standard, whether the language is oral or written. The word *cat* is sounded *k-a-t*, and written in that same sequence.

5. The child learns that words can be chained together into sentences, and that when they are, the order is important. "He hit her" is different from "She hit him" or "He was hit by her."

6. The child learns that certain sequences are acepted in his language and others are not. "The tall man" is acceptable, but in Spanish that order is not.

7. The child learns that, at times, language is read metaphorically, or cannot be translated literally. Written language includes "meanings" which are hinted at, referred to, but not directly expressed. Allegory and metaphor, humor and poetry, are all examples of ways in which language exceeds its literal limits.

8. Finally, if one is to believe the central message of Frank Smith (1971, 1979), good reading requires a mind set—a search for meaning that starts as a psychological process within the child. Smith would probably argue that this item should come at the beginning of the list.

In the field of special education many different approaches have been used which come from reading programs for children in the regular classroom. Those approaches have typically been applied without regard to the official "category" or label. Most teachers of self-contained classrooms use an eclectic approach to reading instruction. They try what seems logical, and if it does not give results then a variation is tried, or a competing strategy is tried.

Some Phonics Approaches

To deal with the aspects of reading which are related to sound–letter correspondences, the field had developed "phonics approaches" in all their variations. It would appear to be logical from the adult point of view to start on the level with the special child being taught the fundamentals of phonics in the English language. However, I would argue that phonics approaches should probably begin with top-down approaches—establishing meaning of passage before individual phonics lessons are introduced. Basic reading series are available from any of the major publishers. Examples would be: the Palo Alto Reading Program— the Harcourt, Brace, Jovanovich series; the Open Court Reading Program; the Phonics Explorer or the Reading Trail; Science Research

Associates; Patterns, Sounds, and Meaning—Allyn and Bacon; and Speech to Print Phonics—Harcourt, Brace, Jovanovich. These programs have been used extensively with special children within the self-contained clasroom. The research on their success or failure is inconclusive. A teacher who really likes to teach phonics and who feels it is an important element in a child's development as a reader will find ways to adapt those basic programs to the needs of the children in his or her classroom—and the children will learn.

The key to the success seems to be the individual teacher's skill in adapting the programs to the individual needs of the children. At times that will mean slowing the instruction down, using more repetitions (a fundamental task of the computer) than are called for in the official system, changing the sequence for some children, or combining the system with a second nonphonics approach. At times the success will come when the reading program is embedded as part of a behavior modification program or part of an "engineered classroom" model as advocated by Hewett (Hewett & Taylor, 1980). In the finaly analysis the experience of the teacher is important, the "clinical" skills of the teacher are as important as the "clinical" skills of any other professional in the application of a commercial program to a particular group of children.

Phonics approaches also fail with some exceptional children. On one level, phonics seems a simple building block to oral reading. On another level, phonics is a very complex set of rules of sound–letter correspondences in the English language. For some retarded children, phonics will become a very difficult maze of sound–letter correspondences. The complexities of English phonics will only confuse a bright learning-disabled child who is already having trouble with understanding and processing language. We marvel at the problem college students have with some phonics rules. For example, why is the word *bow* pronounced differently in the following two sentences: The girl had a bow on her blouse; and, After singing her song the girl took a bow. Smith and his colleagues have estimated that the oral vocabulary of a first-grade child (most primary 2,000 words) includes over 180 sound–letter correspondences. When the rules of phonics in common words are "regular," they seem to help handicapped children learn to read faster. When a teacher has to explain the irregularities of English phonics then it would seem to just add to the learning problems a handicapped child already has.

Because of those irregularities in phonics the field has seen several attempts to approach to the problems of initial reading skills from different perspectives. The initial teaching alphabet (ITA) was introduced in the 1960s (Mazurkiewicz, 1966; Pitman, 1961). It is a "regularized" alphabet with 44 characters, and leads to regularized spelling (*fun, wun,* and *dun* replace *fun, won,* and *done*). It solves some of the problems of the irregularities of English phonics. It also created its own problems, primarily because it is a transitional system. The child must learn the ITA symbols as an intermediate step to learning the "regular" alphabet and all the regular rules of phonics.

As such, the ITA never got off the ground in special education. The system seemed to ask the handicapped child to learn one alphabet only to have it replaced with the "real" alphabet later. Most of the programs that tried the ITA with slow learners or retarded children in the 1960s and early 1970s found that it was simply more for the child to learn. The proponents of the ITA often spoke of the future total acceptance of their system, once touted as the replacement of the standard English alphabet. That replacement never occurred, and the ITA seemed to recede in importance as the 1970s decade progressed.

The other major innovative approach to helping children decode the mysteries of words, letters, and sounds was the "Rebus" method. In this system, the words of the language are replaced by simple pictures or symbols. Such a system would be easy to incorporate on floppy disks so that children could progress through the "Rebus" system at their own rate.

No attempt is made to modify the spelling of the initial words that the student learns to read as was done in the ITA. Instead, a transitional set of pictures is presented which substitute for words, and, at the end of the program, the transition to reading words should be complete. Again, the system tries to help the student to make the transition from an auditory or vocal vocabulary to the written letter system of words. It is considered transitional and could be helpful to special children, when they are having basic problems in the initial stages of learning to read. If a student is a strong visual learner, as many preschool children are, it is a good system to use as an introduction to basic reading skills. Much of children's television, including the newest machine monster adventure series has incorporated these techniques into its programming for preschool children. Surely more children come to school now knowing how to spell words like *POW, WHAM,* and *SMASH* than *dog, cat,* or *tree.*

Teaching the Special Child to Read: Remedial Approaches

As has been noted, most children who are found in self-contained classes in special education are there because they have been failures at learning to read. Coupled with behavior problems, failure to learn to read comprises the two greatest sources of referrals to classes for the handicapped. Consequently, when the child has fallen 2 to 3 years behind in reading skills, the student is referred to the committee on the handicapped, classified, and placed into a self-contained classroom, where the teacher is forced to develop a remedial reading program.

The choices of remedial reading programs seem endless, each promising success to the teacher. Many of the approaches are multisensory and are modifications of systems which go back 50 or 60 years. The reading systems of Montessori (1964), Fernald (1943), and Gillingham and Stillman (1970) all build on the concept of concrete experiences through which the child can learn to master words. All of the senses are brought in to help the child master the processes—visual, auditory, kinesthetic, and tactile. In each case the principle is that, if the student can not master visual symbols, letters, and words, then perhaps the child will be able to do so if the visual, auditory, and kinesthetic processes are actively engaged in a way that is integrated by the child and monitored by the teacher. These systems have been used with learning-disabled students and with brain-injured students before that. Moreover, they have been used with retarded children at all levels for many years, with the assumption that a multisensory approach will help the slow learner master the skill. One sensory modality is meant to offset a weakness in the other. If a child is a good listener, then pair the visual presentation with that of an auditory task. Help him or her compensate for the disability, while at the same time trying to help the student develop stronger skills in the weak areas.

Variations of this approach have been introduced over the years. Gattegno's (1962) Words in Color was an attempt to introduce the phenomena of our language through 39 shades of colors. In 1966, Bannatyne introduced a psycholinguistic "color" system which was designed to help the slow reader. At times the focus was on auditory input—as with the Neurological Impress Method of Heckelman (1969), in which the teacher and child read passages aloud in unison, with the teacher literally reading into the ear of the child. In some magical way the teacher's voice going into the auditory system was throught to strengthen the student's understanding of the words that he was reading aloud.

Many variations of auditory training as a point of language development can be found in the literature. The work of Semel (1970) focused on teaching the child to process the auditory messages in language correctly as a basis for understanding written language. Lindamood and Lindamood (1969) developed a system which taught auditory discrimination skills in great depth. As controversial as it has been over the past 15 years, the work that grew from the ITPA (Illinois Test of Psycholinguistic Abilities) was meant to reinforce the concepts of language being addressed as modalities processes—visual and auditory.

Children were evaluated according to their abilities in receptive and expressive language skills in both visual and auditory modes. While the ITPA as a diagnostic test has been severely criticized, the assumptions underlying the model it represents have never been denigrated. Learners process language in both visual and auditory modes and receptive association and expression are still thought to be of fundamental points of language, and therefore, reading.

Parts of the field have been based on the 'linguistic" understanding of handicapped children. Poor reading skills are seen as an outgrowth of poor linguistic development or indadequate understanding of the linguistic structures in our language. Consequently, sets of readers which focus on the development of linguistic skills have emerged: the Merrill Linguistic Readers, the SRA Reading Skills texts, the Harper and Row Linguistic Readers, the Miami Linguistic Readers, and the Bloomfield and Barnhardt Let's Read Series.

A whole set of reading programs and approaches has emerged in the past 25 years which basically relates to the experience of the child—that is, programs which were to draw heavily from the cultural context of the child's life, teaching the child to read by starting with the reality of the child's home, community, ethnic, or social membership. The late 1960s saw the DISTAR program by Engelmann and Bruner (1969), which was designed to focus on the real experience and needs of the culturally deprived and slow learning student. DISTAR's most fundamental contribution seems to have been to break down the 6.6 phenomenon—that is, it now seems possible with correct methods to start instruction in reading prior to the age of 6.6 years. Englemann suggests that a mental age of 4 years is appropriate for children to begin to learn to read. The academic program of DISTAR also focused on the disadvantaged child. The organic reading approach of Ashton-Warner (1963) also focused on teaching the learner words that had intense meaning for the learner. Reading experiences were built from the day-to-day life experiences of the learner, as opposed to the Dick, Jane, and Spot approach which shows the hypothetical middle class suburban family. Perhaps the bilingual education programs should be considered as a part of this focus in that they try to teach the child to read in two languages—the primary language of the home is retained while the second language (usually in English) is introduced in the school.

Parallel to most of the reading programs which have been introduced to the field as texts, one has to consider the development of computers and computer-like instruction in reading. The initial representation of computer reading programs was in programmed textbooks. These programmed instructional approaches were the forerunners to the floppy disks of the 1980s. The 1960s gave us the Sullivan Programmed

Readers; the 1970s produced modified material in the form of programmed instruction and task analysis approaches such as the Edmark Reading Program. In all of these approaches the constant repetition, immediate feedback, and very small sequential steps dominate the material. Reading skills are broken down into a multitude of small incremental stages. These approaches have long been successful with the slow learner in the self-contained classroom. Anyone who is familiar with computer programming knows that these are essential elements in any program.

The 1980s saw the introduction of the computer to the special education classroom. The apparent leader in these classrooms seems to be the Apple Series, with all of its attendant software, although IBM, Radio Shack (Tandy), and Digital do provide some reading software programs for exceptional children. Computer-assisted instruction, which was introduced in the 1960s and died because of inadequate hardware and software, has been replaced by an overwhelming variety of software programs created and designed for the personal computer (the microcomputer). Often the software is fixed—that is, the programs are prewritten and the teacher cannot modify the instructional sequence very much. Thus, if an exceptional learner needs drill on blends, sight word recognition, or some other specific skill, then usually a teacher can find software which presents that skill.

At this point in time, while many districts have the microcomputers in place, the teachers are not trained to use them, and the software which is needed to cover all of the possible lessons for the handicapped is unavailable. Software is beginning to appear in very well-stocked curriculum laboratories or libraries. The information is there, but it still takes an interested and trained teacher who knows how, why, when, and where to access it, if microcomputers are to live up to their potential as remedial programs for handicapped children.

Summary

The use of microcomputers to teach and/or remediate reading with exceptional children has just begun to be understood. One can envision software which is programmed to teach phonics "families," sounds of letters, and syntax in addition to building concepts and enlarging a child's vocabulary. Already, writing-to-read programs are in place where children learn their basic sight vocabulary through the use of a minicomputer. Prior to coming to school, most childen have accompanied a parent into a store where a computer terminal calculates a bill, checks an account, or does a million other things. We all know that the computer technology will not disappear. Computer literacy is already a basic part of many school districts' demands on the students.

The use of microcomputers as a part of a remedial reading program for handicapped children is a field which must develop. I say it must because it has all the right answers, the capacity to stimulate and motivate the child (at all ages!), and the capacity to program an individual plan, to carry it out, and monitor the child's progress, releasing the teacher for other tasks. With graphics and soon-to-be-added voice responses, the age of the microcomputer is just beginning.

The future will see a greater utilization of the concepts to teach children metacognitive skills, because it is a natural development. Teachers will understand that the computer is a natural tool to develop the metacognitive skills of the child. Working with microcomputers demands that the user constantly assess the limits of his or her knowledge about the computer. It constantly requires the user to monitor what he or she is doing and does and does not know about the computer. That appears to be a basic theme in metacognition—understand what we understand about our own mental processes, what we know about how we think. How often do we hear teachers say, "If only I could teach him or her to think it through," to learn how to learn. Working with microcomputers will be found to help develop cognitive processes in handicapped children.

Finally a few words about what the teachers need to know about this "beast" which has invaded their classrooms. The first time I taught a course about computers to special education teachers, I was stunned at the apprehension in the teachers. I found the book by Michael Behrmann (1984) to be an excellent introduction for the teachers. My conclusions are that teachers need several sets of basic skills, such as the fundamentals of operating a microcomputer, information about simple word processing software which many students can incorporate into their writing and reading programs, perhaps a little information about file management, and fundamental information about evaluating software. For the teacher of handicapped children the Council for Exceptional Children can be an important source of information, if the school district does not already have a specialist who can guide the teacher.

Finally, a word about "attitudes." The microcomputer is a useful machine, one that can help the teacher and motivate the child. It can be very helpful, just as the typewriter was a large step ahead of pens and ink bottles. It calls for imagination from the teacher, and very quickly becomes the friend of the child. It is truly here to stay and will soon become an extension of most teachers which they will find extremely helpful, and perhaps someday they too will join the child in thinking of it as a good "friend."

References

Ashton-Warner, S. (1963). *Teacher*. New York: Simon & Schuster.

Bannatyne, A. D. (1966). *Psycholinguistic color system*. Urbana, IL: Learning Systems Press.

Barsch, R. (1965). *A movigenics curriculum*. Milwaukee, Wisconsin: State Department of Public Instruction.

Behrmann, M. 91984). *Handbook of microcomputers in special education*. San Diego: Ca: College-Hill Press.

Delacato, C. A. (1959). *The treatment and prevention of reading problems: The neurological approach*. Springfield, IL: Charles C. Thomas.

Englemann, S., & Bruner, E. C. (1969). *DISTAR: An instructional system*. Chicago, IL: Science Research Associates.

Fernald, G. (1943). *Remedial techniques in basic school subjects*. New York: McGraw-Hill.

Frostig, M., & Horne, D. (1964). *The Frostig program to the development of visual perception*. Chicago, IL: Follett Publishing Company.

Gattegno, C. (1962). *Words in color*. Chicago, IL: Learning Materials Company.

Gillespie-Silver, P. (1979). *Teaching reading to children with special needs*. Columbus, OH: Charles E. Merrill.

Gillingham, A., & Stillman, B. (1970). *Remedial training for children with specific disability in reading, spelling, and penmanship*. Cambridge, MA: Educators Publishing Service.

Goldenberg, E. P., Russell, S. J., & Carter, C. J. (1984). *Computers, education and special needs*. Reading, MA: Addison-Wesley Publishing Company.

Heckelman, R. G. (1969). The neurological impress method of remedial reading instruction. *Academic Therapy, 4*, 277–282.

Hewett, F. M., & Taylor, F. D. (1980). *The emotionally disturbed child in the classroom: The orchestration of success*. Boston, MA: Allyn & Bacon.

Kephart, N. C. (1971). *The slow learner in the classroom* (2nd ed.). Columbus, OH: Charles Merrill.

Kirk, S. A., McCarthy, J. J., & Kirk, W. (1968). *Illinois Test of Psycholinguistic Abilities*. Urbana, IL: University of Illinois Press.

Lindamood, C., & Lindamood, P. (1969). *Auditory discrimination in depth*. Boston: Teaching Resources.

Lovaas, O. I. (1977). *The autistic child: Language development through behavior modification*. New York: Irvington Publishers, Inc.

Mazurkiewicz, A. J., & Tanyzer, H. J. (1966). *The i/t/a/ handbook for writing and spelling: Early-to-read i/t/ program*. New York: United Teaching Alphabet Publication.

Montessori, M. (1964). *The Montessori method*. New York: Schocken Books.

Richek, M. A., List, L., & Lerner, J. (1983). *Reading problems: diagnosis and remediation*. Englewood Cliffs, NJ: Prentice-Hall.

Salvia, J., & Ysseldyke, J. E. (1985). *Assessment in special and remedial education*. Boston: Houghton Miflin.

Semel, E. M. (1970). *Sound-Order-Sense: A developmental program in auditory perception*. Chicago, IL: Follett.

Smith, F. (1971). *Understanding reading.* New York: Holt, Rinehart, & Winston.
Smith, F. (1979). *Reading without nonsense.* New York: Teachers College Press.
Woodcock, R. W., & Clark, C. R. (1969). *Peabody Rebus Reading Program.* Circle Pines, MN: American Guidance Service.

Chapter 12

Learning with QUILL:
Lessons for Students, Teachers
and Software Designers

Andee Rubin and Bertram C. Bruce

BBN Laboratories

She sat silently in the back of the room. Every line in her scowling face demanded, "Show me! Show me how this computer stuff is going to teach my kids how to write!" At the end of the 3-day training session on QUILL, a set of microcomputer-based writing activities, we were sure that this was one fourth-grade teacher who would never become a successful user. Soon, however, reports started to filter back about a teacher everyone was calling "Mrs. QUILL." It was our scowling resister. By the end of the school year, her class had written letters to their local congressman and to President Reagan, organized a "Face the Students" session with their congressman, and traveled to Washington, where they met with Maureen Reagan. The initial letters, lists of questions for the "Face the Students" session, and thank you letters to the Reagans were all written using QUILL. The project was aided by a local parent who knew the congressman and was impressed by his child's school activities. Several local newspapers carried accounts of the class's letter-writing activities and journey to Washington.

Many people learned important lessons from this teacher's experience. She, herself, learned that computers could enhance her classroom, even in the unlikely area of writing. The students in her class learned that writing could be used to accomplish goals they cared about, even in the unlikely place called school. We, as software designers, learned that even unlikely teachers could use QUILL in educationally exciting and valuable ways, if QUILL was consistent with their educational goals and techniques. In this case the teacher had always valued letter writing as a language arts activity. She ran a well-organized yet flexible classroom into which it was possible to integrate the use of a computer. Using QUILL and the microcomputer, she was able to establish a new and meaningful context for developing literacy in her classroom.

This chapter describes the effects QUILL has had on classroom contexts for communication and literacy. More generally, it investigates the changes an open-ended innovation can bring about for teachers and students. Educational tools that allow significant flexibility require teachers to participate actively in their implementation. Thus, individual classrooms may choose different activities, teachers may focus on their own special interests, and students may use the tools in significantly different ways. Given this freedom, teachers often create educational activities that the innovation developers never considered.

The computer is a particularly interesting medium for investigating these concepts because it is often thought of as an instrument for controlling students and classrooms. We hear about "teacher-proof" software and "individualized instruction." In contrast, open-ended software such as QUILL is teacher-dependent and provides a context in which students can work at their own rate only if teachers provide that opportunity (Bruce, 1985; Levin, 1982; Rubin, 1982; Collins, 1986).

Our contention is that open-ended software—like other flexible educational contexts—provides opportunities for learning that go beyond transferring knowledge from the machine to the student. In this chapter we discuss lessons teachers, students, and software designers learned during the past 2 years of working with QUILL. They span traditional lessons in language arts, lessons about the writing process, lessons about classroom organization, and philosophical lessons about the interaction of purpose and tools in writing. These lessons provide powerful evidence for the educational value of software and other innovations that can provide multiple opportunities for learning.

What is QUILL?

QUILL (Collins, Bruce, & Rubin, 1982; Rubin, Bruce, & The QUILL Project, 1985; Bruce & Rubin, 1984) is a set of microcomputer-based writing activities for students in Grades 2 through 12. The software is based on recent research in composition and encompasses the prewriting, composing, revising, and publishing aspects of the writing process (Bruce, Collins, Rubin & Gentner, 1982; Flower & Hayes, 1981;

Graves, 1982; Newkirk & Atwell, 1982). To aid students in becoming more experienced writers, QUILL includes two tools for writing: PLAN-NER, which helps students plan and organize their pieces, and WRIT-ER'S ASSISTANT (Levin, Boruta, & Vasconcellos, 1982), a text editor that facilitates the revision process by making the addition, deletion, and rearrangement of text easier. QUILL also provides dtudents with two contexts for writing designed to foster communication by providing audiences for student composition. The first, MAILBAG, is an electronic mail system with which students can send messages to individuals, groups, or an electronic bulletin board. The second, LIBRARY, is an information management system in which writing is accessed by title, author, or keywords.

QUILL was used in over 150 classrooms across the country from Massachusetts to Alaska (Barnhardt, 1984) from 1982 to 1984. These sites provide the basis for the examples used throughout this chapter.

Lessons for Students

Student Lesson 1

There are many legitimate reasons for writing and reading, even in school.

Students typically find the purpose of writing in school to be mystifying. The assignment often involves half an hour of sitting alone, writing about a topic that they may find either boring (e.g., compare *Hamlet* and *Huckleberry Finn*) or silly (e.g., describe how it would feel to be an ice cream cone). In most cases everyone in the class must write on the same topic, and the teacher who assigned the topic are then expected to read and evaluate themes on a subject that is not meaningful to them either. The final indignity is that most of the teacher's responses to the writing tend to focus on grammatical or mechanical errors rather than on content.

Students in several QUILL classrooms realized—some for the first time—that writing could be different from this dreary picture. In most cases this came about through teachers consciously setting up a communicative environment where the audience and purpose for writing were both specific and real. QUILL contributed both by providing examples of such contexts and by being an easily adaptable tool around which to build communicative evednts. The examples below illustrate these contexts.

On a trip through Alaska to visit QUILL classrooms, we carried a disk called "Supermail." Students in each classroom wrote messages to children in classrooms they knew we wold later visit. Students in some of the later classrooms read these messages, gaining ideas for messages of their own. Some even set for themselves the task of outdoing their peers. Thus, writing became meaningful as a form of communication, sometimes even as competition for readers from an audience of their peers. One example of this "competition from afar; began with the following piece, written by two eighth graders in McGrath, Alaska (population: 500, reachable only by air).

CALLING ALL MEN

Sheila Forsythe   Althea Jones

Hi, This note is to all you good looking guys out there in the world. There are two of us writing so we'll tell you a little bit about ourselves. Our names are Sheila Forsythe and Althea Jones. We're both 14 and stuck in a small town in Alaska called McGrath. We have a pretty big problem and we hope that you guys will help us out. We have a very short supply of foxy dudes here. So if you are a total fine babe PLEASE I repeat PLEASE write us!!!!

Write:
>   Sheila Forsythe and Althea Jones
>   General Delivery
>   McGrath, Alaska 99627

and hurry!

Keywords: /McGrath/Male Order Men/

The two authors acknowledged that it was important to call attention to their letter by their choice of keywords. The first keyword— McGrath—was an obligatory identification of the source of the message. But the second (including the misspelling) was their own invention. Since the Supermail disk was actually a LIBRARY disk, students chose which entries to read by scanning the list of keywords. These girls were correct in their assessment of their audience: groups of boys in later classrooms did choose their message. Not to be outdone, two girls in the next town, Holy Cross, wrote the following message on the Supermail disk:

GOOD LOOKING JUNEAU BOYS

Two Holy Cross Girls   Josie and Evelyn

Our names are Josie Adams and Evelyn fields. We like skiing, basket-ball, hockey, writing letters to cute boys, and we would be more than pleased if any of you cute boys would write to us. We don't have any boyfriends. So you don't have to worry about that! We also would like you to send a picture when you write. (You are going to write aren't you?) We will send you a picture too. Josie is 14 and Evelyn is 13. Well, please write soon! We are waiting for your letter !!!!!

WE SEND YOU OUR HEARTS!

SINCERELY, JOSIE AND EVELYN.

Keywords: /Juneau Boys/H.C.R. Girls/

These two girls used a slightly different strategy for attracting readers; they knew the disk would be traveling to Juneau next, so they specifically aimed their "personal ad" toward Juneau boys, including them in both the title and keywords. They also spent considerable time and effort drawing the heart (an idea they appropriated from the younger students in the school who had spent the morning making word pictures with QUILL) so their message would compete effectively with the one from McGrath. Incidentally, boys in both Juneau and Oregon, where the disk later traveled, took all four girls' addresses with the intention of writing to them during the summer.

Some students discover that writing can be meaningful for self-expression as well as for communication. This was evident in a poignant episode concerning Peter, a sixth grader in an inner-city school. Peter's home situation was troubled, and he did not do very well in school. In January he ran away from both home and school and spent several nights sleeping in an abandoned car. After a few days he reappeared in his classroom and asked if he could use the computer. When the teacher told him he would have to wait his turn, he offered to use the computer in the morning before classes began. One of the first pieces he wrote after returning to school was the following:

PETER'S ISLAND

PETER

HI SWEET POLLY LOVERS . . . HERE IS A REVIEW OF THE LATEST NEW T. V. SHOW . . . "PETER'S ISLAND."
ONE DAY THERE WAS A BOY NAMED PETER. HE WANTED TO RUN AWAY BECAUSE EVERY BODY DID NOT LIKE HIM SO HE RAN AWAY HE HEARD OF A BOAT GOING OUT TO SEA SO HE WENT TO GET ON THE BOAT AND ON THE SECOUND DAY AT SEA THERE WAS A BAD STORM AND HE WOKEUP HE WAS IN THE SEA LAYING ON A BOARD AND HE WAS GETTING TIRED AND HUNGRY SO

WENT TO SLEEP AND ALL MOST DIED BUT WHEN HE WOKEUP
AND HE WAS ON A ILAND AND HE LOOK AROUND AND SEEN A
DOLPHIN BUT MICHAEL KEEP SAYING WHO SAVED HIM THEN HE
KNOW WHO SAVED HIM THE DOLPHIN AND HE LIVED THE REST
OF HIS LIFE ON THE ISLAND WITH THE DOLPHIN

THE END.

Keywords: /Peter/boat/boy/

In this piece Peter adopted a TV-announcer's role, a strategy that he
had used in the past. There seem to be two plausible purposes for Peter's
piece. It might have been his way to come to terms with running away.
He may in addition have composed it as a message to his teacher asking
for help or understanding. Peter eventually became one of the most
prolific writers in the class. In his classroom girls dominated the
keyboard, yet Peter always made sure he had writing time. Later in the
year he became the food editor of the class newspaper and wrote a book
five typed pages in length.

Student Lesson 2

Revision is both possible and desirable.

According to some, the computer's most important contribution is
that it "takes the sting out of revision" (Romick, 1984). Professional
writers recognize the importance of revision; some analyses of the
writing process suggest that 14% of the time is used in prewriting, only
1% in actually composing, and 85% in rewriting. The distribution of time
allotted to the writing process in schools does not reflect this in any way.
Few teachers give their students the opportunity to revise, and those
who do usually face a chorus of moans from their students who hate
copying over. The students rarely understand all that revision can
entail, perhaps because of their long exposure to a focus on mechanics
and neatness (Scardamalia, 1981). While the presence of a text editor
does not guarantee informed revision, it does make it possible without
the undue hardship that results from rewriting entire texts.

Some students, in fact, carry revision to extremes. One sixth-grade
girl in Hartford was fascinated by the fact that she could potentially
produce a perfect paper. While she had been one of the most prolific
writers in the class, she was slowed down considerably by her habit of
correcting every typo as she noticed it, rather than waiting until she had
completed a chunk of text. However, her meticulousness illustrated her
real concern with the appearance of her writing.

Most teachers who used QUILL were not accustomed to commenting on the content of students' writing; their training and the demands of achievement tests had encouraged them to focus on mechanics. The training they received during workshops on QUILL, combined with the possibility of their students making substantial changes easily using QUILL, led some of them to respond more substantively to their students' writing. The result of such feedback can be seen in the changes on two drafts of a "New Jersey resolution" written by two fourth-grade boys; the assignment was to develop a resolution that the legislature could pass to help improve New Jersey.

Drugs Are Dumb

Benjamin M.   Darren S.

What is bothering us the most in New Jersey is underaged kids are taking drugs. Their not getting enough education. Some kids even get killed!

Adults should educate their children not to take drugs. To get help you should go to a psychiatrist. Try not to take drugs.

It would take a few months or weeks to get over this problem. It is important to solve this problem because sometimes people get killed.

Keywords: /psychiatrist/drugs/children/killed/education/

Their conversation with their teacher about this piece focussed on the need for snappy conclusions and on how long it would really take to kick a drug habit. Benjamin and Darren then produced the following final draft.

Dangerous Damaging Drugs

Benjamin M.   Darren S.

What is bothering us the most in New Jersey is underaged kids are taking drugs. They're not getting enough education. Some kids even get killed! Adults should educate their children not to take drugs or not to get involved with drugs. To get help you should go to a psychiatrist. Try not to take drugs. If you take drugs, go for help! It would take an unlimited amount of time to get over this problem. It is important to solve this problem because sometimes people get killed. So be smart, make sure you don't take drugs!

Keywords: /psychiatrist/drugs/children/killed/education/

In addition to correcting mechanical errors and responding to their teacher's comments, the two boys revised their previous title, extending the alliterative theme, and increasing the chances for it to attract a reader's attention. This use of the text editor for both revision and editing within a number of drafts is an important step beyond the way writing instruction is handled in many classrooms.

Lessons for Teachers

Teacher Lesson 1

Truly communicative writing in school is possible, legitimate, and necessary.

Teachers are sometimes suspicious of the notion of "communicative writing" in school, associating it with surreptitious note passing, giggling, and other disruptive activities. Part of the goal of the QUILL training workshop and teacher's guide was to convince teachers that communicative writing was a legitimate part of writing in school, and that assessing the communicative value of any written piece should be a primary concern. The Cookbook, a handbook of suggestions for teachers on how to use QUILL, suggested sending messages on MAILBAG as a beginning activity, to acquaint both students and teacher with QUILL. A sixth-grade teacher in Oregon discovered that his students took advantage of this opportunity to write him serious notes about their opinions of school. Some typical examples are: "I think it's a good idea to write our schedule for the day on the board," and "I'd like to do more art in school."

A teacher in a combined sixth-, seventh- and eighth-grade class in Holy Cross, Alaska, took advantage of a real-world situation to create a truly communicative task for her class. Villages in Alaska like Holy Cross (population: 275) receive an inordinate number of requests for information about their village. In Holy Cross, the city council gives all such requests to the school. After answering several of the letters individually, this teacher decided to have her class construct a tourism brochure about Holy Cross. They decided what the brochure should include, took responsibility for various sections, did the required research and wrote the text. The finished product includes several hand-done drawings as well as sections on schools, clothes, trapping and hunting, fishing, businesses, government, communication, recreation, and population.

A third way teachers discovered to include functional writing in a school was through class newspapers. Since the computer is a useful aid for the most onerous parts of putting together a newspaper—text preparation, editing, and formatting—many classes published regular editions, as often as monthly. Without the advantages of the computer, the typical pattern one finds is that one or two issues are published with the bulk of the preparation done by the teacher. The issues end when the teacher gets tired of staying up all night typing dittos. Newspapers in QUILL classrooms were produced for both in-school and out-of-school audiences; the assumed readership included the members of the class, friends, and their families. A newspaper produced by a sixth-grade class in Massachusetts included the following column, editorial in nature and clearly directed to other class members.

Kids' Behavior Toward Substitute Teachers

When we have a substitute teacher you are supposed to treat the substitute teacher with any respect. Some of the kids in the classroom don't treat the substitute teacher with any respect. They treat them like another kid. They call the substitute names, or yell out disturbing the teacher. Some of the girls act like it is their regular teacher, but some of them act fresh. You hardly ever see a boy act nice to the substitute teacher. They always for some reason act nice to our regular teacher, but not to substitute teachers.

These writing activities demonstrate, not only the possibility and legitimacy of communicative writing in the classroom, but its necessity. Students contributed enthusiastically to the newspaper and brochure projects in part because they knew there was a real audience for the information they possessed. This crucial element had been missing in many other less successful classroom writing activities.

Teacher Lesson 2

Changes in the classroom social structure that allow more student interaction can lead to better writing.

One of the unsuspected advantages of having only one computer in each classroom is that teachers immediately acknowledge the need for students to work at the computer in pairs or small groups. In most classes, individual work during writing is the rule; with QUILL it has become the exception. The need to have students work on the computer together has led several teachers to realize the potential benefit of collaborative work. A sixth-grade teacher from Oregon commented that papers produced by pairs of students have fewer grammatical errors; he hypothesized that both students' independent writing would improve as a result of working with another student. The following conversation, observed in another sixth-grade class, illustrates one benefit of student collaboration. The first student had written a message to students in other cities using the Supermail disk: "We are in Mr. Kinder's class." His partner immediately reminded him that "the kids who read that won't know who Mr. Kinder is!"

One of the most dramatic examples of the influence of social structure on writing occurred in a sixth-grade classroom in Hartford. Students had seen a Black History show given by the younger classes in the school. Upon returning to their room, several students opted to write reviews of the show. Once they had completed a draft at their desks, students were assigned consecutive numbers that designated their turn to enter their draft on the computer. A backlog soon developed, and several students ended up standing around the computer reading each other's first drafts. One girl, named Margaret, had written a lukewarm review of the show. Part of her piece read:

> The scenery was pretty good, and the light was bright enough, but the sound was not that good. Mr. Hodges was speaking very loudly and was good on the stage. I think the show deserves three stars because it was very good.

While she was waiting to use the computer, Margaret read a first draft by her friend Marines. Marines's review claimed that "the light was a little dull." She also complained about the glee club: "They were almost all weak. The audience couldn't hear them. They sounded soft then they went loud. It was a disaster!"

Margaret was aware that her review and Marines's expressed different opinions—and that hers might be ignored in the face of Marines's strong views. She also had an explanation for Marines's criticism of the glee club. This explanation was included in her final draft:

> The scenery wasn't very much, and the light was kind of dull, and the sound wasn't very good. Mr. Hodges was speaking loud and clearly, and he was great on the stage. When the Glee Club was singing so nice, Marines got very jealous and asked Mrs. Evens to be in the Glee Club. But when Mrs. Evens said no she wrote bad things about the Glee Club on the computer up-stairs.

Notice that, while she had undermined Marines's opinion of the glee club, she has also changed her own description of the lightning to agree with the other girl's (see Bruce, Michaels, & Watson-Gegeo, 1984, for a more detailed analysis).

None of these incidents would have occurred in the traditional model of writing instruction—students sitting alone, writing, turning in a paper, and receiving a grade. The presence of QUILL in the classroom contributed to creating a positive context for writing by shaking up the teaching of writing, making it necessary for students to write together in order to have sufficient computer time. The challenge for teachers is to channel these social interactions to improve students' writing.

Lessons for Software Designers

Software Designer Lesson 1

A teacher's instructional philosophy is a more powerful determinant of software use than the software itself; that is, the teacher's contribution overwhelms that of the software.

Many software designers overestimate the effect their software will have on education. On a global scale, predictions are made of revolutions in education and a technologically literate citizenry due largely to the use of new software (Papert, 1980). Our experience has shown that, especially in the case of open-ended software like QUILL, the software makes an important but not an enormous contribution to what happens in the classroom. A much more potent effect comes from the teacher.

One example can be found in teachers' use of MAILBAG in their classrooms. One of our most successful classrooms, particularly in their use of electronic mail, was a fourth-grade class who used the QUILL software in its very early stages. Even using a relatively primitive system, messages flew among the students and between students and their teacher. The teacher made it clear to her students that she believed this written exchange among the students served an important educational purpose.

In contrast, a teacher in another class later in the project viewed students' use of MAILBAG as illegitimate writing once they started using it to write love notes, and immediately made it unavailable. By this time, the MAILBAG had been polished and was easier to use, but the teacher clearly indicated that she felt it lacked any educational value.

The process of educational change involving QUILL seemed to proceed in two stages. First, the software made possible a new writing genre (written conversations, in the case of MAILBAG). Second, the teacher responded to this new genre in her own way. In most positive cases teachers transferred the children's new-found sense of communicative writing to other genres and modalities. In the most negative cases teachers rejected the new genre as illegitimate.

Teachers demonstrated interesting differences in communicating with students using MAILBAG. A sixth-grade teacher in Hartford adopted two separate personae in writing to his students. The first was a perfectly serious one used when he carried on straightforward—and sometimes quite personal—written conversations with his students. The following exchange is typical:

Bathroom

Marlowe B.
   There is a lot of trouble in the bathrooms. There's been writing on the new paint job, and there's been someone who's been peeling the paint off the radiator.
   If people keep messing up the bathroom, Ducky said that she was going to close the bathroom until we learn not to write in it. And there's been plenty of noise in there. If we don't have to go to the bathroom, don't go in.

Keywords: /bathroom/clean/
Girls' Bathroom
Dr. A.
Dear Pee Wee,
   Thank you for being concerned about the girls' bathroom. I feel sorry for the girls who are messing it up. They must be a little "messed up" themselves.
   When I see Ducky, I'll try to remember to tell her what you did.
Dr. A.

When he was not being serious, this teacher adopted a frivolous personality called Dunedeen, a mischievous monster who sent anonymous messages to several students each week. These messages, predictably, provoked similar unserious replies. Both sets of messages were filled with "hahahaha" and epithets such as "Squarehead." The point to emphasize is that students responded in kind to whatever personality the teacher adopted. The teacher was careful to separate the two because they required such different responses from his students.
   A fourth-grade teacher in New Jersey used MAILBAG quite differently. One of the suggestions in the teacher's guide for using MAILBAG is Classroom Chat. By sending anonymous messages students can discuss personal problems with other chatters in the class without revealing their identity. In the newspaper prototype writers usually adopt a pseudonym that refers to their problem (e.g., Hassled Mom or Concerned Commuter). This teacher decided to use this idea to give her class an assignment. She sent the following message, complete with pseudonym:

The Shower Problem

I. Needabath
Dear Classy Computer Kids,

There are five members in my family and only one shower. Because I'm the youngest member of our family, I'm the last one in line to take a shower. By then, there's usually no more hot water and not too much time for me to wash behind my ears! It's a horrible way to start a day. What can I do to solve this problem?

Cold, late, and dirty,
I. Needabath

The assignment produced the following predictably tongue-in-cheek responses, which hover between reality and fantasy much as the original letter did.

Buying a Shower

Jill Y.   Suzanne H.

Dear Ichabod Needabath,

The next time your parents have a garage sale, go to your room and pick out things you don't use anymore. Put them with the rest of the items that are going to be sold. (Make sure you ask your parents first.) Take the money that you make from the sale and dig deep into your piggy bank for more. Go to your parents and give them your money. Ask them (nicely) if they will buy a shower with the money you have. (Some other family members can use it after you.) If at first they say no, tell them it will be better for the whole family. Good luck, Icky!!

Showers

Dear I. Needabath,

I think you should tell the first person that takes a shower you have to go the bathroom. Then they should let you go before they take a shower. Quickly lock the door and take your shower. You will have enough of time to wash behind your ears.

Sneaky and Desparate,
Kerry N. and Jenny B.

An interesting problem emerged in this activity: The form of the teacher's message mimicked that of the standard Confidential Chat letter, but the students in the class all knew who had sent the letter and, even more important, that it posed a fake problem. Thus, their assignment was to pretend they were answering a real letter from a needy person, yet they knew it was an imaginary letter from their teacher. While students produced imaginative pieces, observers in the classroom reported they were confused about their audience (their teacher or I. Needabath) and their purpose (real or fantasy) while they were writing. This lack of clarity was most obvious when they were signing their names; many were not sure whether to use their own names or to make up pseudonyms.

While the software was identical in our two examples, the outcome was notably different. These differences can be attributed to the teacher's style and values. QUILL contributed the concept of MAILBAG and a medium through which students could send messages, but the content of the writing belonged to the teacher and the students.

Software Designer Lesson 2

There is an important difference between using a computer for editing and for communication.

When we began designing QUILL we underestimated the importance of this distinction. We knew there were text editors available for schools but thought they were insufficient. We wanted to create software informed by recent work on the writing process. In fact, one of our early designs required children to access the text editor by declaring the part of the writing process (drafting, revising, editing, etc.) on which they were working. It seemed clear to us that an effective writing curriculum should be embedded in the writing process. A corollary was that a piece of writing software had to embody writing process concepts.

We were surprised later to find that the usefulness of QUILL in many classrooms derived, not from our (perhaps insufficient) attempts to reflect the writing process, but from its ability to support the establishment of environments for communication, for example, the exchange of personal mail, sharing writing with others, and publishing newspapers. In contrast, we found some classrooms where QUILL's communication environments were not used. For example, in one junior high classroom the teacher did not want to allow direct communication among students since she feared it might encourage obscene language. In that case a simple text editor, such as WRITER'S ASSISTANT, would have been more appropriate.

While QUILL includes a text editor as a tool, it is only part of a larger environment that provides purposes and audiences for writing. For private writing (e.g., diaries) or public writing that is only to be shared in printed form (e.g., professional papers), a text editor might be sufficient. In fact, in those cases the environments of QUILL could be cumbersome and interfere with writing. Students in many situations, however, would benefit from more attention to the social aspects of writing. Social environments and interactions with peers and teachers provide a sense of purpose and audience for young writers, especially if they have access to software that can provide support for the processes of drafting, editing, and publishing their work.

Summary

These six lessons arose during 2 years of field testing QUILL in second-through eighth-grade classrooms. During that time we also learned much about the importance of administrative support to the success of educational innovations. Teachers taught us a great many lessons about creative and effective uses of QUILL that we had never imagined. Had we designed a program that required multiple-choice answers or merely asked students to edit a flawed piece, we would have missed important aspects of the learning process. The final lesson for software designers is just this: We will all learn more if the software is flexible and adaptable. Put in less computer-oriented terms, it applies to other educational innovations as well. QUILL's open-ended nature and attention to process provided a context in which both students and teachers increased their awareness of literacy. Similarly, other flexible contexts for language instruction can lead to significant and truly individualized learning for all the participants.

References

Barnhardt, C. (1984, April). The Quill Microcomputer Writing Program in Alaska. In R. V. Dusseldorp (Ed.), *Proceedings of the third annual statewide conference of Alaska Association for Computers in Education* (pp. 1–10). Anchorage, AK: Alaska Association for Computers in Education.

Bruce, B. (1985). Taking control of educational technology. *Science for the People, 17,* 37–40.

Bruce, B., Michaels, S., & Watson-Gegeo, K. (1985). How computers can change the writing process. *Language Arts, 62,* 142–149.

Bruce, B. C., Collins, A., Rubin, A. D., & Gentner, D. (1982). Three perspectives on writing. *Educational Psychologist, 17,* 131–145.

Bruce, B., & Rubin, A. (1984, September). *Final report on the utilization of technology in the development of basic skills instruction: Written communications.* Washington, DC: U.S. Department of Education.

Collins, A. (1986). Teaching reading and writing with personal computers. In J. Orasanu (Ed.), *A decade of reading research: Implication for practice* (pp. 171–187). Hillsdale, NJ: Erlbaum.

Collins, A., Bruce, B. C., & Rubin, A.D. (1982). Microcomputer-based writing activities for the upper elementary grades. In *Proceedings of the Fourth International Learning Technology Congress and Exposition* (pp. 134–140). Warrenton, VA: Society for Applied Learning Technology.

Flower, L. S., & Hayes, J. R. (1981). Problem solving and the cognitive process of writing. In C. H. Frederiksen, & J. F. Dominic (Eds.), *Writing: The nature, development and teaching of written communication* (pp. 39–58). Hillsdale, NJ: Erlbaum.

Graves, D. H. (1982). *Writing: Teachers and children at work.* Exeter, NH: Heinemann.

Levin, J. A. (1982). Microcomputers as interactive communication media: An interactive text interpreter. *The Quarterly Newsletter of the Laboratory of Comparative Human Cognition, 4,* 34–36.

Levin, J. A., Boruta, M. J., & Vasconcellos, M. T. (1982). Microcomputer-based environments for writing: A writer's assistant. In A. C. Wilkinson (Ed.), *Classroom computers and cognitive science* (pp. 219–232). New York: Academic.

Newkirk, T., & Atwell, N. (1982). *Understanding writing.* Chelmsford, MA: The Northeast Regional Exchange.

Papert, S. (1980). *Mindstorms.* New York: Basic Books.

Romick, M. (1984, April). The computer chronicles. In R. V. Dusseldorp (Ed.), *Proceedings of the third annual statewide conference of Alaska Association for Computers in Education.* Anchorage, AK: Alaska Association for Computers in Education.

Rubin, A. D. (1982). The computer confronts language arts: Cans and shoulds for education. In A. C. Wilkinson (Ed.), *Classroom computers and cognitive science* (pp. 201–217). New York: Academic.

Rubin, A. D., & Bruce, B. C., & The QUILL Project. (1985). QUILL: Reading and writing with a microcomputer. In B. A. Hutson (Ed.), *Advances in reading and language research* (pp. 97–117). Greenwich, CT: JAI Press. (Also published in 1981: Reading Education Rep. No. 48. Urbana, IL: Center for the Study of Reading.)

Scardamalia, M. (1981). How children cope with the cognitive demands of writing. In C. H. Frederiksen, & J. F. Dominic (Eds.), *Writing: The nature, development and teaching of written communication* (p. 81–104). Hillsdale, NJ: Erlbaum.

Author Index

Subject Index

DATE DUE

MY 24 '9			
DE 1 8 '92			
MR 20'93			
MY 18 '9			
MY 30 '96			
MY 28 '99			
MY 04 '00			